genius series

Olympiad Excellence SCIENCE GUIDE

Salient Features of the Book

- In-depth analysis of each topic, followed by relevant practical and illustrative examples
- Meant for International/National Olympiads, Quizzes, Inter school competitions
- Comprising questions prepared by teachers from various schools of India and abroad
- Selected questions of various National and International Olympiads
- Model Test Paper
- All the questions are in MCQ format
- Practice exercises
- Special emphasis on concept and problem solving skills

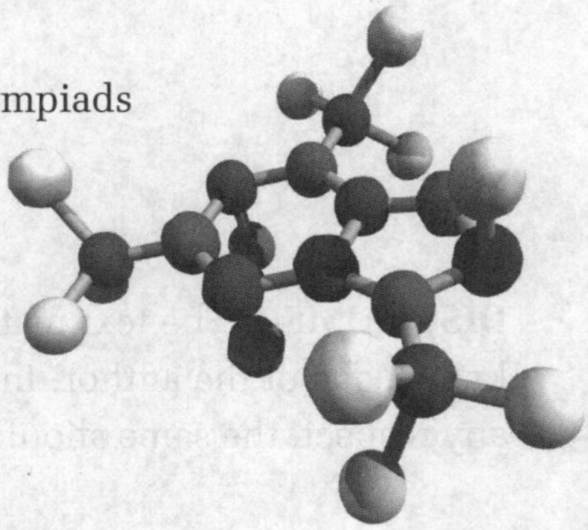

CLASS IVth

Prepared & Published by: **Silverzone Enterprises India Pvt. Ltd.**
B-2 | Ansal Chamber-II, Bhikaji Cama Place
New Delhi-110066(India)
E-mail : info@silverzone.org

DISCLAIMER: The text material of this book is completely based on the original self-ideas and knowledge of the author. In case, any part of this book is found similar with any other book in any respect, the same should be treated as mere coincidence only.

ALSO RECOMMENDED

Olympiad Comprehensive Book

From the past many years Silverzone Enterprises Pvt. Ltd. has been publishing books for Olympiads on National/International level. The motive behind conducting such an examination is to enhance the knowledge or ability that is gained through learning. For gaining mastery over such an examination, Comprehensive books are highly recommended. These books are highly beneficial to students as these contain questions that enhance the participant's ability to think and reason abstractly. These books cover chapter-wise study material, one sample test paper, OMR sheet sample with answers and many more features. Students participating in such examination can purchase these books and attain a remarkable score. With this Book, you will also be getting many key points to gain success as these books contain sufficient material that is apt for cracking such competitive examination. These books are apt for summarised, quick revision of all topics.

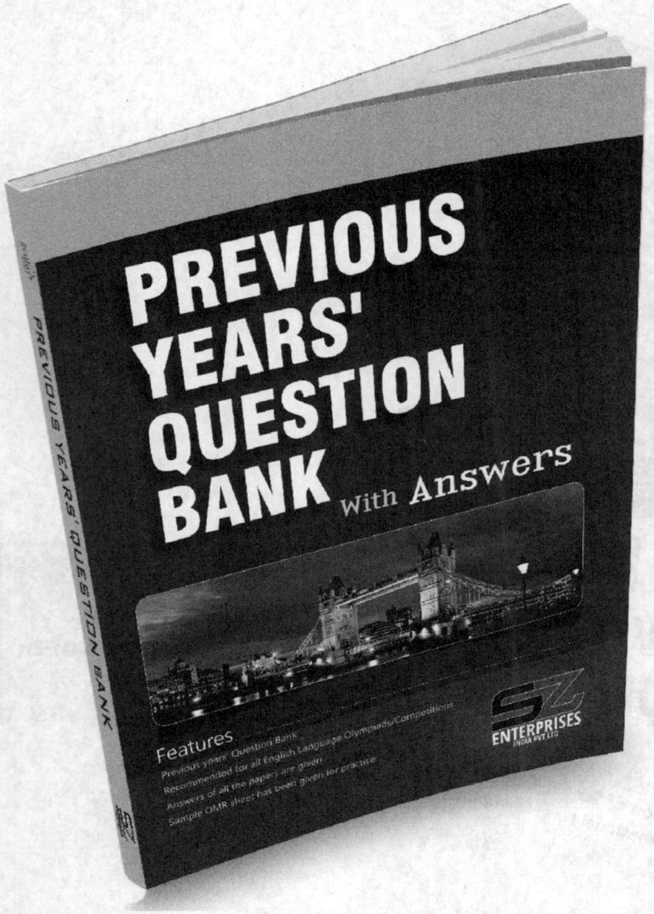

ALSO RECOMMENDED

Previous Year's Question Bank

National/International level competitions and Olympiads have made a major contribution to enhance the student's growth academically. These Olympiads serve as a boon for participants as these help in developing their confidence level to a great extent. The result of the exam does not indicate pass or fail for the participants so the fear of losing or failing in a particular exam does not bother the children and they give the exam without stress. This adds to encouragement of the children to participate in various competitive examinations as by studying Previous Year papers, their morale is boosted. These papers are of great help as by solving these papers the students are encouraged to give exams fearlessly as they are aware about the pattern of the exam conducted in previous year. These papers serve as a kind of rehearsal for participants to a certain level. These will also help you to understand the syllabus, pattern and how the pattern and difficulty levels have evolved over the years. By solving these papers the participant can find out your shortcomings and accordingly prepare for the current exam he/she wishes to crack this year. Thus, previous year papers are the best way to get a clear idea of the exam pattern and level of difficulty of questions as these contain all questions with answers and detailed explanation.

Olympiad Excellence Guide

genius series

Science

TABLE OF CONTENTS

Part I

CHAPTERS

Part II

PRACTICE EXERCISE

Olympiad Excellence Guide

genius series

Science

TABLE OF CONTENTS

Part III

ANSWERS

SELF EVALUATION TESTS

Part IV

ANSWERS

PRACTICE EXERCISE

Chapter 1 Plant Kingdom

Learning Objectives

- Plants as Autotrophs
- Photosynthesis
- Respiration in Plants
- Aquatic Plants
- Non Green Plants
- Terrestrial Plants

Introduction

Living things on the Earth are mainly divided into two major groups, the plant kingdom and the animal kingdom.

Plant Kingdom

Animal Kingdom

The plant kingdom comprises of all the green plants present on the land, in the water and even those which are non-green in colour. The green colour of the plant is due to the presence of chlorophyll, which aid in photosynthesis. Nature has a wide variety of plants. Each variety has its own uniqueness. We see most of the plants that are green. But there are plants which has coloured leaves. Some plants have small flowers, while some have tiny one. Yet another group doesn't have any flower at all. Some plants have thorns while some are soft, delicate, beautiful and great to smell. We can also see plant life in and on water. Some plants live in dry places, while others need maximum rainfall.

Plant as Autotrophs

Auto means self and trophs means nourishment. Autotrophs are living organisms which can make their own food. They make their food by taking water and minerals from the soil, carbon dioxide from the atmosphere and sunlight from the Sun. Algae, some bacteria and large trees belong to this category. This mode of nutrition is called autotrophic nutrition. All green plants can make their own food. They are also known as producers.

Plants as Autotrophs

Algae as Autotroph

Sun is the ultimate source of energy for all living organisms. Autotrophs can capture the energy of the sunlight to synthesize food. It is a unique process. The survival of almost all living organisms directly or indirectly depends on the food made by the plants. Autotrophs are fundamental to all in the food chains. All animals, almost all fungi, as well as most bacteria and protozoa, depend on autotrophs for the energy and raw materials.

Commonly Asked Question

1. **Look at the following figure of coleus plants.**

Coleus Plant

Coleus plant obtain its food by which one of the following process?

(A) Evaporation
(B) Photosynthesis
(C) Transpiration
(D) All of these
(E) None of these

Answer (B)

Explanation: Green plants obtain their food by the process of photosynthesis.

2. **Which one of the following cannot perform the process of photosynthesis?**

(A) Wheat plant
(B) Cactus plant
(C) Peepal tree
(D) Hyena
(E) None of these

Answer (D)

Explanation: Only plants can perform photosynthesis but hyena is an animal, so it doesn't perform photosynthesis.

Photosynthesis

Photosynthesis is the process by which plants make their own food. It is the process of converting carbon dioxide into organic compound, especially sugar using water and sunlight. Oxygen is a by-product of this process. Photosynthesis is vital for life on Earth, as it maintains the normal level of oxygen in the atmosphere. All life depends on photosynthesis directly as a source of energy or indirectly as the ultimate source of the energy for their food. Photosynthesis is also the source of carbon in all the living forms. Most of the plants have green pigment called, chlorophyll, in their leaves. Chlorophyll gives the green colour of the leaf, helps in photosynthesis. It is the chlorophyll that helps the plants to trap the energy from the sunlight for making their food. Oxygen, which is produced during photosynthesis is essential for all living organisms for their survival. In the absence of photosynthesis life would be impossible on the Earth.

Process of Photosynthesis

$$\text{Carbon dioxide} + \text{Water} \xrightarrow[\text{Chlorophyll}]{\text{Sunlight}} \text{Carbohydrates} + \text{Oxygen}$$

Commonly Asked Question

1. **Air enters plants through which part?**

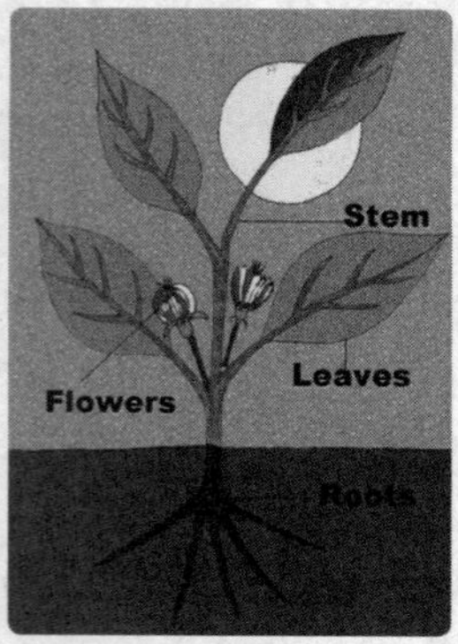

(A) Stem
(B) Stomata
(C) Fruit
(D) Flower
(E) None of these

Answer (B)

Explanation: Air enters into the plants through tiny pores present on the leaves, called Stomata.

2. **The food, synthesized by the plants in the process of photosynthesis, is stored as ______.**

(A) Vitamins
(B) Water
(C) Starch
(D) Both (A) and (C)
(E) None of these

Answer (C)

Explanation: The food synthesized by the plants is stored as starch.

Respiration

Like all living organisms, plants also go through the process of respiration. This process is essential, as it provides energy and the carbon escalation for growth and maintenance. Plants consume about 25 – 75% of all the carbohydrates produced in photosynthesis.

Sugar + Oxygen → Carbon dioxide + Water + energy.

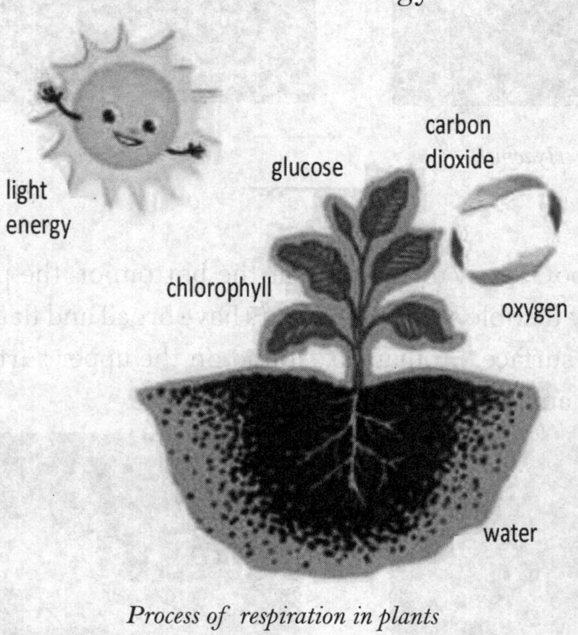

Process of respiration in plants

Plants, like other living things use atmospheric oxygen to breakdown glucose (food produced in photosynthesis) into carbon dioxide and water for the release of energy. This energy is used for its growth and maintenance. In plants, all living cells of root, stem and leaf take in oxygen independently and give out carbon dioxide and water. Hence in plants, there is little transport of gases, from one part to another, occurs . Respiration in plants occur at a much slower rate as compared to animals.

Aquatic Plants

The plants that grow in water are called aquatic plants. Such plants are adapted so that they can survive in the water. These are three types of aquatic plants:

Floating Plants

These plants are like sponge. There are numbers of empty spaces throughout their body, which is filled with air. This makes the plant light enough to float on the water. For example, duckweed, water hyacinth, etc.

Water Hyacinth

Duckweed

Fixed Plants

These plants have roots fixed to the mud at the bottom of the pond. They have thin, long, hollow and very flexible stem. The plants have broad and flat, plate like leaves with waxy coating on the surface. Stomata are found on the upper surface of the leaves. For example, water lilies and lotus.

Lotus

Water lily

Underwater Plants

These plants live and grow under water. Their roots fix the plant to the muddy soil. They have narrow thin leaves with no stomata. The leaves absorb carbon dioxide and oxygen directly through their surface. The stems are flexible and have air spaces. For example, tape grass, hydrilla and pond weed.

Tapegrass

Hydrilla

Commonly Asked Question

1. **What are the aquatic plants?**

   (A) The plants which grow in water

   (B) The plants which grow in desert

   (C) The plants which grow in plain

   (D) The plants which grow on mountains

   (E) None of these

   Answer (A)

   Explanation: The plants which grow in water are called aquatic plants.

2. **Lemna, Eichhornia, Wolffia, Pistia are example of which type of hydrophytes?**

   (A) Fixed hydrophytes

   (B) Floating hydrophytes

   (C) Under water hydrophytes

   (D) Both (A) and (B)

   (E) None of these

   Answer (B)

   Explanation: The plants given above are the example of floating plants.

Non-Green Plants

Plants which do not have chlorophyll are called non-green plants. They cannot make their own food and usually absorb food from other plants, dead animals or stale food. One type of non-green plant is fungus. Mushroom, toadstools and moulds are some examples of non-green plants.

Mushroom

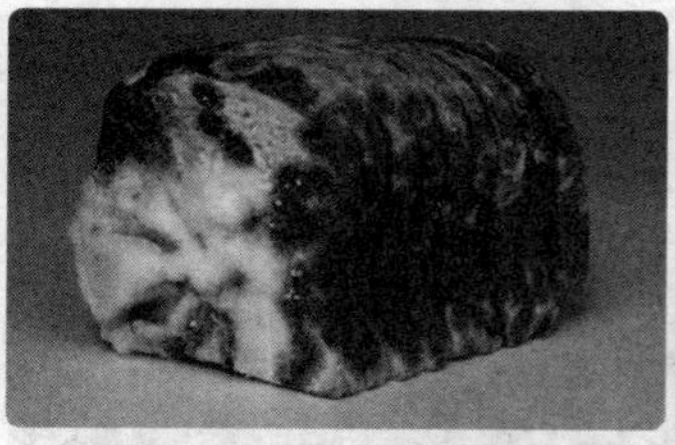

Mould

Commonly Asked Question

1. **Fill in the blank with the appropriate answer.**

   Non-green plants have ______ type of nutrition.

   (A) Autotrophic
   (B) Heterotrophic
   (C) Symbiotic
   (D) All of these
   (E) None of these

   Answer (B)

   Explanation: Non-green plants depend on other organisms for their food, so they have heterotrophic type of nutrition.

2. **Name a non-green edible plant that cannot prepare their own food but provide us with high nutrition.**

   (A) Yeast
   (B) Mushroom
   (C) Mould
   (D) All the above
   (E) None of these

   Answer (D)

   Explanation: The above given non-green plants are example of non-green edible plants.

Terrestrial Plants

Plants that grow on land are called terrestrial plants. Terrestrial plants are of different types depending on the condition they grow in.

Plants on Mountains

Plants on mountains and hills are tall, straight and have slopping shape to make the snow fall off easily. They are usually flowerless and have cones with seeds inside them. The leaves are needle like with waxy coating. For example, fir, deodar, pine, cedar, small flowerless plants like ferns, lichens and mosses etc.

Pine tree

Deodar tree

Lichens

Plants in Plain

These plants grow in plain, flat, surface of the Earth. Trees have several branches and leaves. Many of these plants grow in warmer climate of the plains and shed most of their leaves in autumn. For example, Neem, Peepal, Ashoka and Mango.

Mango tree

Peepal tree

Ashoka tree

Evergreen Plants

The evergreen plants of the plain are those which grow in hot and wet climate. For example, Tea, Coffee, Rubber, etc.

Tea Plants

Coffee Plant

Rubber Plants

Plants in Deserts

Desert is a place with hot weather, very little water and scanty rainfall. Plants growing in these places are called desert plants. These plants develop certain features that help them to survive the harsh conditions of the desert. Roots are spread out just under the surface of the soil to catch the smallest amount of water. These plants have leaves in the form of spines or don't have any leaf at all to prevent water loss. Desert plants store water in its stem. Stem carry out photosynthesis. The plants use water stored in their stem when no water is available. For example, cactus, babul, kikar

Cactus

Babul

Plants on Sea Cost

These are the plants that grow on the sea cost. Here the water is very salty and area has high rainfall. For example, coconut.

Coconut tree

Plants in Area with Heavy Rainfall

They are the evergreen plants and remain green almost round the year. For example, rubber, teak, rice, cotton and sugarcane.

Orchid

Cotton

Rice

Plants in Marshy/Swampy Area

The place, where the soil is very clayey and sticky is called marshy area and the plants growing there are the marshy plants. Major problem for the growth of plant here is oxygen, which cannot reach the roots of the plants. To over come this problem, plants here have breathing roots to absorb air. For example, mangroves.

Mangroves

DID YOU KNOW?

- A notch in a tree will remain at the same height from the ground, as the tree grows.
- Both George Washington and Thomas Jefferson grew cannabis sativa (marijuana) on their plantations.
- The first diesel engine ran on peanut oil.
- Brazilian engineers have developed a way to produce bio-diesel using coffee oil extracted from bad quality coffee beans.

SUMMARY

- **Autotrophs:** Organisms capable of making their own food.
- **Photosynthesis:** Process by which green plants make their food using carbon dioxide, water and sunlight.
- **Respiration:** Process that provides energy and the carbon skeleton for the growth and maintenance of plants.
- **Aquatic plants:** Plants which live in or on the water surface.
- **Non green plants:** Plants which do not have chlorophyll are called non green plants.
- **Terrestrial plants**: Plants that live and grow on the land.

Self Evaluation Test–1

1. **Identify the autotroph from the following.**
   (A) Peepal tree
   (B) Zebra
   (C) Mushroom
   (D) Buffalo
   (E) None of these

2. **Which one of the following is fixed aquatic plant?**
   (A)  Duckweed
   (B)  Water Hyacinth
   (C)  Hydrilla
   (D)  Lotus
   (E) None of these

3. **Plants make their own food. This process is known as _______.**
   (A) Evaporation
   (B) Photosynthesis
   (C) Respiration
   (D) Transpiration
   (E) None of these

4. **Spines of cactus are modified ______.**

(A) Leaves
(B) Stems
(C) Roots
(D) Flowers
(E) Fruit

5. **If a plant is placed in a dark room it will soon**

(A) Bear fruits
(B) Bear flowers
(C) Grow bigger
(D) Become weak and die
(E) Grow stronger

6. **Which one of the following is an aquatic plant?**

(A) Peepal
(B) Coconut
(C) Wheat
(D) Vallisneria
(E) None of these

7. Match the following.

1. Is an evergreen tree (a) 

2. Is a non-green plant (b) 

3. Is an aquatic plant (c) 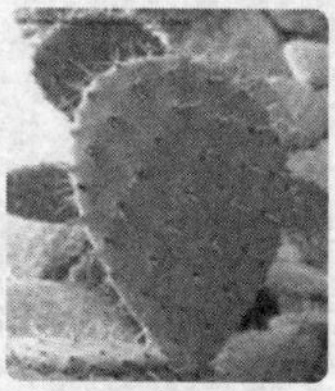

4. Is a desert plant (d) 

5. Grows along the sea coast (e) 

(A) 1- d, 2- a, 3- b, 4- c, 5- e
(B) 1- e, 2- d, 3- a, 4- c, 5- b
(C) 1- b, 2- d, 3- a, 4- c, 5- e
(D) 1- a, 2- c, 3- d, 4- b, 5- e
(E) None of these

8. Breathing roots are special modification of which tree?

(A) 

(B) 

(C) 

(D) 

(E) None of these

9. Which one of the following statements is correct?

Statement 1 : Aquatic plants can't perform the process of photosynthesis.

Statement 2 : Aquatic plants can perform the process of photosynthesis.

(A) Statement 1
(B) Statement 2
(C) Both statements are correct
(D) Both statements are incorrect
(E) None of these

10. Which one of the following plants have spines instead of leaves?

(A) Lotus
(B) Cactus
(C) Peepal
(D) Coconut
(E) None of these

Chapter 2

Animal Kingdom

Learning Objectives

- Classification of Animals
- Animals and Their Habitat
- Food of Animals
- Adaptation for Protection
- Reproduction in Animals

Introduction

Every organism living on this Earth is unique in itself. This uniqueness of each living individual is the basis of the great differences or diversity of the living world. The type of living organism found in one place is entirely different from organisms found in another place. For example, animals found in plains is different from the animals found in mountains or hilly regions. In fact different places, in different part of the world have their own typical kind of living organisms. The degree of diversity in the living world is endless.

Different Types of Animals

With such vast differences and large number, it is very difficult to study each and every living organism separately, at the individual level. Therefore to study and understand the life of animals effectively they have been classified into different groups, on the basis of certain criteria.

Classification of Animal kingdom

The animals are broadly divided into two major groups based on the presence or absence of the major characteristic feature, that is, the backbone.

Invertebrates

Invertebrates are those animals which do not have a backbone or vertebral column. They are considered to be primitive form of life on the Earth. A large variety of small animals like insects, worms, slugs, snail, spider and scorpion, etc. belong to this group. A surprising fact is that the Earth is home to more insects than any other kind of animal. Insects are very unique, among all living creatures on the Earth.

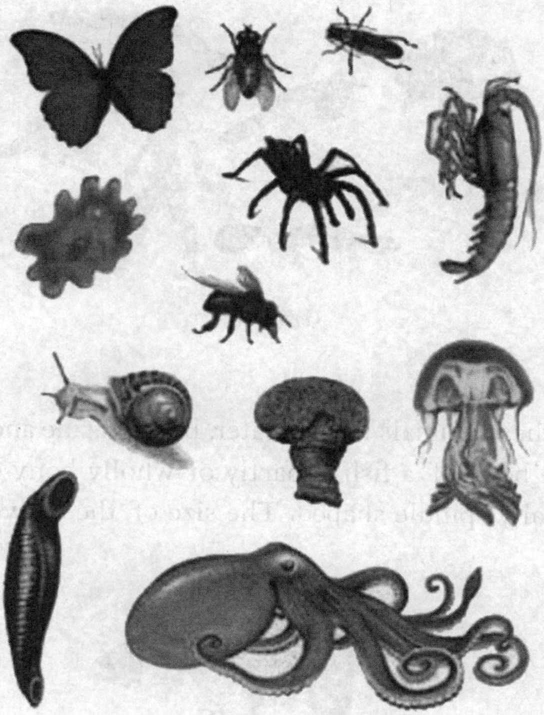

Different Types of Invertebrates

The body of an insect is divided into three parts head, thorax and the abdomen. The head contains the mouth, the eyes and the antennas. Some insects use their antennas for smelling. The thorax of an insect is similar to our chest. If an insect has wings, they are attached to this portion of the body i.e. thorax. The abdomen contains the large part of the digestive system. As the invertebrates lack bones, they have hard outer covering to support the body called chitin. This outer layer is waxy and waterproof. All insects have six legs. Invertebrates are found everywhere on the Earth, land, water, air, etc.

Vertebrates

The animals which have a backbone or a vertebral column are called vertebrates. These animals are highly evolved and have well developed organ system. Vertebrate is a large group. To study and understand the animals in this group, vertebrates are further divided into five major groups.

Vertebrates

Fish

As the name suggest, these animals live in water. Both marine and fresh water fish come under this group. The body of a fish is partly or wholly bony endoskeleton (internal skeleton) and is generally spindle shaped. The size of the body varies from 10 mm to 4 meters.

Rohu Fish

The body of the fish is either naked or covered with scales. These animals breathe through gills. They swim in water with the help of their fins. Some common example are labeo (rohu), mackerel, shark, etc.

Amphibians

Amphibian, as clearly indicated by the word amphi means double and bios means life. Amphibians are animals that live both on land and in water. The body of these animals is divided into head, trunk and their heart is of three chambers. Respiration in amphibians takes place through gills, lungs, moist skin or the mouth lining. These animals do not maintain their body temperature (cold blooded). Their body temperature changes with the environment.

Frog

Some common examples of this group are frog, toad, newt and salamanders, etc.

Reptiles

Reptiles are the group of animals living mainly on land. 'Reaper' is a Latin word meaning 'crawl'. Reptiles are known as creeping vertebrates. They are cold blooded, mainly terrestrial, but some may be aquatic. The body of the reptiles is covered with dry, water proof skin having horny scales.

King Cobra

Body of the reptiles is usually divided into head, neck, trunk and tail, though the structure of the body may vary. Teeth are present in almost all reptiles except a few. Heart of these animals is three chambered. Most reptiles lay eggs on land. For example, snake, lizards, tortoise, crocodile, etc.

Birds

Birds are the most magnificent and easily differentiated group. This group is scientifically called AVES, a Latin word meaning bird. Animals of this group are highly evolved with well developed organs and complex organ systems. Bird are warm blooded (maintain their body temperature) vertebrates with several flight adaptations.

Bird

The size of this group of animals varies from the smallest humming bird to largest ostrich. Feathers cover most of the body. They have two legs and a pair of wings that help them to fly. Some birds such as kiwi, ostrich and penguin cannot fly. These birds are called flightless birds. The heart of the birds is fully formed with four chambers. Birds lay eggs. For example, Sparrow, Crow, Eagle, Peacock, etc.

Mammals

Mammals are the most evolved species of the animal's kingdom. They are the group of animals that give birth to their babies and mother suckle their young ones.

Elephant

Mammals breathe through their lungs. Heart is completely formed with four chambers. They are warm blooded animals. Hair is present on the body of the mammals. They show the highest degree of parental care i.e. parents taking care of their young ones. Mammals are mostly terrestrial but they are also found in water, on the trees, etc.

Primary example of mammals are human beings. Other example of this group are rat, monkey, tiger, elephant, whale, etc.

Commonly Asked Question

1. **Which one of the following animals belongs to the group of amphibians?**

   (A) Dog (B) Frog

   (C) Whale (D) Cat

   (E) None of these

   Answer: (B)

   Explanation: Frog belongs to the group of amphibians.

2. **Animals which give birth to their young ones are __________**

   (A) Aves (B) Amphibians

   (C) Insects (D) Mammals

   (E) None of these

   Answer: (D)

   Explanation: Aves, Amphibians, Insects and Reptiles lays eggs.

Animals and Their Habitat

Animals are found everywhere on the Earth. They are found on the highest of mountains and in the deepest of the sea. They are found in the hottest deserts or in the coldest poles (Antarctica). Animals live in the wild and even in our homes. They live in air too. The surrounding or the environment in which an animal lives and survive is called its **habitat**. Animals develop certain features, which help them to survive in their specific environment, or habitat. If they are not properly adapted to their surrounding, they either die or they move to places where they are better suited and can adjust in a much better way for survival and growth. The process of developing special features in order to adjust to the changes in the surrounding or the habitat of an animal is called **adaptation.** Depending on the habitat of animals, they can be differentiated from one another into five different groups.

Terrestrial Animals

Terrestrial animals are animals which live on land. These animals have developed specific features that help them to survive and live on land. Most of these animals have legs, which help them to run fast. They have to run fast to catch their prey or to protect themselves from becoming prey of other animals (predators). They breathe through well developed lungs.

Tiger

Some terrestrial animals have sharp teeth with pointed canines and sharp claws to catch their prey. These animals have well developed sense organ, which helps them to look for food in the dark night or by mere movement of their prey. These special adaptive features are common to most of the terrestrial animals.

Conditions on the land are not uniform everywhere. It varies from place to place. Mountain regions and the Polar regions are very cold. Animals living there have developed several adaptations to adjust to these climatic conditions. Polar bear living in the polar region and Yak living at high mountain range have thick coat of fur on their body, which protects them from the chilling cold. Animals like Walrus, Seals and Penguins also live in freezing conditions. These animals have special adaptation called blubber (thick layer of fat).

Polar bear

Conditions in the deserts are also very harsh. Here the temperature is very hot during the day but the nights are cold. Animals living here has to adapt to the changing temperature and scarcity (i.e. very little) of food and water. Camel is the very good example of an animal which has very well adapted itself to the life in a desert.

Camel

Camel has thick skin and very little hair on its body. This thick skin protects it from scorching sun during the day and also from the nights that are cold. Camel has a hump at its back. It can live on its fat in the hump and can survive without food or water for several days.

A very special adaptation to combat winter by many animals is **hibernation**. Some animals such as snake, lizards, frog, etc. cannot bear the cold winter. They stuff themselves with lots of food during the summer and get fat. These animals become inactive during the winter. This winter sleep is called hibernation. Animals in the desert go for a long summer sleep, as the summer is hot and with very little water and food. Animals, wade of the harsh summer heat, to save water and to combat scarcity of food, sleep in their holes and burrows. This summer sleep is called **aestivation**. These are few of special adaptations of animals living in their specific habitat.

Aquatic Animals

Animals living in water are called aquatic animals. All aquatic animals are not found in the same type of water. Many kinds of fish, snails, snake are found in fresh water i.e. streams, lakes, etc. Animals like dolphins, sharks, seals, starfish, jellyfish are found in salty water i.e. the sea and oceans.

Fish

Most of the aquatic animals breathe the air dissolved in water, through organs called gills. Animals like dolphins and whale breathe through their lungs. Aquatic animals have special body shape like spindle shaped, flattened or disc shape. Dog fish, spindle shaped sting ray has a flattened shape. Aquatic animals swim in water. They have special organs called fins or paddles, which help them in swimming.

Amphibians

Amphibians are animals, which can live both on land and in water. They have special adaptations for their life in both habitats. The best example of an amphibian is frog and toad.

Amphibians

Special features that make them a perfect amphibian is the lungs to breathe on land and moist skin to breathe in water. The back legs of frogs, are stronger than their front legs, this help them to jump. They have webbed feet which help them to swim in water. Frogs lay eggs in water. Early stages in the life cycle of frog (tadpole) cannot survive on the land.

Arboreal Animals

Animals that spent most of their life time on trees are called arboreal animals. These animals have sharp and strong claws to cling or hold on tightly to the branches of the trees. Arboreal animals have strong arms and legs to climb up and down the branches. Monkeys use their long muscular tail to coil around branches when they move from one branch to the other. Arboreal animals feed on the food from the tree. Koala bear found in Australia is another good example of arboreal animal.

Monkey

Aerial Animals

Aerial animals are those which spent a greater part of their lives in the air. Flying is the main characteristic of this group. Most of the adaptations of aerial animals revolve around their flying. Most of the birds and bats belong to this group. The body of the birds is made light with hollow light bones. Their front legs (fore limbs) are modified into wings, which help them to fly. Their bodies are covered with feathers. They have well developed lungs to breathe air. They have sharp claws to hold branches. Claws of eagle are specially designed to catch prey. Birds living in cold places like Siberia come to India during winter season as the climatic condition there is very harsh and also there is scarcity of food. Siberian crane travel thousands of miles and come to India in search of food, warmth and to give birth to their young ones. They travel in large groups. At the end of the winter they travel back to their original home land. This mass movement of the birds from their home to the comfort region in the harsh climatic condition and back is called **migration.**

Aerial Animals

Commonly Asked Question

1. **Long winter sleep is ______.**

   (A) Aestivation (B) Hibernation
   (C) Migration (D) Rotation
   (E) None of the above

   Answer: (B)

   Explanation: Winter sleep is hibernation. Summer sleep is aestivation. Mass movement of birds is migration.

2. Bat can fly, It is aerial in nature. To which group does it belong?

(A) Reptiles (B) Birds

(C) Mammal (D) Aves

(E) None of the above

Answer: (C)

Explanation: Bat is a mammal.

Food of Animals

We all need food to live and grow. Animals cannot prepare their own food like plants. Hence they have a heterotrophic form of nutrition. The large and the diverse groups of animals living in this world have different food habits. It is for this difference that all the forms of life are surviving. Can you guess what will happen if all the animals eat the same type of food?

Different animals eat different kinds of food and their body parts are accordingly adapted. Adaptability and availability are the two main reasons for an animal to have a specific food habit. Based on the type of food that an animal eats, they have been divided into five major groups.

Herbivores

Plants i.e. herbs, bushes, leaves, grasses, fruits or seeds, etc., of a plant are eaten by animals. These plant eating animals are called herbivores. Herbivores have adaptation to break, graze, chew and digest plant products. These animals have sharp front teeth which help them to cut grass or leaves and very strong flat grinding teeth at the back. These grinding teeth help to chew the grass.

Cow

Buffalo

Herbivore like cows continuously eat grass and store it in their stomach. The partially digested grass, called cud, is stored in stomach. Later the cud is returned to the mouth in small lumps and the animal chew it. This is the reason why a cow continuously chewing even when they are not eating. The grass is rich in cellulose, a type of carbohydrate. Cellulose cannot be digested by all the animals. The special adaptation of the cow to digest cellulose is that they have a large sac between large intestine and small intestine. Cellulose is digested in this sac by the action of certain bacteria present there. Common examples of herbivores animals are cow, sheep, goat, zebra, etc.

Carnivores

Carnivores are animals that eat the flesh of other animals. Latin word 'carne' means flesh. Carnivores are solely dependent on animal's tissues (flesh) for their need of energy and nutrients. Lion, a carnivore has developed special characteristics which help them to adopt the life that they lead. Lions have sharp canines for hunting and tearing out the flesh of its prey. Eyes of lions are faced in front of the face, which allows it to have a correct idea about the location of the prey. They have sharp, pointed long claws in their front legs, this help them to pounce and hold on to their prey. The light brown colour of the body help it to hide in dry glasslands when it hunts. Lions have strong legs which help them to run very-very fast to catch their prey.

Lion

Tiger

Snakes use the scales on their body to move fast on the ground. Snakes kill the prey by injecting venom (poison) into the body of the prey. Then they swallow their prey. Carnivores birds like eagle have sharp claws to catch their prey and strong hooked beak to tear the flesh. Eagles have very strong and good pair of eye. These help them to site their prey far from up in the sky.

Omnivores

Animals, which eat both plants and animals are called omnivores. Latin word 'omni' means everything. They are opportunistic, general feeders and not specially adopted to eat and digest either meat or plant material primarily. They eat what they can find easily.

Human beings are best example. We eat fruits and vegetables when they are widely available and eat meat also. We neither have sharp claws nor sharp canines, because we don't go for hunting.

Human Being

Bear

We neither have very broad flat grinding teeth like herbivores. Omnivores can switch over from plant to animals food depending on the availability of the kind of food.

They have the highest degree of survival in the toughest condition like scarcity of food. Herbivorous cannot survive if there is no plant, neither a carnivores without flesh. Omnivores can survive in the absence of any one kind of food. If plant is available they eat that and if meat is available they can live on it.

Scavengers

Scavengers are those animals, which eat the flesh of dead animals. Scavengers are carnivores. Their feeding behavior include the flesh of animals not killed by them. Scavengers play an important role in the environment by eating the dead remains of other animals. Thus they help to keep the surrounding clean.

Hyena

Vulture

The adaptation of scavengers is also like those of the carnivores. They have sharp teeth and claws. Birds like vultures have strong, sharp, pointed beak to tear the flesh. Some common examples of scavengers are jackals, hyenas, burying beetles.

Parasites

Some small animals depend on other animals for food and sometimes even for shelter. They suck the blood of their host animals for their food and nutritional requirement. In return they cause harm to the host body by making it diseased or sometimes even killing the host. Such animals are called parasites. Parasites do not have teeth, instead they have sucking tube in their mouth.

Depending on the place where a parasite lives, it is grouped into 2 major groups, **Endoparasite** and **Ectoparasite**. Endoparasites are those parasites which live inside the body of the host, for example, roundworm, tapeworm, etc. Ectoparasites are those parasites, which live on the body of the host. For example, lice, bed bug, mosquito, leech, etc. Endoparasite is always more dangerous than Ectoparasite. Parasites have special mechanisms, which help them to hop from one host to another.

Leech

Bed Bug

Commonly Asked Question

1. **Which one of the following is a carnivorous animal?**

(A) Cow (B) Giraffe
(C) Panther (D) Zebra
(E) None of these

Answer: (C)

Explanation: Panther is a carnivorous animal.

2. **Scavengers eat:**

(A) Grasses (B) Leaves of plants

(C) Fruits and vegetables (D) Flesh of dead animals

(E) None of these

Answer: (D)

Explanation: Scavengers eat flesh of dead animals.

Adaptation For Protection

The living world is full of challenges. Organisms have to adopt all the harsh conditions of the environment, in order to live and reproduce. Apart from the harsh environmental conditions like high and low temperature, little or lots of water etc., a major struggle of the animals is for food. Many of the animals are the food for other animals. Mostly the carnivores or omnivores hunt herbivores for their requirement of foods. However, many of the animals have adopted special features that help them to protect themselves from enemies. Let us look and understand at some of the special adaptive features of animal that have evolved specially for their protection against their enemies.

Large Size

Huge sizes of some animals are enough to scare away their enemies. For example, bear, elephant and hippopotamus are so gigantic that their mere sizes scare away most of their enemies. It is not a common that a lion is attacking an elephant.

Hippopotamus

Strong Legs

Some animals have very strong legs and are able to run very fast. These animals due to their great speed run away from their enemies. For example, Deer.

Deer

Position of Eyes and Ear

The long ears help them to hear the slightest of the movement. Hearing the slightest of movement they run for their life. The position of eyes on the side of its head allow them to look in all direction for danger. The large ear of the elephant helps them to hear even very soft sounds. This alarms them much in advance and they move away from danger. The position of eyes and ears help deer to move quickly away from the enemies.

Move in Herds

Most of the animals protect themselves from their enemies by moving in large groups. This large group is known as herd. It becomes difficult for the enemies to attack such a large group. Hence animals remain safe. For example, deer, wild buffaloes, monkeys, elephants move in herd.

Elephant Herd

Different Body Covering

Many animals such as tortoise, turtle, snail, crab have hard outer covering on their body known as **shell.** This shell protects their soft body parts from injury and also from the attack of the enemies. These animals also have a special characteristic of withdrawing their body parts into their shell at the time of danger. Some animals such as porcupines or hedgehogs have spines covering their body. When a hedgehogs sense danger, it rolls up into a ball. This ball of spines is not easy for the enemy to attack and they remain safe.

Tortoise

Camouflage

Camouflage is a phenomenon in which an animal's body colour merge or blends with their surroundings. This makes it very difficult for the enemy to spot. The chameleon, a lizard like animal can also change the colour of their skins to match their surroundings.

Grasshopper

Chameleon

A stick insect looks almost like a twig. Grasshopper is also a perfect example of camouflage. The colour of the polar bear and the arctic fox matches with the surrounding snow and thus makes it very difficult to spot. The stripes of zebra and tiger make it difficult to be easily spotted in the forest.

Apart from these, some animals have their unique way of protecting themselves from enemies. For example, some snakes and opossums pretend to be dead when they are in danger. If a flying fish is chased by an enemy, it jumps out of the water and flies by spreading its large fins. Globefish blows itself upto twice its normal size. So that it looks much bigger and scares away its enemy.

Rhinoceros

Wild buffalo

Rhinoceros and wild buffalo when confronted with their enemy stand and fight them. They use their horns while fighting. These are only a few of the adaptations that we know about them. There must be many more about them which we don't know. The living world is so vast, fascinating and mysterious that we may never be able to understand and open up all the secrets that it holds.

Commonly Asked Question

1. **Which one of the following animals has a shell to protect it from enemies?**

(A) Turtle (B) Lion
(C) Man (D) Rat
(E) None of these

Answer: (A)

Explanation: Turtle has a shell to protect it from enemies.

2. **Kiwi fight their enemy using____________**

(A) Hair (B) Wings
(C) Claws (D) Both (A) and (B)
(E) None of these

Answer: (C)

Explanation: Kiwi is a fiery fighter and fight with the claws in their legs.

Reproduction in Animals

Like any other living thing, animals are born, grow, give birth to their own kinds, get old and die. The ability to produce more of their own kind is known as **reproduction**. Reproduction is very essential for the continuation of a species or a group of animal. It ensures the continuation of similar kind of individuals (animals) generation after generation. Animals have mainly two different ways of reproduction. Animals, which give birth to their young one, the baby develops inside the body of the mother. Second group of animals are those which lays eggs, baby hatches out from the egg. Now let us understand these two ways of reproduction in detail.

Reproduction

Reptile-Egg laying animal

Human-giving birth to young one

Egg Laying Animals

Many of the animals reproduce by laying eggs. The eggs are laid in a safe place like nest, borrows, holes, etc. Either of the parent sit on the egg to keep it warm. After a fixed period of time the egg gets matured and the young one hatches out. In the centre of the egg, is a yellow portion called yolk. It contains the developing baby called **embryo**. Yolk is rich in fats, vitamins and minerals which is the food for the growing embryo.

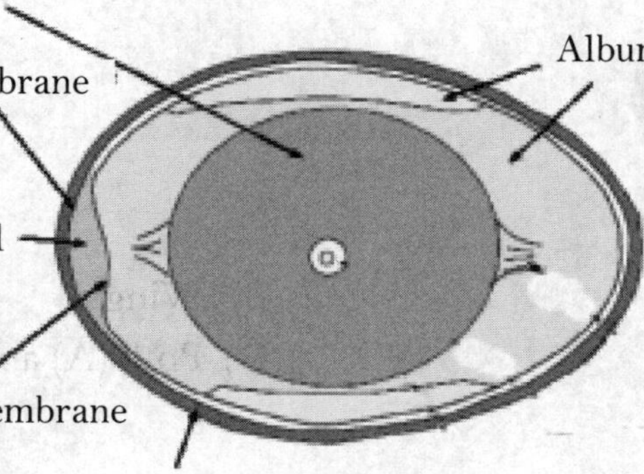

Hen's Egg

Yolk is surrounded by a white jelly like substances called albumen. It is rich in protein. Albumen protects the embryo and provides water to it. These substances are protected all together in a thin protective shell called the egg shell. The embryo develops into a chick.

Birds

All birds reproduce by laying eggs. Birds build nests to lay eggs and to raise their young ones. Within the egg, embryo goes through various developmental stages. Mostly the mother sits on the egg to keep it warm. The baby bird hatches out. The parent birds feed and protect the young bird until they can look after themselves. The baby bird grows into an adult. All the stages of development from the embryo to a mature adult make up a complete cycle. This cycle is called life cycle of an animal.

Frog

Female frog lays hundreds of eggs at a time in a lake or pound. These large clusters of eggs are called **spawns**. Tiny tadpoles hatch out of the egg. They swim in water and look like fish. A tadpole starts to grow legs after a few weeks. Tadpole's tails becomes shorter and shorter and finally disappear, and they develop into an adult frog.

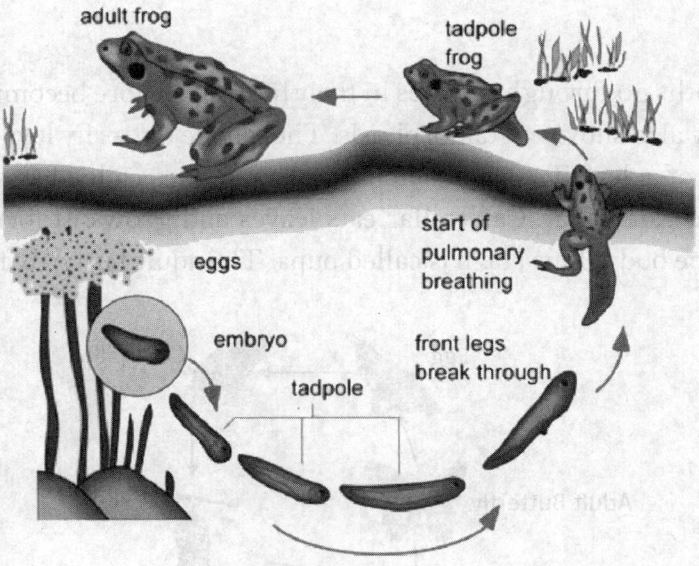

Life cycle of Frog

Tadpole undergoes several changes (as we have seen), before it becomes an adult. This process is called **Metamorphosis.**

Insects

All insects lay eggs. Many of them go through several stages before growing into adults. Let us look at the life cycle of cockroaches. The baby cockroach that hatches out from the egg looks like an adult but has no wings. This is called **nymph**. It sheds its skin several times before developing into an adult. Shedding of old skin is called moulting. Grasshoppers, locusts and termites also go through the same stages of development.

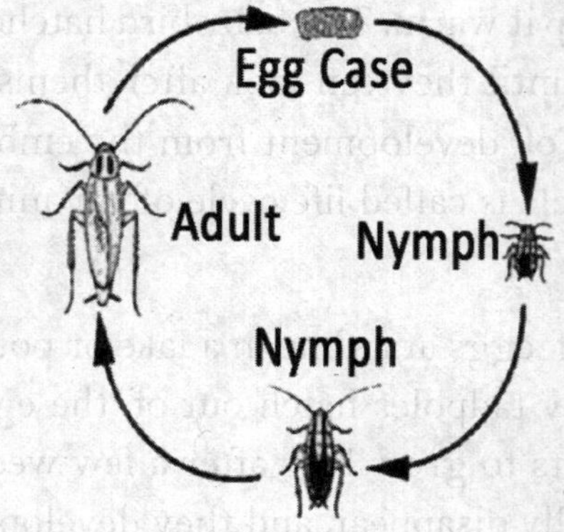

Life cycle of Cockroach

Butterfly

Butterfly and moths go through 4 stages in their life cycle before becoming an adult. Life cycle of butterfly also shows metamorphosis. The female butterfly lays eggs in a cluster on the back part of a leaf. The eggs hatch into young ones called larva. The larva of a butterfly is called caterpillar. Caterpillar eats leaves and grows. It forms a shell called cocoon around the body. This stage is called pupa. The adult butterfly finally comes out of the pupa.

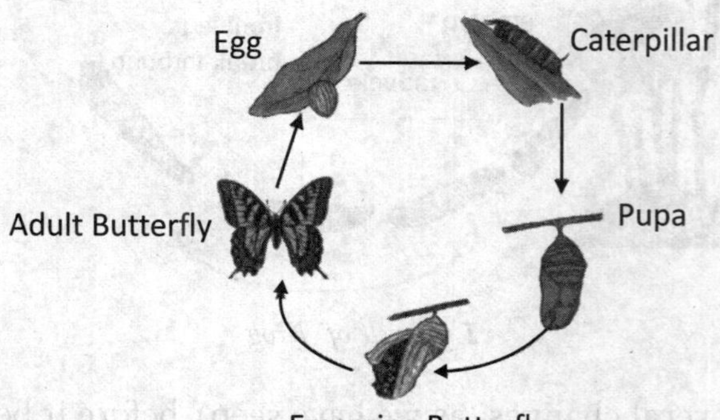

Life cycle of Butterfly

Fish

Fish lay thousands of eggs in water. Baby fish hatch out of the eggs. The eggs and the baby fish are eaten by other fish.

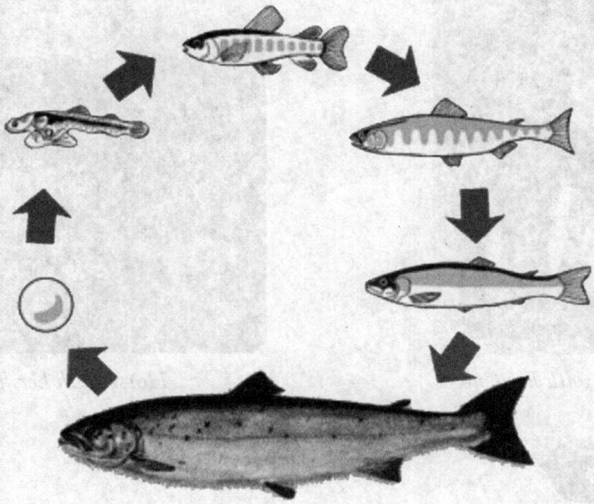

Life cycle of Fish

Turtles

Turtles and tortoises dig holes in the sand and lay their eggs there. They cover them with the sand and leave them to hatch. Young ones hatch out and move to the nearest water.

Crocodiles

Mother crocodile digs shallow pits in sandy river banks to lay eggs. Then they cover the eggs with the sand and guard them. When the babies hatch, it digs away the sand and sets them free.

Animals that Give Birth to Babies

Highly evolved animals have developed a much complex process of reproduction. Here the babies develop in the mother's womb. They stay in the mother's womb for fixed period of time. The baby born looks like his/her parents. When the babies are born they are weak and helpless. Mother takes proper care of her babies and protects them from all odds till they can look after themselves well and lead their life independently. The mother feeds her babies with her own milk. Such animals which give birth to their babies and feed them their own milk are called **mammals**. They are highly evolved animals, with well developed brains. They have hair on their body. Most mammals live on land and breathe through lungs. Whale and dolphins are aquatic mammals. For examples, horse, deer, man, cat dog, elephant, etc.

Leopard with her Cub

Horse with her foal

DID YOU KNOW?

- Turtles have been inhabiting our planet for more than 150 million years.
- Green Turtles can stay under water for up to five hours with the air of one breath in their lungs.
- Green Turtles can reduce their heart rate to a minimum of one pulse per nine minutes when diving.
- An elephant can smell water three miles away.

SUMMARY

- **Classification of Animals:** Animals are broadly classified into invertebrates and vertebrates.
- **Habitat of Animals**: Environment in which an animal lives.
- **Food of Animals:** Things eaten by animals to get energy and nutrition.
- **Adaptation:** Process of adapting some characteristics to survive in a particular environment.
- **Reproduction:** Process by which new young ones are produced.

Self Evaluation Test–2

1. **Which one of the following is an insect?**
   (A) Lizard
   (B) Snake
   (C) Man
   (D) Mosquito
   (E) Dear

2. **Identify the reptile from the following.**
   (A) Lizard
   (B) Crocodile
   (C) Tortoise
   (D) Snake
   (E) All of these

3. **Which one of the following is an invertebrate?**
   (A) 
   (B) 
   (C) 
   (D) 
   (E) None of these

4. **Which one of the following can live both on land and in water?**
   (A) Fish
   (B) Mammals
   (C) Birds
   (D) Amphibians
   (E) None of these

5. Choose the animal from the following which lays eggs to produce its offsprings.

(A) 

(B) 

(C) 

(D) 

(E) None of these

6. Which one of the following is a cold blooded animal?

(A) 

(B) 

(C) 

(D) 

(E) None of these

7. Which one of the following is a scavenger?

(A) 

(B) 

(C)  (D) 

(E) None of these

8. **Animals in the desert go for a long summer sleep, as the summer is hot and with very little water and food. This summer sleep is called:**

(A) Aestivation (B) Hibernation

(C) Adaptation (D) Migration

(E) None of these

9. **Which one of the following process has been shown with the help of given figure?**

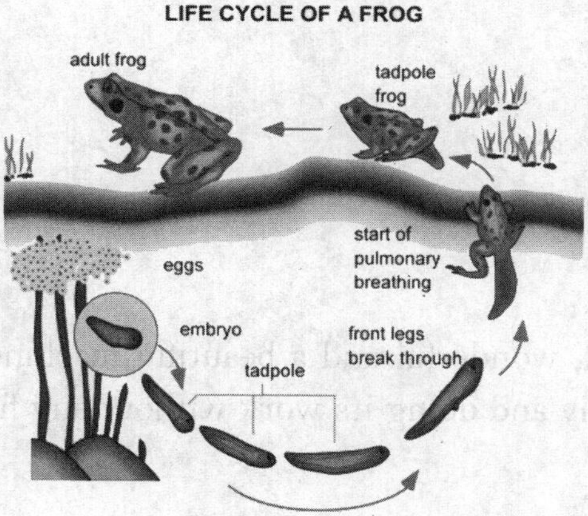

(A) Adaptation (B) Metamorphosis

(C) Reproduction (D) Hibernation

(E) None of these

10. **Which one of the following parts of the egg contains embryo?**

(A) Albumen (B) Yolk

(C) Egg shell (D) All of these

(E) None of these

Chapter 3

Functioning of Human Body

Learning Objectives

- Functioning of Human Body
- Nutrients
- Digestion
- Respiration
- Circulatory System
- Excretory System
- Nervous System

Functioning of Human Body

Human body is a complex, well coordinated, wonderful and a beautiful machine. We have different systems working independently and doing its work without any fuss or irregularities.

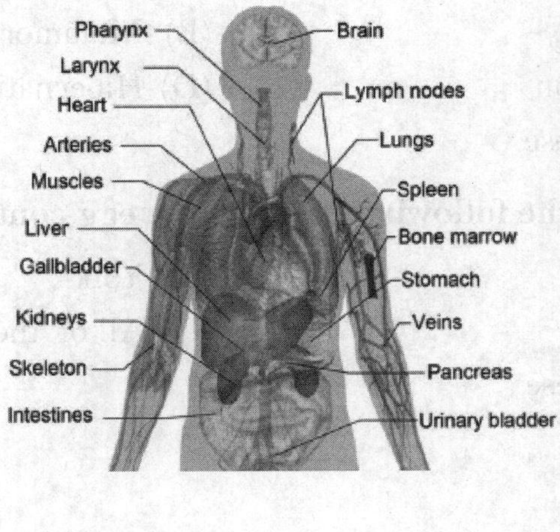

We can say that our body follow the rule of division of labour. We have different systems like the digestive system whose function is to digest the food, circulatory system which supplies food and oxygen to the required cells and collects waste from all body parts. Nervous System which coordinates all our body function. Respiratory system is concerned with the release of energy from the food. Excretory System excretes the waste material from our body. Reproductive system is involved in reproduction, i.e., producing young ones. The functions of these systems are monitored by the brain.

These systems are made up of many organs working together for a common function. For example, digestive system consists of mouth, salivary glands, oesophagus, stomach, liver, gall bladder, pancreas, small intestine, large intestine, rectum and anus. Other than organs of the systems we have the sense organs which helps us to see, feel, hear, smell and taste. The human body is also wonderfully packed with each organ placed at proper point with all care and protection. The soft organs of the body are protected by the hard outer covering of the rib cage and the bones. The organs of our body function all the time.

Nutrients

All living things needs food for its growth, maintenance and development. Food has different components. These components are called nutrients. Each nutrient is required in specific amount and has a specific function. Food is divided into different groups according to the function they perform in the body.

Carbohydrates

Carbohydrates provide energy to our body. We need energy to do any kind of work. For example, bread, chocolates, sweet Potatoes and Banana.

Carbohydrate Rich Food

Proteins

They are the body building nutrients. We need protein for our growth. They build muscles and repair the damaged parts of our body. Children need more protein than adult because their body parts need to grow and get bigger. Milk, egg, fish, meat, cheese, curd, pulses and beans etc. are protein rich food.

Protein Rich Food

Fat

Fat gives energy and warmth. They give us more energy and heat than carbohydrates. Fats are stored in the body for future use. This stored energy is used when the body does not get enough food to eat. For example, cheese, butter, oil, nuts are all rich in fat.

Fat Rich Food

Vitamins and Minerals

Vitamins and minerals are the protective nutrients. These food nutrients protect us from diseases and keep us healthy and fit. These are needed in very small amount. For example, fresh fruits, vegetables, eggs, milk are rich source of vitamins and minerals.

Food Items Rich in Vitamins and Minerals

Roughage and Water

Apart from nutrients, our body also needs dietary fibers, which helps us to keep our bowel clean by adding bulk to it. These dietary fibers also known as roughage. Roughage is mainly provided by plant products in our food. Fresh fruits and vegetables, whole grain pulses are the main sources of roughage. It does not provide any nutrient value to the body but still it is very important. It helps us to get rid of undigested food with ease. Water helps in absorption of nutrients from the food. It also plays a major role in throwing out wastes like sweat, urine from the body. Most of the water requirement is fulfilled by the liquids we drink. Fruits and vegetables also provide water.

Roughage and Water

Commonly Asked Question

1. **Which one of the following food is a rich source of carbohydrates?**

(A) Bread
(B) Egg
(C) Milk
(D) All of these
(E) None of these

Answer: (A)

Explanation: Bread is a rich source of carbohydrates whereas other options are rich source of proteins.

2. **Roughage has no food value yet it is an important part of a balanced diet. Why?**

(A) Roughage has water holding capacity
(B) Roughage add bulk to the food
(C) Roughage make the food tasty
(D) Both (A) and (B)
(E) All of the above

Answer: (D)

Explanation: Roughage helps us in regulating our digestion.

Sense Organs

Sense organs are the organs, which help us to sense the outside world. They are the external organs of our body. We have five sense organs.

Eye

Eyes are the organ, which help us to see the beautiful world around us. The eye is connected to the brain.

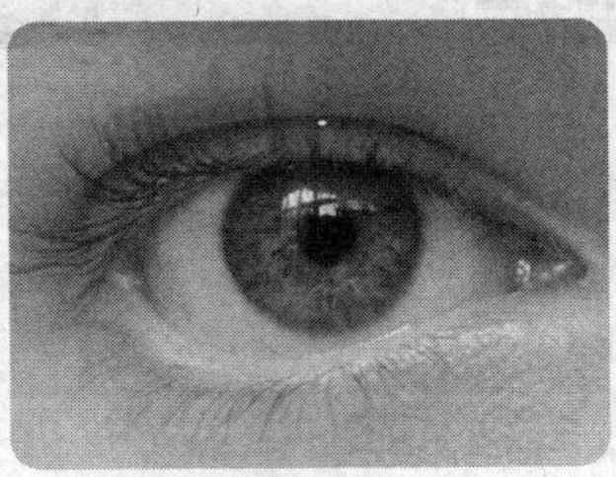

Human Eye

Ear

Ear is the organ, which helps us to listen to all kinds of sound, whether it is music, chirping of birds, moving of waves or laughter of children. The ear is connected to the brain. The brain combines the input of both the ears and then determines the distance and the direction of sound.

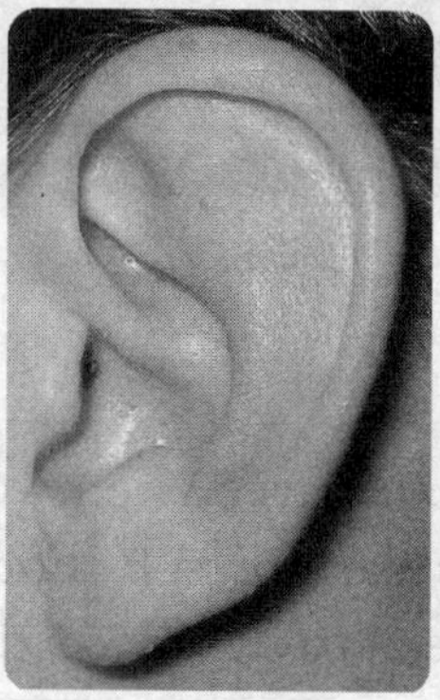

Human Ear

Nose

Nose apart from breathing helps us to smell things. It helps us to smell the fragrance of perfume and the smell of the rotten eggs, decay garbage.

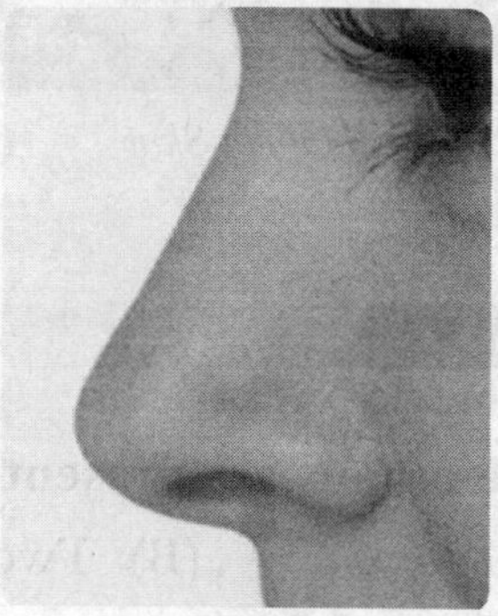

Human Nose

Tongue

Tongue is the organ of taste, it also helps us to talk. The taste of the things that we eat is due to tongue. Tongue is sensitive to different types of taste like salty, sour, bitter or sweet.

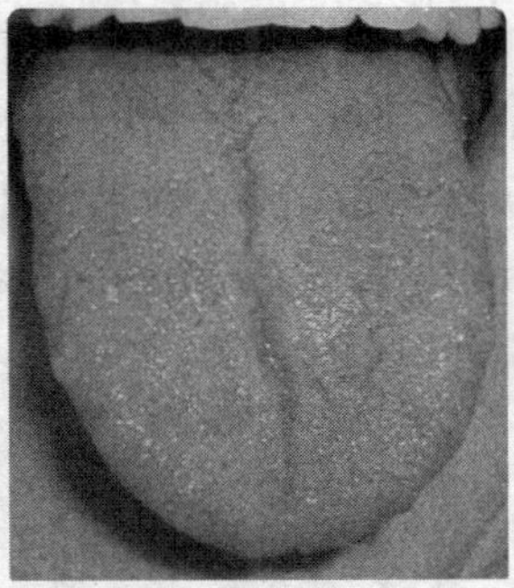

Human Tongue

Skin

Skin help us to feel the things around us. When we touch something we get a lot of information, such as whether it is hard or soft, hot or cold, sharp or blunt, rough or smooth etc. Skin covers us from head to the tip of the toe.

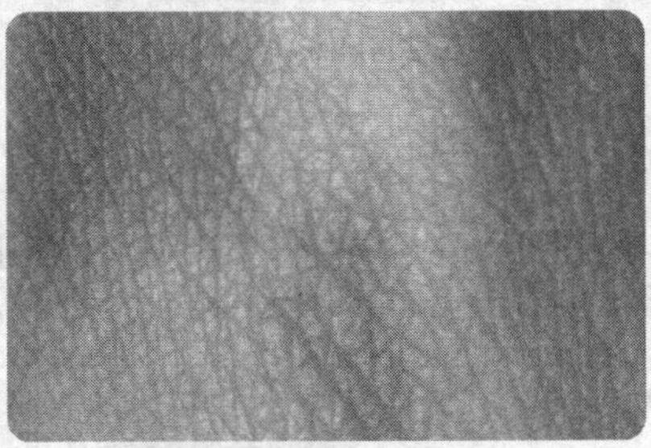

Human Skin

Commonly Asked Question

1. **How many types of sense organs are present in our body?**

   (A) Five　　(B) Two

   (C) Six　　(D) Ten

   (E) None of these

   Answer: (A)

   Explanation: There are five types of sense organs present in our body.

2. **The biggest sense organ of our body is:**

   (A) Eye　　(B) Nose

(C) Skin
(D) Ear
(E) None of these

Answer: (C)

Explanation: Biggest sense organ present in human body is skin.

Digestion of Food

Digestion is the process of breaking down food into simple form so that it is easily absorbed by the body. Digestion of food takes place in a number of steps. There are several organs of our body, which are involved in this process. They all together make up our digestive system. Digestion of food starts in the mouth. The food is broken down by chewing and grinding into a paste. The paste next moves to the stomach through the food pipe. Food is churned by the stomach muscles with more digestive juices. It is then broken down into simple soluble form. The simpler food now passes to the intestine. Here the food is mixed with more digestive juices and breaks down further. Some of these digestive juices come from the intestine, while other is made in other body organs such as liver and pancreas. These juices complete the digestion of food. The food is now in simple soluble form, which can easily be absorbed into the blood through the walls of the small intestine. The undigested food pass through the large intestine and thrown out of the body through the anus.

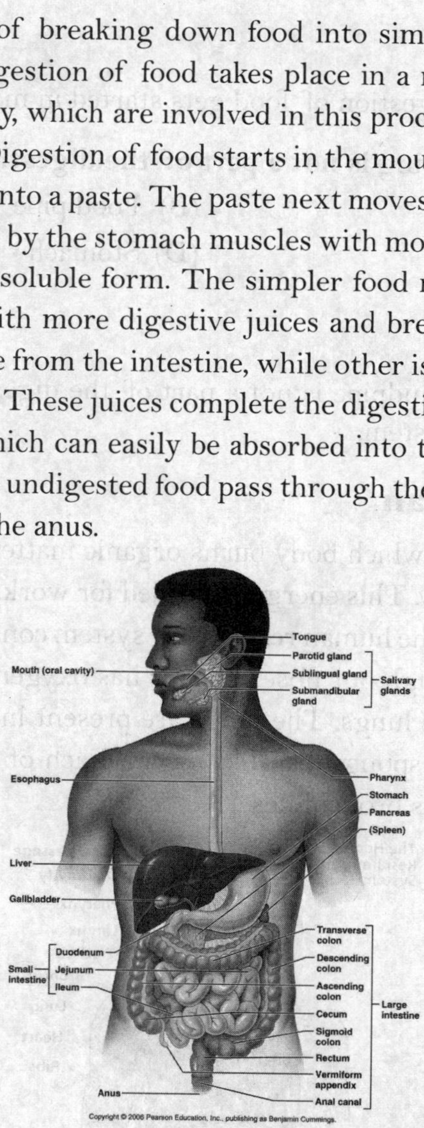

Digestion of Food in Human Body

Commonly Asked Question

1. **Where does the digestion of food start in our body?**

(A) Stomach (B) Small intestine

(C) Large intestine (D) Mouth

(E) None of these

Answer: (D)

Explanation: Digestion of food gets started in mouth.

2. **Which of the following is not a part of the digestive system?**

(A) Mouth (B) Food pipe

(C) Windpipe (D) Stomach

(E) Intestine

Answer: (C)

Explanation: Windpipe is not a part of the digestive system as it is a part of respiratory system.

Respiration in Human

Respiration is a process by which body burns organic matter (glucose) in the presence of oxygen to release energy. This energy is needed for work, growth, development and maintenance of the body. The human respiratory system consists of nose, windpipe and lungs. We breathe air through our nose. The air has oxygen in it. This air now moves down from windpipe to the lungs. The lungs are present inside our rib cage. We have a pair of them. It is a soft spongy bag like organ. Each of our lungs has millions of branching air sacs known as bronchioles.

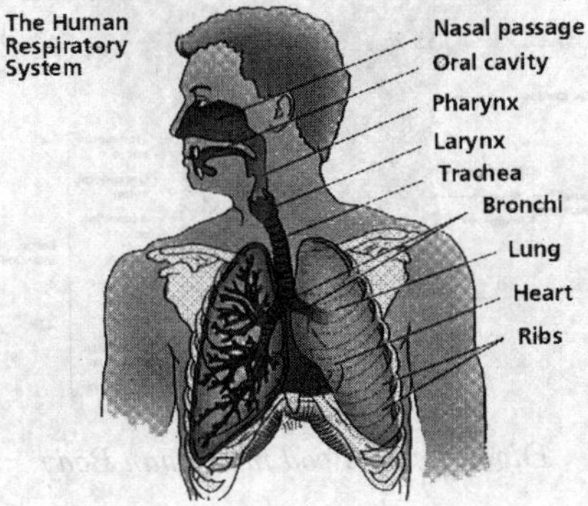

Respiration in Human

At the end of each bronchioles there are bunches of air sacs known as alveoli. During the process of respiration, oxygen from the air seeps through the air sacs into the blood and at the same time carbon dioxide seeps back into the air sac and is thrown out when we breathe out.

Commonly Asked Question

1. **When a person runs or does some hard physical work, what happens to his breathing?**
   (A) Breathes faster (B) Breathes slow
   (C) Breathes at the normal rate (D) None of these
   (E) All of these
   Answer: (A)
   Explanation: Breathing gets faster when we run or perform some hard physical activity.

2. **Name the gas that all animals breathe in to remain alive.**
   (A) Oxygen (B) Carbon dioxide
   (C) Hydrogen (D) Nitrogen
   (E) All of these
   Answer: (A)
   Explanation: We all breathe in oxygen to remain alive.

Circulatory System

Circulatory system circulates blood throughout the body. It takes oxygen and food to every body cell and sweeps out carbon dioxide and other waste materials. It also helps in fighting infection and keeps our body warm. The circulatory system consists of the heart, blood vessels and the blood.

Our heart is a powerful pump made of muscles. It contracts and relaxes automatically about 72 times in a minute to pump blood around the body. Our heart is placed in the middle of our chest, slightly to the left.

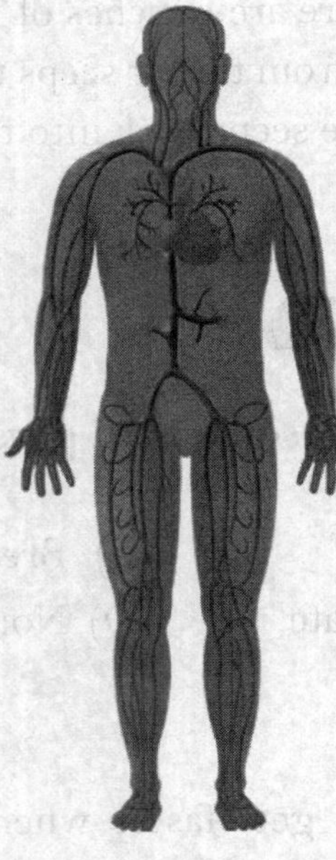

Circulatory System

Our Heart

Our heart has two sides, the right and the left one. The right side pumps blood only to the lungs. The left side, which is the bigger of the two sides pumps blood throughout the body. Blood vessels are thin tube through which blood travels throughout the body.

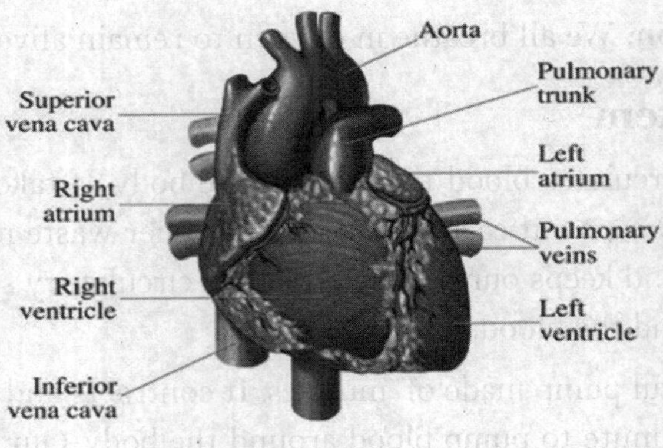

Our Heart

Commonly Asked Question

1. **Which one of the following is a part of circulatory system?**
   (A) Heart (B) Blood
   (C) Blood vessels (D) All of these
   (E) None of these

   Answer: (D)

   Explanation: Heart, Blood and Blood vessels they all help in circulating the blood in our body.

2. **Which one of the following can be termed as "pumping machine"?**
   (A) Lung (B) Nerves
   (C) Kidney (D) Heart
   (E) None of these

   Answer: (D)

   Explanation: Heart acts as a pump in circulatory system.

Excretory System

Excretory system throws out waste from our body. Human excretory system consists of kidneys, ureter, urinary bladder and urethra.

We have a pair of kidneys which is bean shaped. When the blood reaches the kidney it has both useful and harmful substances present in it. The kidneys absorb harmful substances from the blood. The waste is dissolved in water and is removed as urine. The skin also helps in removing waste from our body in the form of sweat.

Lungs act as excretory organ by removing carbon dioxide (harmful gas) from the body.

Commonly Asked Question

1. **A person has been put on dialysis. Which one of his following organs has failed to work?**

(A) 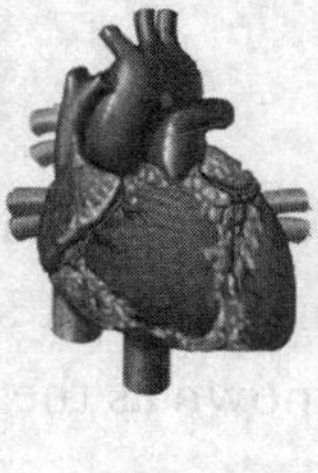

(B) 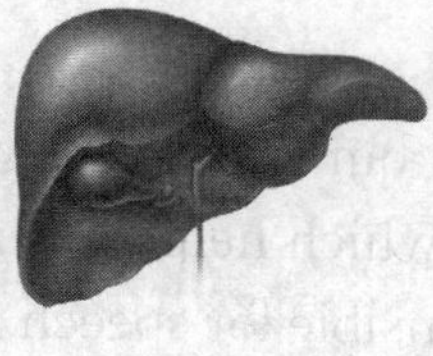

(C) 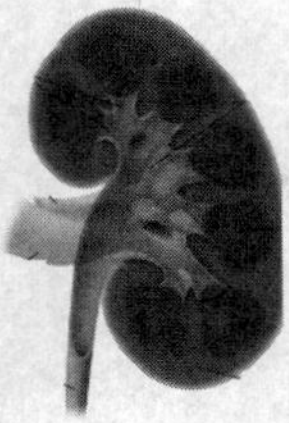 (D) 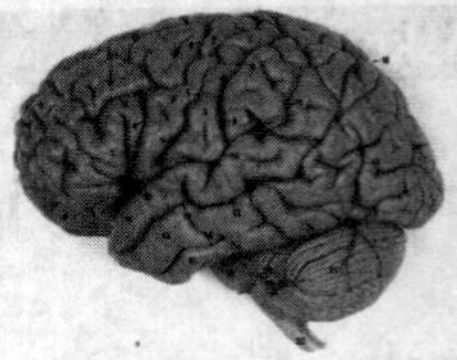

(E) None of these

Answer: (C)

Explanation: Kidneys separate waste from blood when it gets failed to work then the person is put on dialysis.

2. **Which one of the following is a part of excretory system?**

(A) Stomach (B) Liver

(C) Heart (D) Kidney

(E) All of these

Answer: (D)

Explanation: Kidneys extract waste from blood so it is a part of excretory system.

Nervous System

Nervous system co-ordinates all our body functions. It consists of brain, spinal cord and the nerves. Brain is our body's control system. Brain sends messages and receives them from all organs, all over the body. Brain is divided into 3 parts.

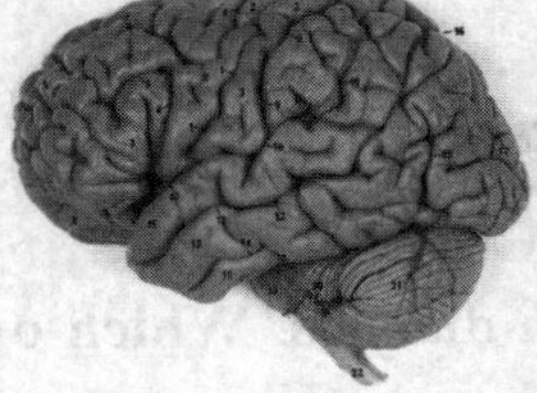

Human Brain

Cerebrum

Accounts for 85% of our brain's weight. It consists of two -halves, right half and left half. The right half, which helps to think about things like colour, different shapes, etc. The left half is responsible for speech, maths, and logic. It is also known as the **forebrain.**

Cerebellum

It is also called the **Hindbrain,** and is much smaller than forebrain. It is responsible for the movement of our body and maintaining body balance.

Medulla Oblongata

It joins the brain and the spinal cord. Functions like digestion, blood pressure, breathing, etc. is controlled by this organ.

Nerve

Spinal cord is a mass of nerves running down the middle of the backbone. A fine network of nerves connects the brain and the spinal cord to every part of our body.

They carry messages to and from the brain to the body part. Nerves present in our body are of two main types. The **sensory nerves,** which carries messages from the sense organs to the spinal cord or the brain. **Motor nerves** which carries messages from the brain or the spinal cord to various parts of the body. 90% of full weight of the brain is achieved at the age of 5 years.

Commonly Asked Question

1. **Human nervous system consists of**

(A) Brain (B) Spinal cord

(C) Nerves (D) All of these

(E) None of the above

Answer: (D)

Explanation: Brain, Spinal cord and Nerves they all are a part of human nervous system.

2. **Nerves which carry the messages from the sense organs to the spinal cord or brain are:**

(A) motor nerves

(B) sensory nerves

(C) both type of nerves carry messages to the brain

(D) All of the above

(E) None of the above

Answer: (B)

Explanation: Sensory nerves carry the message from sense organs to the spinal cord for further processing.

DID YOU KNOW?

- The stomach's digestive acids are strong enough to dissolve zinc. Fortunately for us, the cells in the stomach lining renew so quickly that the acids don't have time to dissolve it.
- The lungs contain over 300,000 million capillaries (tiny blood vessels). If they were laid end to end, they would stretch 2400 km.

SUMMARY

- **Nutrients:** The component of food which is necessary for our body.
- **Sense Organs:** The organs which helps us to sense the outside world.
- **Digestion:** The process of breaking down of the complex food materials into simple form.
- **Respiration:** It is a process of releasing energy from the food.
- **Circulatory system:** It transports oxygen and nutrients to all parts of the body and bring back carbon dioxide and waste from the body.
- **Excretory system:** Removes the waste materials from the body.
- **Nervous system:** Coordinates between the body parts and brain.

Self Evaluation Test–3

1. Which one of the following organs helps in digestion of food?

(A) 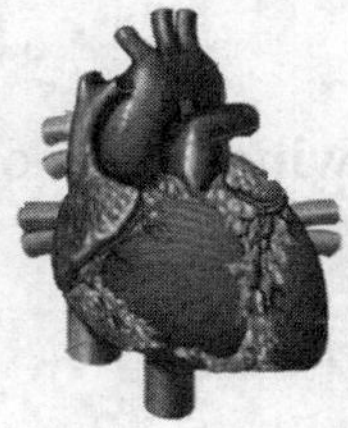

(B) 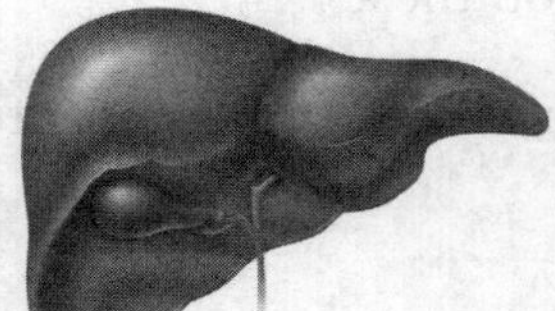

(C) 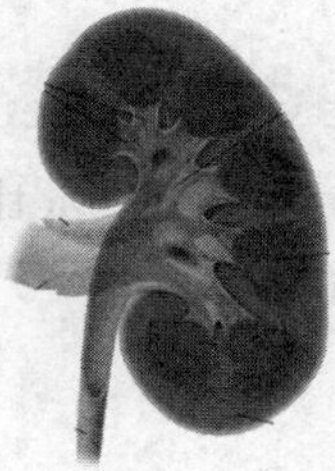

(D) 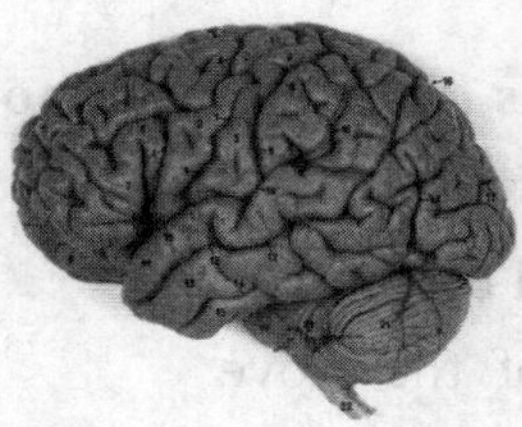

(E) None of these

2. Which one of the following is a sense organ?

(A) 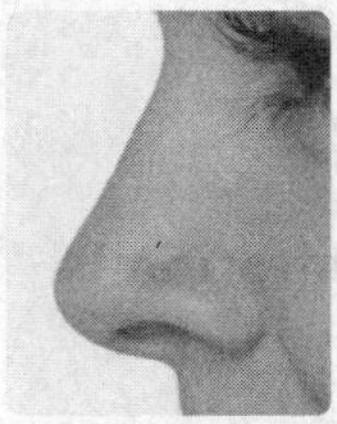

(B) 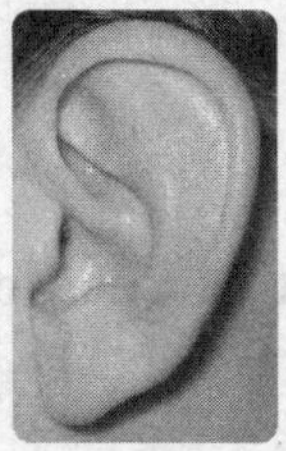

(C) 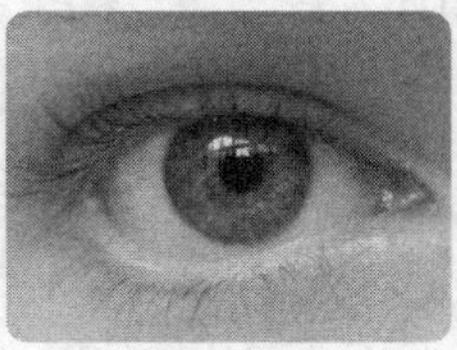

(D) 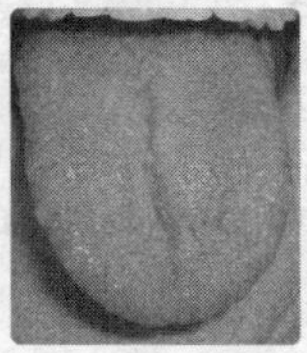

(E) All of these

3. Which one of the following is called body building food?

(A) Carbohydrates
(B) Fats
(C) Proteins
(D) Vitamins and minerals
(E) None of these

4. **Anaemia is a disease caused due to lack of:**
   (A) Calcium (B) Iron
   (C) Iodine (D) Potassium
   (E) None of these

5. **Taste of a food can be detected by which of the following sense organs?**
   (A) Eye (B) Ear
   (C) Nose (D) Tongue
   (E) Rectum

6. **If a child is given fat rich food on a daily basis, what will happen to him?**
   (A) He will become healthier (B) He will become more active
   (C) He will become weak (D) He will become obese
   (E) None of the above

7. **Protective food items are rich in _____ nutrients. Fill in the blank with the appropriate choices.**
   (A) Carbohydrate (B) Proteins
   (C) Vitamins (D) Minerals
   (E) Both (C) and (D)

8. **The gas thrown out of the body in the process of respiration is**
   (A) Oxygen (B) Nitrogen
   (C) Carbon dioxide (D) Hydrogen
   (E) None of the above

9. **Lung is a part of which one of the following systems?**
   (A) Nervous system (B) Respiratory system
   (C) Excretory system (D) Digestive system
   (E) None of these

10. **What is the colour of the blood?**
   (A) White (B) Yellow
   (C) Red (D) Pink
   (E) Green

Chapter 4 Matter

Learning Objectives

- Atoms
- Molecules
- States of Matter
- Chemical Change
- Physical Change

Introduction

All the things that we can see around us, whether living or non-living, are matter if it takes up space and has weight. It can be dog, cat, bat, ball, air, water, etc.

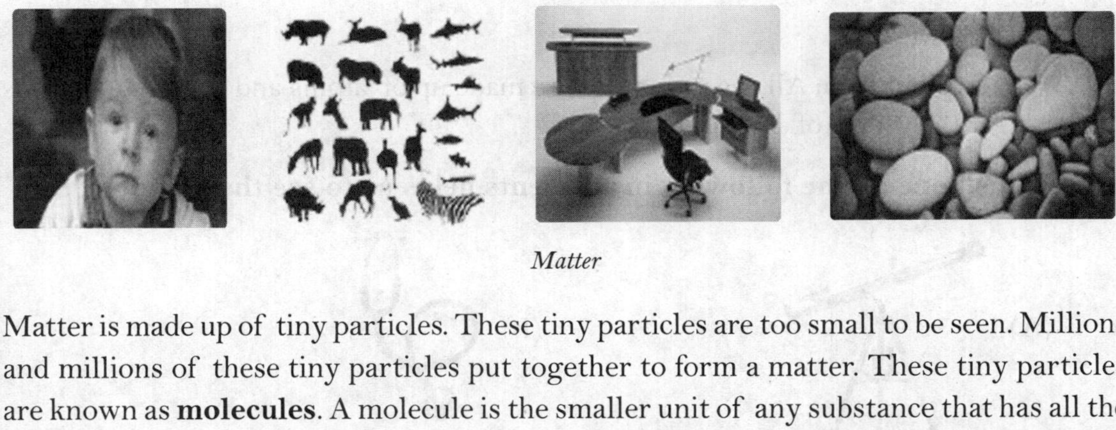

Matter

Matter is made up of tiny particles. These tiny particles are too small to be seen. Millions and millions of these tiny particles put together to form a matter. These tiny particles are known as **molecules**. A molecule is the smaller unit of any substance that has all the properties of that particular substance. A molecule of aluminium has all the properties of aluminium. The molecule of different substances are different from each other. For example molecule of aluminium is different from the molecule of iron. The amount of space that a matter takes up is called its **volume**.

Atoms

Atoms are made up of fundamental particles electrons, protons and neutrons.

All materials of the universe are made up of minute particles called **atoms**.

Atoms are the basic building blocks of matter. Atoms can join together to form molecules, which in turn form the objects around us. It is not possible to breakdown the atom further retaining the properties of the element. Atoms are not visible to the naked eye. For example, the atoms of the element carbon cannot be further broken down and each part has the properties of carbon.

Commonly Asked Question

1. **Consider the statements given below and select the right answer.**

   Statement A: Molecules are made up of atoms.

   Statement B: At the centre of an atom is the nucleus.

   (A) Statement: A is True

   (B) Statement: B is True

   (C) Both Statement: A and B are True

   (D) Both Statement: A and B are false

   (E) None of these

   Answer: (C)

   Explanation: All the molecules are made up of atoms and there is a nucleus at the centre of an atom.

2. **Which one of the following instruments helps us to see the tiny objects?**

   (A) 

   (B) 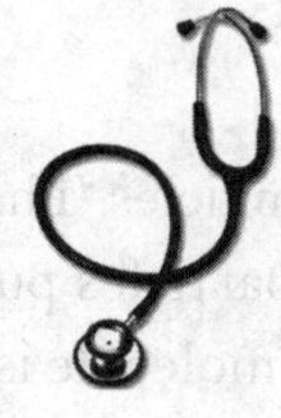

(C) 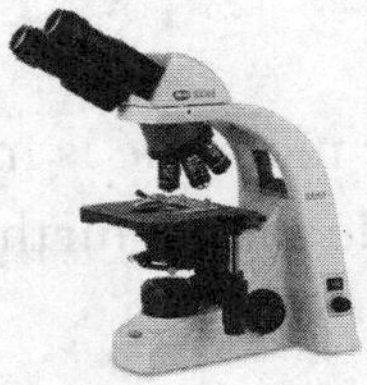

(D) All of these

(E) None of these

Answer: (C)

Explanation: Microscope helps us to see the tiny objects by magnifying them.

Molecules

The smallest particle of matter, which can exist in a free state is called a molecule. Structure of molecules of some elements has been given below.

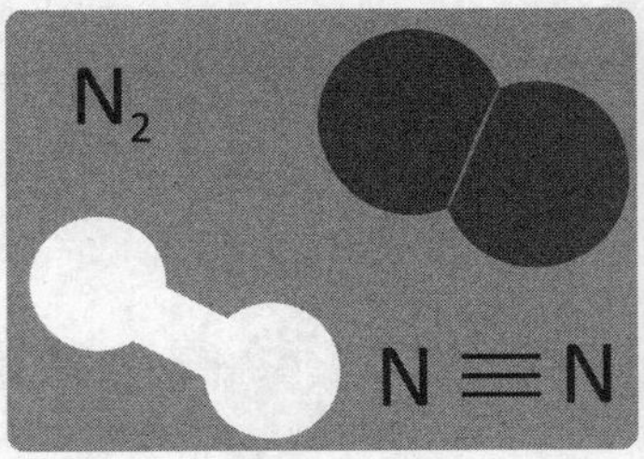

Molecules of nitrogen

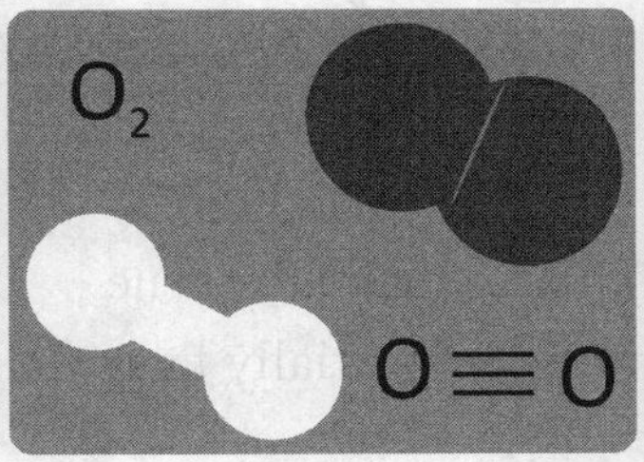

Molecules of oxygen

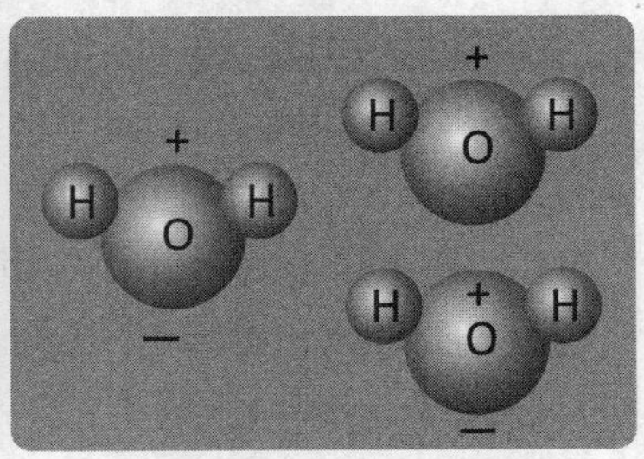

Molecules of water

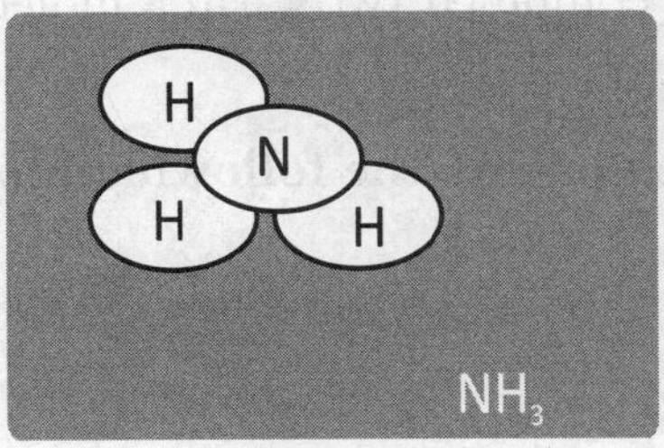

Molecules of ammonia

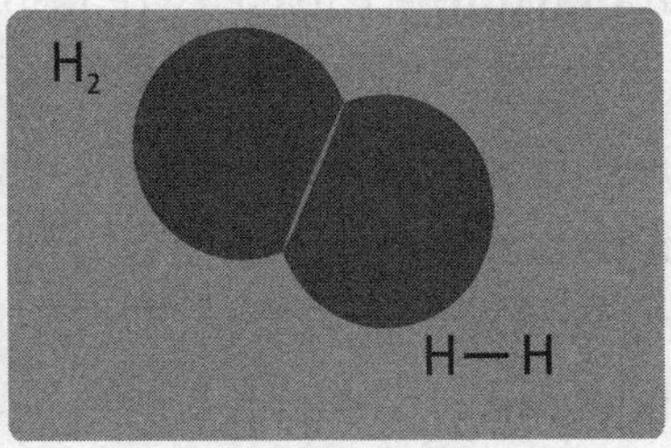

Molecules of hydrogen

Molecules of any given substance are all similar. A molecule is defined as a group of at least two atoms in a definite arrangement. Molecules are formed by the combination of two or more atoms. The Properties of a substance are the properties of its molecule. Molecules can be subdivided to individual atoms. The atoms are bounded together in a molecule. Molecules also are not visible to the naked eye. It can be seen through highly magnifying microscopes and other scientific devices.

Example:

Water is comprised of numerous water molecules. Each water molecule is made up of one oxygen atom and two hydrogen atoms. So a water molecule can be further divided into oxygen and hydrogen atoms.

$$\underset{\text{Hydrogen}}{2H_2} + \underset{\text{Oxygen}}{O_2} \longrightarrow \underset{\text{Water}}{2H_2O}$$

Commonly Asked Question

1. **Consider the statements given below and select the right answer.**

   Statement A: A molecule is defined as a group of at least two atoms.

   Statement B: Molecules are visible to the naked eye.

   (A) Statement: A is true
   (B) Statement: B is true
   (C) Both Statement: A and B are partially true
   (D) Both Statement: A and B are partially false
   (E) None of these

   Answer: (A)

   Explanation: At least two atoms combined two form a molecule which are not seen by the naked eye.

2. **Molecules of water is made of which one of the following kind of atoms?**

   (A) Helium and Oxygen
   (B) Nitrogen only
   (C) Carbon and Hydrogen
   (D) Oxygen and Hydrogen
   (E) None of these

   Answer: (D)

   Explanation: A molecule of water is composed of atoms of oxygen and hydrogen.

States of Matter

Matter is divided into three groups according to the state in which they exist.

Solid

In solids, the molecules are very close to one another and the force of attraction among the molecules is great.

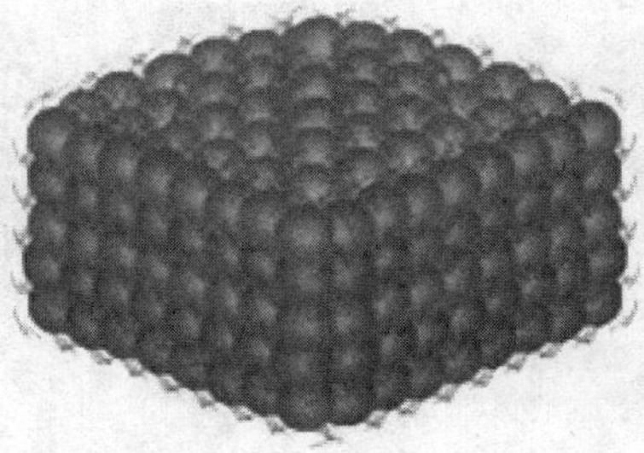

Arrangement of molecules in solid

Because of this close packing and great attraction among the molecules, solids are hard and have a definite volume and definite shape. For example, ice, book, table, etc.

Books

Bag

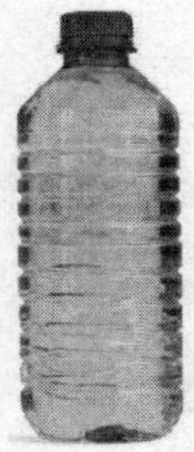

Bottle

Liquid

In liquids, the molecules are not packed very close. They can move about more freely because of less attraction among them.

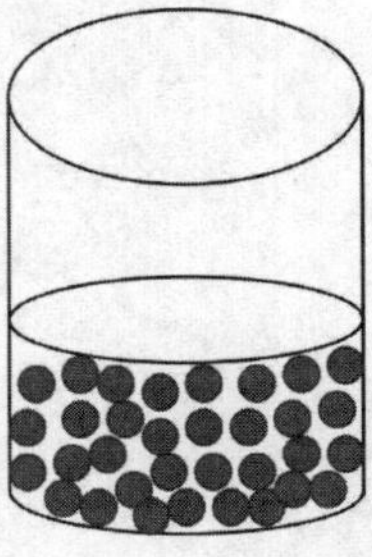

Arrangement of molecules in liquid

This is the reason for the liquid to flow. So liquid has no definite shape but a definite volume. It takes the shape of the container in which it is poured. For example, water, milk, cold drink, petrol, etc.

Water

Milk

Cold drink

Gas

In gases, the molecules are far apart from one another. They have lots of freedom to move. Hence gas has neither fixed shape nor fixed volume.

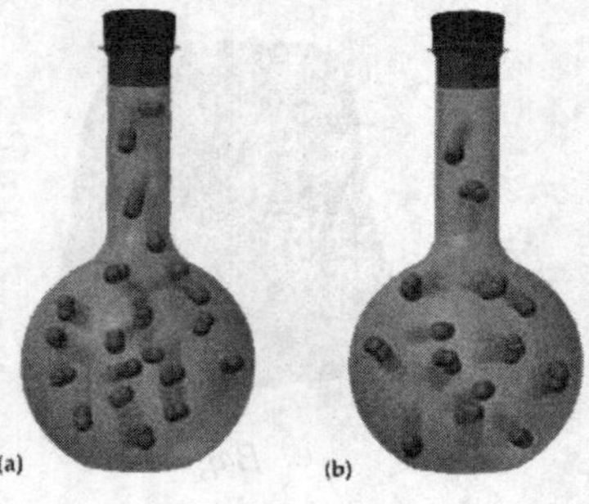

Arrangement of molecules in gas

⏩ Example:

Water vapour, oxygen, nitrogen, smoke, etc.

Water vapour

Smoke

Commonly Asked Question

1. Look at the following figure carefully and choose the correct option for it.

(A) Gas (B) Liquid
(C) Solid (D) Both A and C
(E) All the above

Answer: (C)

Explanation: The picture shown in the question is a solid.

2. In gases, the molecules are separated by large spaces and they have freedom to move about. This gives them their character that is:

(A) No definite shape (B) No definite volume
(C) Definite volume (D) (A) and (B)
(E) None of these

Answer: (D)

Explanation: Gases do not have definite shape and volume.

Physical Change

Physical change is the change in which a substance undergoes the change in its physical properties (shape, size, colour or the state of the substance). A physical change is only a temporary change. This change can be reversed. For example, tear a page from your note book into 4 square pieces. Now lay these pieces on the table in such a manner that it occupies the shape of the original piece of paper. The physical change, brought about by tearing the paper, is back by putting it in order. There is no change in the property of the paper.

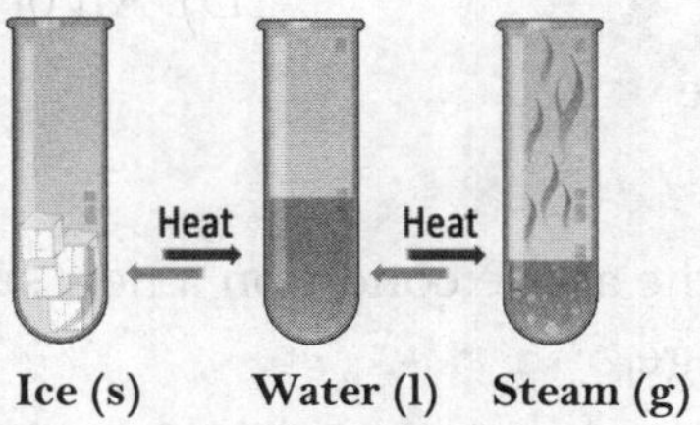

Change in states of water (physical change)

Chemical Change

A chemical change is the change in which new substances are formed and the original substance can't be get back. The change is permanent. For example burning of a cracker is a chemical change in which heat, sound, light and gases are produced and we cannot get back crackers.

Burning of a cracker (chemical change)

Commonly Asked Question

1. Coconut oil in winter solidifies. We leave it in the sunlight and it liquefies again. This type of change in property is called:

(A) No change
(B) Chemical change
(C) Physical change
(D) Biological change
(E) Both (A) and (C)

Answer: (C)

Explanation: In the above condition no new substance is being formed so it is a physical change.

2. Iron gate of a park is exposed to moist air. It gets rusted. Can you name the type of change?

(A) Chemical change
(B) Reversible change
(C) Physical change
(D) All of the above
(E) None of the above

Answer: (A)

Explanation: In the above condition a new substance i.e. rust is formed so it is a chemical change.

DID YOU KNOW?

- ❖ It is believed that an atom is made of 200 or more than 200 subatomic particles.
- ❖ A human hair is about 1 million carbon atoms.
- ❖ A speck of dust might contain 3 trillion atoms.

DID YOU KNOW?

- ❖ **Atom:** Smallest particle of an element.
- ❖ **Molecule:** A molecule is defined as a group of at least two atoms.
- ❖ **States of Matter:** Matter exist in three different states.
- ❖ **Physical Change:** Change in physical property.
- ❖ **Chemical Change:** Change in chemical property.

Self Evaluation Test–4

1. **Which one of the following is a matter?**
   (A) Love (B) Emotion
   (C) Anger (D) Flower
   (E) None of these

2. **We know that all the substances are made up of small particles and the particles are connected with each other with a force. In which one of the following the particles are connected with the greatest force?**
   (A) Bricks (B) Oil
   (C) Smoke (D) All of these
   (E) None of these

3. **Water can exist in which state of matter?**
   (A) Solid (B) Liquid
   (C) Gas (D) All the above
   (E) None of these

4. **In which one of the following molecules, atoms of different elements are joined together?**
   (A) Molecules of hydrogen (B) Molecules of gold

(C) Molecules of water
(D) Molecules of carbon
(E) None of these

5. When we cool a substance to a certain temperature, state of the substance gets changed. If the substance is gas then on cooling it will convert into______.

(A) Solid
(B) Liquid
(C) Gas
(D) All of these
(E) None of these

6. How many atoms of hydrogen are there in one molecule of water?

(A) 1
(B) 2
(C) 3
(D) 4
(E) None of these

7. When we heat a substance, force of attraction among the particles gets______.

(A) Weaker
(B) Strengthen
(C) Remains same
(D) All of these
(E) None of these

8. Which one of the following properties is correct for liquid?

(A) It has fixed volume and fixed shape
(B) It has fixed volume but not fixed shape
(C) It has neither fixed volume nor fixed shape
(D) All of these
(E) None of these

9. Neutron is one of the three basic fundamental particles by which a metal is made up of. Where does neutron lie in the atom?

(A) In the nucleus
(B) Outside the nucleus
(C) Neutron doesn't lie anywhere in the atom
(D) All of these
(E) None of these

10. Which one of the following statements is true?

Statement 1: In physical change, original substance we can get back.
Statement 2: In chemical change, original substance we cannot get back.

(A) Statement 1
(B) Statement 2
(C) Both statements are correct
(D) Both statements are incorrect
(E) None of these

Chapter 5

Force and Energy

Learning Objectives

- Force
- Types of Force
- Work
- Types of Energy
- Sources of Energy

Introduction

To do any kind of work we have to apply force and to apply force we require energy. It shows that these three terms (Work, Force and Energy) are related and dependent on one another.

Work	Force	Energy
Done <————	Applied <————	Needed

Thus we can say that work is only done, when we have the energy to apply force.

Force

Think of the normal activities like catching a ball, throwing a ball, pulling or pushing a chair. Have you ever thought, why a chair moves when we push it or pull it? The chair moves because we apply a force on it.

Force – push or pull an object

Force is push or pull acting on an object. Force is used not only to move an object, but also to stop it. Force is also used to change the direction and position of an object. It is also used to increase or decrease the speed of moving object. While playing cricket, many of you must have been given caught out. The friend of yours who caught the ball has applied force to stop the ball, which was moving in the air by your hitting. The force applied by you is to move the ball and the force applied by your friend is to stop the ball. Both you and your friend has applied force but to do different kinds of work.

Force is applied to hit the ball

Everyone of you must have enjoyed your bicycle ride. You can increase or decrease the speed of the bicycle when you want to. The speed of the bicycle depends on the rider. The rider apply force to increase or decrease the speed of the cycle.

Force is used to increase or decrease the speed of moving object. Children, while playing with football or basketball have the habit of sitting on it or pushing it against the hard surfaces. While doing so shape of ball gets changed. Force is used to change the shape of the object. Therefore, force is push or pull acting on an object. Force is used to move objects, to stop the moving objects, to change the direction of the moving objects, to decrease or increase the speed of the object and also to change the shape of the object.

Commonly Asked Question

1. **Force applied can make the ____________.**

(A) Body move (B) Body stop

(C) Change the direction of motion (D) Change shape

(E) All of the above

Answer: (E)

Explanation: Force applied can move the object, stop the moving object, change the direction of motion and change the shape of the object.

2. **Which one of the following statements is correct?**

Statement 1: Force is used to increase or decrease the speed of a moving object.

Statement 2: Force is not used to increase or decrease the speed of a moving object.

(A) Statement 1

(B) Statement 2

(C) Both statements are correct

(D) Both statements are incorrect

(E) None of these

Answer: (A)

Explanation: Force is used to increase or decrease the speed of an object.

Types of Force

In this chapter, we will study about two types of forces:

(i) Frictional force

(ii) Gravitational force

Friction

Friction is a type of force exerted when two surfaces are in contact with each other. Let us understand it in a simpler way with an example.

Example:

A bicycle gradually slows down and finally stops, when we stop pedalling. A ball that you have rolled, gradually slows down and then comes to rest. When you push your toy, it moves for some distance and then slows down and finally stops after some time. These are few of the events that most of you have experienced. Can you guess why the moving object comes to rest automatically? In all the above cases there is no force that appears to act on the object, then why the object's speed slows down and finally stops? Or, is there some force acting on these objects? Yes, the force is known as **friction.**

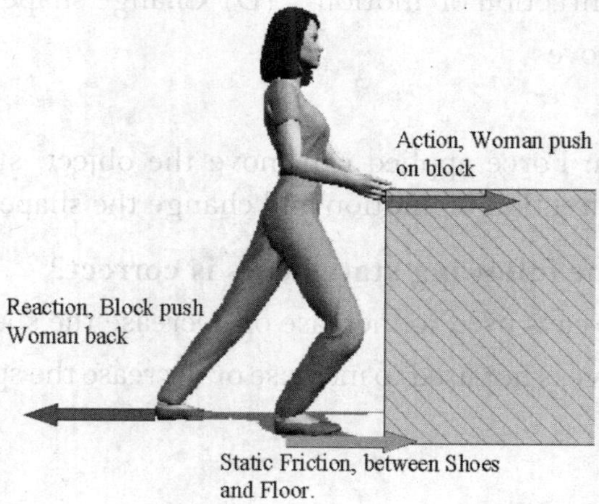

Friction always acts on all the moving objects, but the direction of force of friction is always opposite to the direction of motion of the object. In all the above cases, it is the force of friction which slows down the speed and finally stops the moving objects, like a moving ball, bicycle or a moving toy. Surfaces in contact with each other, exert force on each other. This force exerted by the surface is in the opposite direction to the other. This causes resistance of motion of one surface on the other. This opposing force is called the **force of friction** or even as force of resistance. This opposing force is the main cause of slowing down of the movement of the object.

We need this force of friction in all our actions. If there was no friction we would not be able to walk, run, play or doing any such activities. Anything that started to move would never stop, a toy would keep moving or the ball would keep rolling. Imagine how the world would be with object once set in motion always remaining in the same condition.

Force of friction depends on the surface of the moving object. In general, rough surfaces like, stoned or kacha road, floor with carpet has more friction as compared to smooth floor.

Gravity

Gravity is the force with which objects are pulled downwards towards the centre of the Earth. Let us understand it better with an example.

Ball falling down due to the force of gravity

▶▶ Example:

You must have observed that when you throw a ball up, it acquires certain height and then comes back toward the surface of the Earth. Have you ever given it a thought why this happens? Well, this happens because of the force of gravity. Actually what happens is, when you toss the ball up in the air, you apply a force on the ball. This moves the ball up against the gravitational force applied by the Earth. But due to the force of gravity, speed of the ball gradually slows down and finally stops for a while. And then it returns toward the centre of the Earth. Thus we can say that force of gravity is an attractive force that pulls all the objects towards the centre of the Earth. The force of gravity acts on all of us and on all object, all the time, without our being aware of it. It was **Sir Isaac Newton** who discovered this force of gravity.

Fruits or leaves of the plants fall towards the ground, the water comes downwards from the tap, a pen or a note book falls downwards only, are the examples showing the force of gravity working on them.

Commonly Asked Question

1. **When we push an object it covers some distance and finally gets stopped. Which one of the following forces causes this?**

   (A) Gravity (B) Friction

   (C) Muscular force (D) Nuclear force

   (E) None of the above

   Answer: (B)

   Explanation: Friction is the resisting force which stops the movement of moving object.

2. **Name the force by which Earth attracts all other objects.**

   (A) Magnetic force (B) Frictional force

   (C) Electrostatic force (D) Gravitational force

   (E) All of the above

   Answer: (D)

   Explanation: Gravitation force acts on all the objects all the time.

Work

When force is used to move an object from its position, we say that work is done.

To move a table from one position to another, we require to apply force on the table. You must have pushed a chair many a times. Why the chair moves? The chair moves because of the force applied by you. You apply the force on the chair and move it from its original position to a new position of your choice. This is the process of doing work.

Work done by moving an object

Work is always done by a force. We often name the agent that has applied this force and say that the agent has done work.

When a girl pushes a notebook on the table, we say that the girl has done work on the notebook. Actually the work is done by the force exerted by the girl.

Energy

Any kind of work can only be done when we have the energy to apply force. Energy can also be defined as the ability to apply force which in turn does the work.

Reading, writing, sitting, eating, playing these are some activities that we all do. Now think of activities like climbing, riding a bicycle, carrying load, lifting heavy items. To do all those works, even the simplest one, we need energy. We use energy even while we are sleeping.

Energy is also required by matter to change its states. We need heat energy to change water into vapour. Ice is changed into water, which again requires energy.

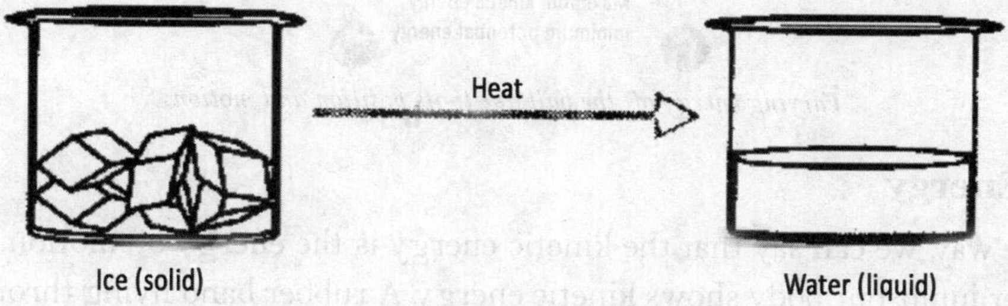

Changing state of matter

Energy is present in different forms like heat energy, light energy, sound energy, electrical energy, mechanical energy, chemical energy and nuclear energy. Energy has the ability to be converted from one form to another.

Types of Energy

There are two major types of energy. The energy present in a resting body is the **potential energy** and the other is the **kinetic energy,** which is present in the objects in motion.

Potential Energy

Potential energy is the energy of an object due to the position of its body. The S.I. unit of potential energy is 'joule'.

Example:

When a rubber band is stretched to the left, it exerts a force to the right so as to return to its original un-stretched position. When a mass is lifted up, the force of gravity on the object brings it back to the ground. Roller coaster climbs a hill, it has maximum potential energy at the top of the hill. When the Roller coaster speeds down the hill it starts to loose potential energy.

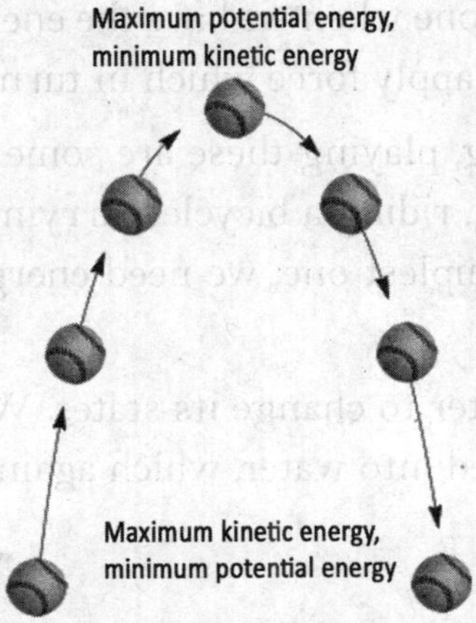

Varying energy of the ball due to its position and motion

Kinetic Energy

In a simple way, we can say that the kinetic energy is the energy of motion. When we walk, run or jump, our body shows kinetic energy. A rubber band flying through the air has kinetic energy. You all must have played with yoyo. How does it work? A yoyo at the rest position has potential energy, at the top has the maximum potential energy. When the yoyo starts to fall, the potential energy begin to change into kinetic energy. At the bottom, its all potential energy has been converted into kinetic energy.

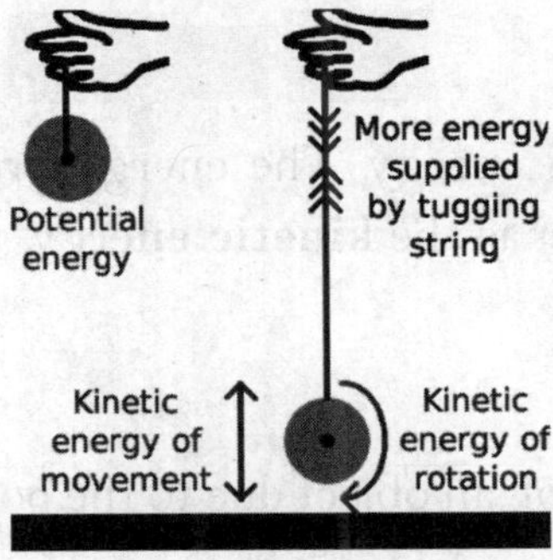

Yoyo at different position.

Example:

In the game of billiards the players give kinetic energy to the cue ball by striking it with the cue stick. If the ball, which is hit, collides with another ball, it slows down, and the ball it collided with, starts to move. This is because the kinetic energy is passed on to it.

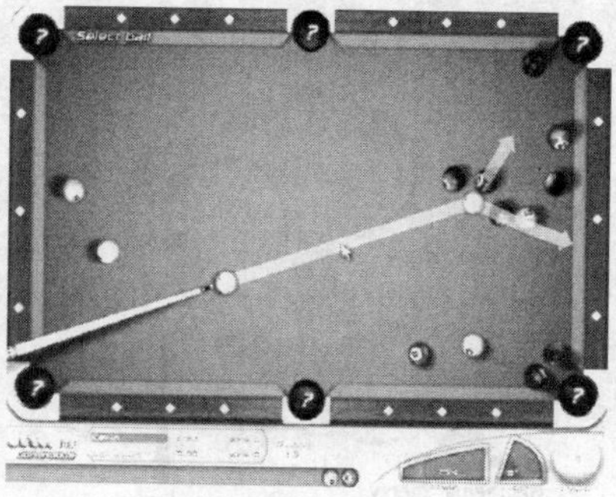

Billiard Board

Commonly Asked Question

1. **A brick lying on the roof of a house, which is 10 m up from the ground, possess:**

(A) Potential energy (B) Kinetic energy
(C) Heat energy (D) All of these
(E) None of these

Answer: (A)

Explanation: The brick lying on the roof of a house possesses potential energy due to it is position.

2. **As a ball rolls down on an inclined plane, it has:**

(A) Only kinetic energy
(B) Only potential energy
(C) Both potential energy and kinetic energy
(D) Has no energy
(E) None of these

Answer: (C)

Explanation: A ball rolling down on an inclined plane possesses both potential as well as kinetic energy due to its position and motion.

Sources of Energy

Any system from where energy is trapped is called a source of energy. Sun is the ultimate source of almost all energy. Energy that the Earth receives from the Sun is in the form of heat and light. Some of the main sources from where we get energy are as follows:

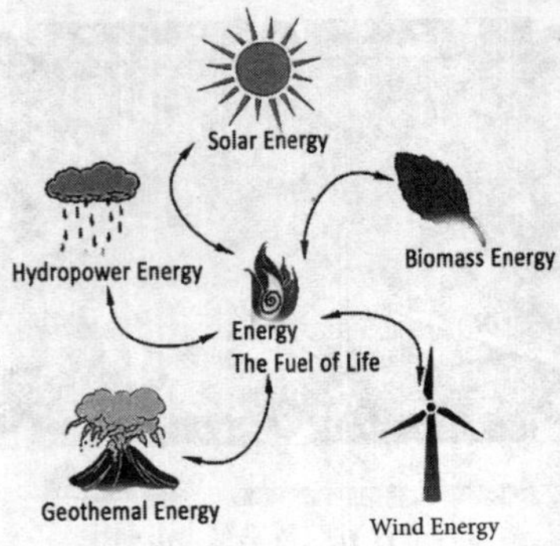

Different sources of energy

Solar Energy

Solar energy is the energy that we get from the Sun. It is in the form of heat and light. The green plants use this solar energy to make food for all living things on the earth. Animals eat the food made by the plants and get energy to do work. Animals can't use the solar energy directly. We depend on plants for this process. Thus we can say that all living things are dependent on solar energy directly or indirectly for their energy need.

Energy from the sun

Wind Energy

Wind, as we understand, is the movement of air around us. As we have seen earlier in this chapter that any moving substance has energy, so wind also has energy. The energy of the blowing wind is called wind energy. As the energy is due to movement of substance, the energy associated is the kinetic energy. Wind energy is also used by boatman to sail boats and to generate electricity.

Windmill used to harness wind energy to produce electricity

Tamil Nadu is the state in our country, which produces largest amount of electricity using wind energy. Wind energy is an eco-friendly and efficient mode of production of electricity.

Water Energy

Moving water like any moving substance has energy. Many natural processes like weathering of rocks and pebble formation is due to moving water. We use this energy of moving water to produce electricity. Electricity, produced by this process is environment friendly and pollution free.

Use of moving water to produce electricity

Atomic or Nuclear Energy

Each atom has a centrally located nucleus, which consists of protons and neutrons. When nucleus of an atom breaks down or two or more nuclei combines together to form a single nucleus, huge amount of energy is released. This energy is called atomic energy.

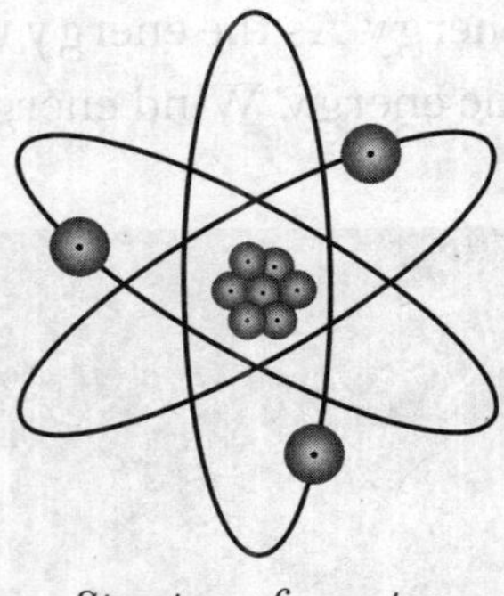

Structure of an atom

Energy of the atoms can be used to produce electricity for our use. In India Nuclear Power Corporation (NPC) produces electricity from the energy of the atoms. The sun also gets its heat and light energy from the atomic energy.

Energy From the Fossil Fuels

Fossil fuels are the fuels, which are obtained from the remains of plants and animals that got buried inside the Earth millions of years ago. Examples of fossil fuels are coal, petrol and natural gas. Fossil fuels are excellent source of energy for the mankind. They have energy stored in them, which is released by burning them.

Different uses of fossil fuels

The energy from the fossil fuels is used to run machines in the factories. Vehicles on the road move using petrol or diesel. Our cooking gas (L.P.G.) is also a fossil fuel. Coal is used in thermal power plants to produce electricity. The modern lifestyle that we lead today can't be thought without these fossil fuels. We need them for everything, right from cooking at home to our movement on road and air, to the things that we produce in our factories and the electricity that we use to lighten our houses. Fossil fuel is available only in limited quantity. We should use them carefully and wisely . Burning of fossil fuel cause air pollution.

There are also some other sources of energy. For example, tidal energy, geothermal energy, ocean thermal energy, chemical energy, etc.

Commonly Asked Question

1. **Solar Energy is the energy that we get from the ________.**

   (A) Wind (B) Electricity
   (C) Tide (D) Atoms
   (E) Sun

   Answer: (E)

   Explanation: Energy from the Sun is called as solar energy.

2. **Which one of the following statements is correct?**

   Statement 1: Fossil fuels are sources of energy.

   Statement 2: Wind is a source of energy.

   (A) Statement 1 (B) Statement 2
   (C) Both statements are correct (D) Both statements are incorrect
   (E) None of these

   Answer: (C)

   Explanation: Fossil fuels and wind both are the sources of energy.

Measurement

We need to measure different things in our daily life like length of objects, height, weight (fruits, vegetables, etc.) quantity of milk, water and so on.

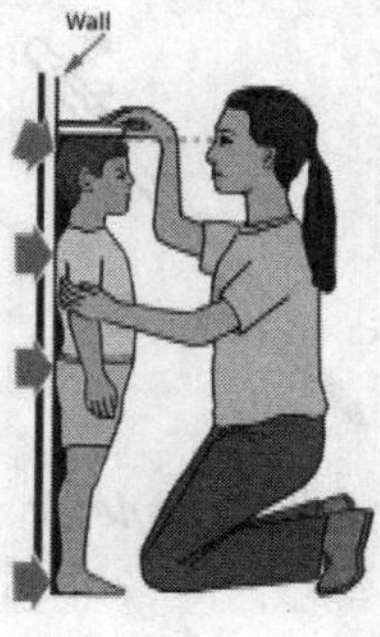

Measurement of Length

In early days, people used body parts to measure lengths.

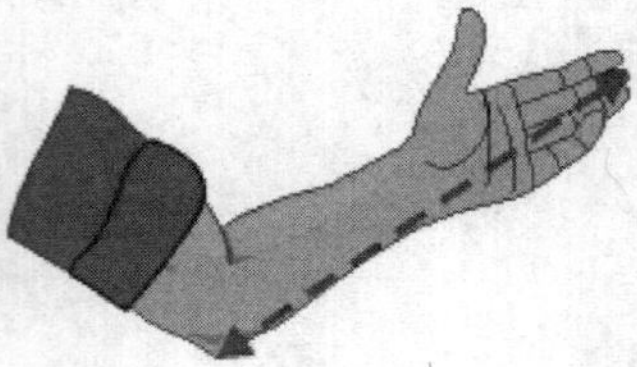

Cubit

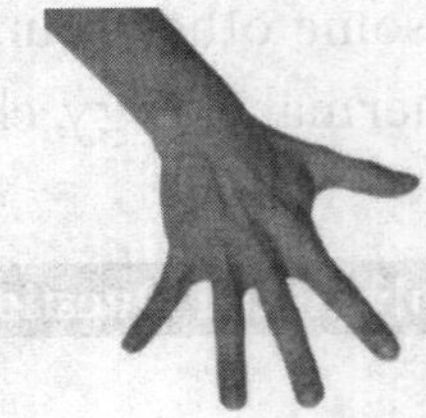

Hand span

The metre is what we normally use for measuring lengths. Smaller lengths are measured in centimetres. Metre is written as **m** and centimetre as **cm**.

Measurement of Mass

Mass tells us how heavy or light an object is. We use weighing scales to find the mass of an object.

Just as we use metre for measuring length, we use kilogram for measuring mass. Smaller weights are measured in grams. Kilogram is written as **kg** and gram is written as **g**.

Measurement of Capacity

Capacity of a container is the amount of liquid it can hold.

Litre is the commonly used unit for measuring capacity. Smaller units are measured in millilitres. Litre is written as **l** and millilitres as **ml**.

Some Other Units of Measurement

In everyday life we also need to measure things that do not involve length, mass, and capacity. Time and temperature are two such examples.

Time is measured in seconds. The measurement of hotness or coldness of an object is called temperature. Temperature can be measured with the help of a thermometer.

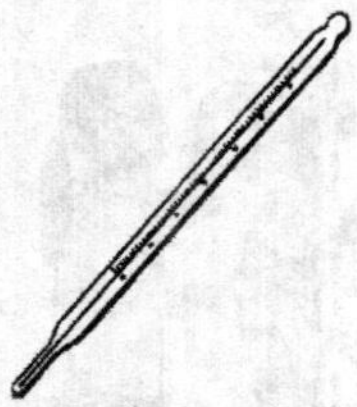

Thermometer

Commonly Asked Question

1. **Which of the following is a unit for measuring length?**

(A) Metre (B) Litres
(C) Millilitres (D) Kilogram
(E) None of these

Answer: (A)

Explanation: For measuring length we normally use metre.

2. **Which of the following tells us how heavy an object is?**

(A) Mass (B) Volume
(C) Length (D) Temperature
(E) None of these

Answer: (A)

Explanation: Mass tells us how heavy or light an object is.

DID YOU KNOW?

- Mars has a lower gravity than Earth, therefore a person weighing 100 kg (220 pounds) on Earth would only weigh 38kg (84 pounds) on Mars.
- Only one third of the energy in burning coal reaches the consumer as electricity.
- If 10,000 schools turned off their lights for one minute it could save $81,885.

SUMMARY

- **Force:** It is pull or push acting on an object.
- **Friction:** Frictional force opposes the motion of a moving object.
- **Work:** Work is said to be done when force is applied to move an object.
- **Types of Energy:** There are two types of energy depending on the object at rest or motion i.e. potential energy and kinetic energy.
- **Source of energy**: It is the system from which energy can be obtained.

Self Evaluation Test–5

1. **The energy of an object which it possesses due to its motion is called:**
(A) Potential energy (B) Kinetic energy
(C) Magnetic energy (D) Electrical energy
(E) All of these

2. **In the following figure, the direction of the ball changed on colliding with the wall because:**

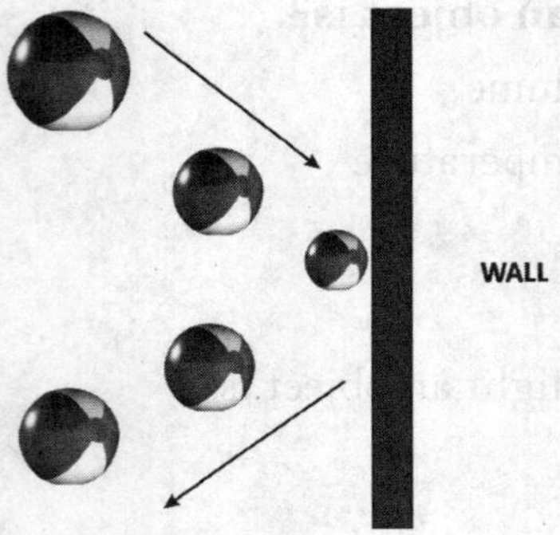

(A) Wall applied force on the ball
(B) Ball automatically changed its direction
(C) Softness of the wall
(D) All of these
(E) None of these

3. **We sprinkle powder on the carrom board. Why?**
(A) To increase friction
(B) To get pleasant smell
(C) To decrease friction
(D) To make the carrom board white so that it looks beautiful.
(E) None of these

4. **Objects fall down towards the earth due to the force of _______.**

(A) Friction (B) Gravity

(C) Force of our muscle (D) Air

(E) None of these

5. **What name has been given to the energy which lights the bulbs in our houses?**

(A) Electrical energy (B) Chemical energy

(C) Magnetic energy (D) All of these

(E) None of these

6. **Work is said to be done when _______ moves an object from one position to another.**

(A) Friction

(B) Resistance

(C) Force

(D) All of these

(E) None of these

7. **We suspend an object to the end of the hook of a spring. The spring is stretched.**

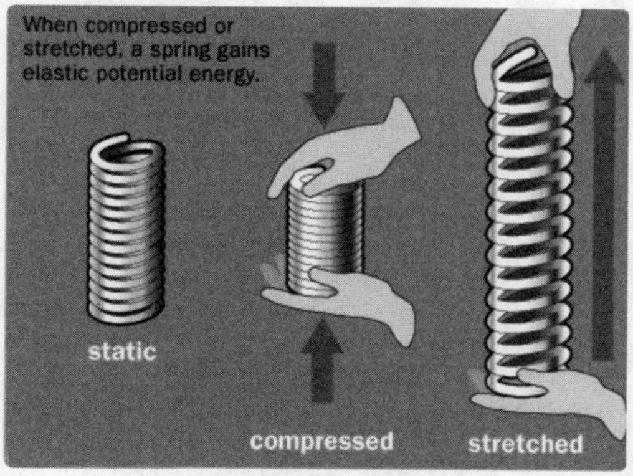

What type of energy is stored in the stretched spring?

(A) Pull energy (B) Push energy

(C) Potential Energy (D) Kinetic Energy

(E) Solar Energy

8. **A ball, which is thrown up always comes down. Falling ball is losing its potential energy and gaining up which type of energy?**

(A) Kinetic energy
(B) Solar energy
(C) Atomic energy
(D) Heat energy
(E) None of these

9. **Solar cooker uses _______ energy to cook food.**

(A) Wind
(B) Water
(C) Atomic
(D) Solar
(E) None of these

10. **Use of fossil fuels should be reduced as the burning of it causes ____.**

(A) Water pollution
(B) Air pollution
(C) Noise pollution
(D) All of these
(E) None of these

Chapter 6

Rocks and Soil

Learning Objectives

- Types of Rocks and Their Uses
- Layers of Soil
- Soil Erosion
- Soil Conservation

Introduction

The Earth as we see it is made up of rocks, soil, and minerals.

Rocks

Soil

Minerals

The lower layers of the soil are the rocks. If you observe a rock closely you will see small grains on it. A single rock may have grains of different colour. These grains are the minerals occurring naturally. Many rocks that contain metals are called ores. We get iron, copper, aluminium from their respective ores. Gemstones are the minerals in the form of crystals e.g. diamond, emeralds, rubies, etc. Soil is the uppermost layer of the Earth's surface. Soil is responsible for the greenery and life on the Earth's surface. It supports the plants, which produces food for the entire living world. Soil is also home to many microorganisms and insects. There are different kinds of soil. Sandy soil, clayey soil and loamy soil.

Types of Rocks and Their Uses

Our Earth is made up of rocks. There are 3 kinds of rocks. They are:

(A) Igneous rocks

(B) Sedimentary rocks

(C) Metamorphic rocks

Igneous Rocks

Igneous rocks are formed from the molten rock material. The hot liquid material comes out on the Earth surface, from deep inside the Earth, through cracks and then cools down. These rocks contain minerals such as quartz, mica, silica, iron, etc. Granite and pumice are two types of igneous rocks.

Granite

Pumice

Sedimentary Rocks

Sedimentary rocks are formed by splitting up of materials, such as gravels and pebbles, by wind, water and snow of the surface of the soil. As the materials pile up on the top, the pressure hardens the lower layer and converts it into rocks. For example, sandstone and limestone.

Sandstone

Limestone

Metamorphic Rocks

Metamorphic rocks are formed by the action of heat and pressure on sedimentary and igneous rocks. They are the rocks that have gone through changes. As the name suggests metamorphic means change. These rocks were originally sedimentary or igneous rocks. The changes make them tougher and harder, for example, slate and marble.

Slate

Marble

Commonly Asked Question

1. **How many kinds of rocks are there?**

   (A) 5 kinds (B) 3 kinds

   (C) 10 kinds (D) 8 kinds

   (E) None of these

   Answer: (B)

   Explanation: There are 3 kinds of rocks: Igneous, Sedimentary and Metamorphic.

2. Pumice is an example of which one of the following kind of rocks?

(A) Sedimentary rocks (B) Metamorphic rocks

(C) Igneous rocks (D) Both (A) and (B)

(E) None of these

Answer: (C)

Explanation: Pumice is an Igneous rock.

Layers of Soil

Soil is defined as the upper layer of the Earth's surface, which contains sand, organic matter (dead animals or plants), minerals with little amount of water and air. It is one of the most important natural resources, which is capable of supporting life on Earth. Soil supports and nourish plant life. It is also home to many small animals and microorganisms.

Soil profile is the vertical section of the soil, from the surface to the bedrock below. Each layer of the soil has different colour and texture. These layers are called **horizons**. A typical soil profile has four different layers.

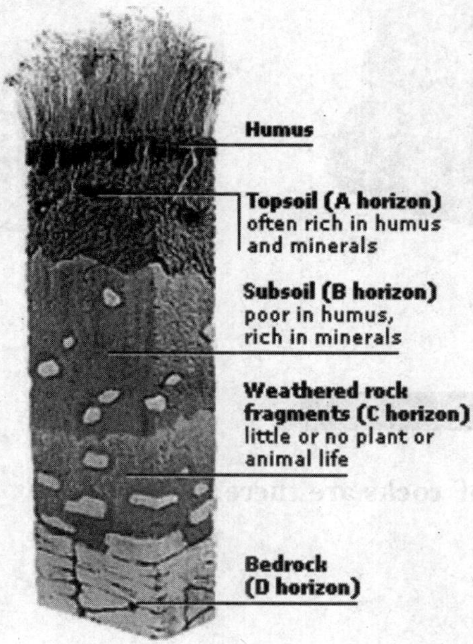

Different Layers of Soil

A Horizon or Topsoil

This is the dark coloured uppermost layer rich in humus.

B Horizon or Subsoil

This is middle layer generally coarse and rich in minerals. It is light in colour due to very less amount of humus.

C Horizon or Weathered Rocks

This is the third layer which is made up of small lumps of rocks crevices cracks. It is the zone of infertility.

D Horizon or Bedrocks

The fourth layer is made up of unweathered, non porous and impervious parent rocks. This is the bedrock. This layer is hard and very difficult to dig. This layer provides the base for the upper three layers.

Commonly Asked Question

1. **Which one of the following is the uppermost layer of the soil?**

   (A) A-horizon (B) B-horizon
   (C) C-horizon (D) D-horizon
   (E) All of these

   Answer: (A)

   Explanation: Topsoil i.e. A-horizon is the uppermost layer of the soil.

2. **Julia took some soil in a covered container. She heated it slowly, after some time she observed some droplets of water under the cover of the container. What does this show?**

   (A) Soil has humus (B) Soil has sand
   (C) Soil has gravel (D) Soil has moisture
   (E) Soil has air

   Answer: (D)

   Explanation: Water is also an ingredient of soil that is why Julia observed droplets of water under the cover of the container.

Soil Erosion

Soil erosion means the removal of the topsoil (the fertile layer) by the action of natural forces, like, wind and water. It is a slow and steady process where the top layer is lost and the land becomes barren and unfit for agriculture. Soil erosion is a natural process but the rate of this process has greatly increased by human activities, which are discussed below.

Soil Erosion

Deforestation

Cutting down of trees on large scale is called deforestation. We cut down trees, clear up forests to build our farms, hotels, houses. This provides us both space and the wood for our need. But in the process, as land gets cleared of vegetation, no roots remained to hold the top soil. This leads to an increase in soil erosion.

Deforestation

Overgrazing by Animals

Overgrazing of the land by cattle, goat, sheep, which is reared by humans beings for their needs, is another cause of soil erosion. Overgrazing exposes the soil by removing the plants shield that protects it. This in turn causes an increase in soil erosion.

Overgrazing by the animals

Commonly Asked Question

1. **The carrying away of the topsoil by natural agents like wind and water is called:**

   (A) Degradation (B) Soil pollution

   (C) Soil erosion (D) Leaching

   (E) None of these

   Answer: (C)

   Explanation: Loss of the topsoil by natural or unnatural agents is called soil erosion.

2. **Deforestation is:**

   (A) Growing of trees (B) Cutting of trees

   (C) Trimming trees (D) Caring of trees

   (E) None of the above

   Answer: (B)

   Explanation: Cutting of trees on large scale is called deforestation.

Soil Conservation

Soil conservation is the process in which we use techniques that will protect the soil from agents like wind and water. This also takes into account the methods that add to the fertility and protects the natural qualities of the soil.

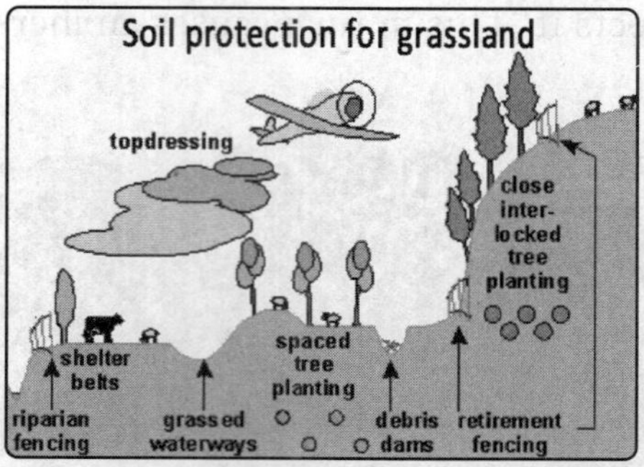

The Technique and the Methods of Soil Conservation are

Afforestation

Afforestation is also known as planting of trees. This is a major check on the rate of soil erosion. Trees and grasses grown on hilly areas prevents soil erosion by water flowing down the slope.

Afforestation

Soil Cover

The farmland should be covered with grasses or dried trees and bushes after harvesting of a crop. This will ensure that the soil is not bare and wind cannot easily carry it away.

Soil Cover

Shelter Belts

Soil erosion can be reduced by reducing the speed of the wind. Hedges and small bushy trees can be grown along the edge of the farmland as wind breakers.

Shelter Belts

Crop Rotation

Crop rotation simply means rotation of the crops. Different crops should be grown on the farmland, one alternating the other. This gives soil the time to recover the minerals that earlier crops have used. It also helps to maintain the quality and fertility of the soil.

Crop Rotation

Terrace or Step Farming

Terrace or step farming is done in hills by cutting steps in the slopes. This type of farming reduces the speed of water as it flow down. As a result erosion of soil gets reduced. The soil removed from one step is deposited on the next step. This helps in further slowing down of erosion.

Terrace or Step Farming

Construction of Embankments

Rivers constantly remove soil of their banks. Strong embankments of rocks so that it can bind the soil or by building dams along the banks can prevent the soil erosion from flooding.

Construction of Embankments

Commonly Asked Question

1. **Method used to retain the quality of soil and its mineral content:**

(A) Step farming (B) Crop rotation
(C) Afforestation (D) Deforestation
(E) None of these

Answer: (B)

Explanation: The quality and mineral content of the soil can be maintained by crop rotation method.

2. **Protection of soil from erosion is known as_____.**

(A) Soil erosion (B) Crop rotation
(C) Afforestation (D) Soil conservation
(E) None of these

Answer: (D)

Explanation: Soil can be conserved by preventing soil erosion.

DID YOU KNOW?

- The average quarter acre lawn contains 50 to 250 earthworms.
- It can take 100 to 500 years to create one-inch of soil.
- Just one gram of soil contains 5000 to 7000 different species of bacteria.
- The first recorded use of turquoise dates back to 5000 BC in Mesopotamia, where people used the gemstone to make beads.

SUMMARY

- **Rock:** Earth's crust is made up of rocks which has minerals.
- **Soil:** The uppermost layer of the Earth.
- **Type of rock:** There are 3 different types of rocks igneous, sedimentary and metamorphic.
- **Layer of soil:** There are four different layers of soil according to their composition.
- **Soil erosion:** Removal of top and fertile layer of soil by natural agents like wind and water.
- **Soil conservation:** Protection of soil from erosion.

Self Evaluation Test–6

1. **Quartzite is a type of which form of rock?**
(A) Metamorphic (B) Sedimentary
(C) Igneous (D) Both (A) and (C)
(E) None of these

2. **Marble is a metamorphic rock formed from intense squeeze and heated________.**
(A) Granite (B) Pumice
(C) Limestone (D) Sandstone
(E) Slate

3. **Fossils of plants and animals are commonly found in which types of rocks?**
(A) Igneous rocks (B) Metamorphic
(C) Sedimentary rocks (D) Both A and B
(E) None of the above

4. **Cutting down of trees on large scale is known as:**
(A) Afforestation (B) Deforestation
(C) Conservation (D) All of these
(E) None of the above

5. **In addition to rocks, soil particles also has______.**
(A) Minerals (B) Organic matter
(C) Water (D) Air
(E) All the above

6. **Breaking up of rocks by natural agents like wind, rain and temperature is called:**
(A) Erosion (B) Gradation
(C) Denudation (D) Weathering
(E) Pollution

7. Which one of the following layers of soil contains maximum amount of humus?

(A) A horizon
(B) B horizon
(C) C horizon
(D) D horizon
(E) Rocks

8. The process of soil formation is known as ______.

(A) Soil erosion
(B) Soil conservation
(C) Pedogenesis
(D) Heterogenesis
(E) None of the above

9. Granite is an example of which one of the following kind of rocks?

(A) Igneous rock
(B) Sedimentary rock
(C) Metamorphic rock
(D) All of these
(E) None of these

10. Tea farming is done in hilly areas. Which type of farming is this?

(A) Land Farming
(B) Terrace Farming
(C) Alternate Farming
(D) Crop rotation
(E) None of these

Chapter 7 Our Environment

Learning Objectives

- Environment
- Types of Pollution
- Effects of pollution in Our Environment
- Acid Rain
- Global Warming
- Remedies of Pollution

Environment

Environment is the natural surrounding of a living thing in which it lives and survives. Environment is everything that makes up the surrounding of a living thing.

Natural Environment

Environment comprises of both living (biotic) and non-living things (abiotic). The non-living things in the environment are sunlight, water, air, temperature, etc. The living things in the environment are human, plants, animals, etc. Each living thing has its own environment where it lives and grows. For example, environment of a plant are sunlight, weather, air, water, soil in which it grows and the animal that consumes it. We, human beings, depend on our environment for all our needs. Each of the living things depends on the other living and non-living thing in its environment for its survival.

Humans, while making life more comfortable for themselves, have damaged the environment in which they live, in many ways. Our actions are causing disastrous changes in the environment. We exploit our environment to our maximum utility and in turn do nothing for its good. The condition is very alarming and needs proper thinking and action. We should do everything possible to save our environment before it is too late.

Types of Pollution

Pollution is spoiling of natural resources like air, water and soil by releasing harmful substances. Pollution of air, water and soil has had harmful effects not only on us but on the entire living world.

Air Pollution

Harmful substances in the air causing bad effect on the living things, is called air pollution. Most of the air pollution comes from the smoke of factories, vehicles, burning of fuels, etc.

Air pollution

Water Pollution

When harmful substances from factories, farms, hospitals, sewage from homes are thrown into the water bodies like river, pond, lake and ocean, this causes water pollution. Mixing of unwanted substances, which makes water unfit for drinking and other purposes, is called water pollution. The release of harmful substances kills the living organisms present in water. The balance of the living things in the water bodies is destroyed and the water becomes unfit for use.

Water Pollution

Land or Soil Pollution

When harmful and poisonous substances are released into the soil, it pollutes the soil. This is known as soil pollution. The use of chemical fertilizer and chemical pesticides (kill pest) in the farmland pollutes the soil. Throwing of the waste is also a major cause of soil pollution. The waste like plastic bags, tyre-tube (non-biodegradable) remains on the surface of the soil for a very long time, because non-biodegradable substances are not easily disintegrated into soil. Thus non-biodegradable substances are one of the major causes of soil pollution.

Land pollution

Commonly Asked Question

1. The substances that cause pollution are called________.

(A) Dirt
(B) Pollutants
(C) Smoke
(D) Both (A) and (C)
(E) None of the above

Answer: (B)

Explanation: Pollutants are the substances which cause the pollution.

2. **Consider the statements given below and select the right answer.**

   Statement A: Pollution is caused by natural factors also.

   Statement B: Human being also contributes to pollution in a large way.

   (A) Statement A is correct

   (B) Statement B is correct

   (C) Both Statement A and B are correct

   (D) Statement A is correct but B is false

   (E) Both Statement A and B are false

   Answer: (C)

   Explanation: Pollution can be caused by natural as well as artificial factors and we also contribute in causing pollution.

Effects of Pollution

Any type of pollution is very harmful for the living things. Let's know about them.

Effects of Air Pollution

Air pollution makes air unfit for breathing. Taking in this air causes breathing problems and lung diseases. Global warming and acid rain are other major effects of air pollution. Air pollution also has been damaging ozone layer which protects us from ultra violet rays coming from space and save the life on the Earth.

Effects of air pollution on plants

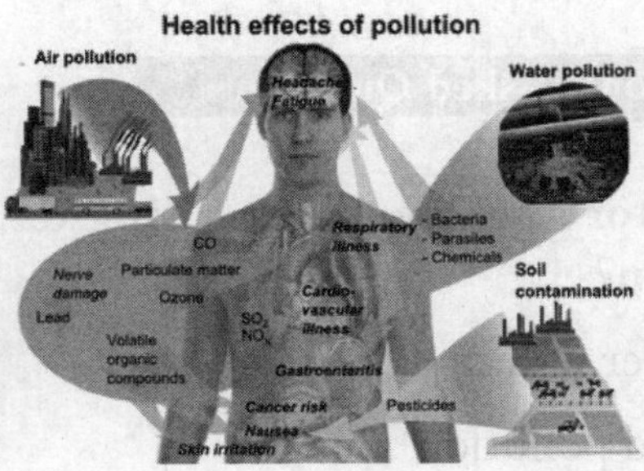

Effects of air pollution on human health

Effects of Water Pollution

The unfit or polluted water if used for drinking, can cause dysentery, diarrhea, typhoid and many other diseases. The living organisms present in the water bodies, where chemical waste is thrown, too becomes poisonous. If we consume these fish, crab, etc. we are likely to fall sick.

Effects of water pollution

Effect of Soil Pollution

Soil gets polluted by the chemicals used to kill pest and weeds (unwanted plants). Chemical fertilizers used for higher productivity, seeps slowly into the soil layers. Crops grown on these soils is not good for our health. These chemicals are slowly getting into the food chain.

Effects of land pollution

Commonly Asked Question

1. **Respiratory problems are rising day by day. This is due to which type of pollution?**

   (A) Water pollution (B) Air pollution

   (C) Land pollution (D) Both (A) and (B)

   (E) All of the above

   Answer: (B)

   Explanation: Air pollution contributes in increasing respiratory problems.

2. **Look at the following picture carefully**

It is one of the major source of______.

(A) Air pollution
(B) Land pollution
(C) Water pollution
(D) A and B
(E) None of these

Answer: (A)

Explanation: The picture given above is showing air pollution.

Acid Rain

Harmful gases released by the burning of coal, by automobiles, factories, oil refinery mix with water vapour present in the air to form harmful substance called **acid.** The acid comes down with rain making the rain acidic. This is called **acid rain**. This acid rain can cause damage to soil, plants, organisms that lives in the rivers, streams, lakes, etc. Acid rain even causes damage to the buildings and results in harmful diseases in humans. The damaging effect of acid rain can best be seen in our great heritage building, Taj Mahal. The white marbles of Taj Mahal are getting discoloured by the effect of acid rain. The monument does not look as white as it used to look some 30-40 years back. Government of India is taking several steps to save the Taj.

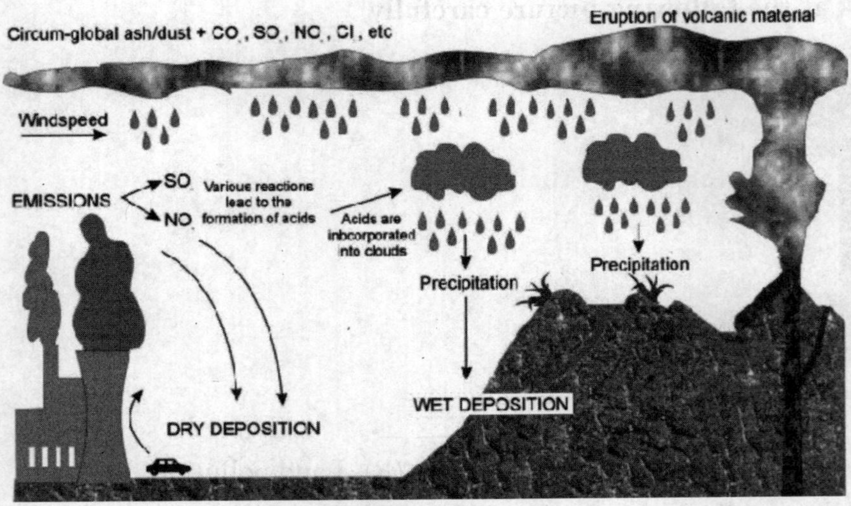

Formation of acid rain

Commonly Asked Question

1. Acid rain a very dangerous phenomenon is mainly due to which type of pollution?

(A) Water (B) Soil

(C) Air (D) Food

(E) None of these

Answer: (C)

Explanation: Poisonous gases when get mixed with rain causes acid rain.

2. Acid rain is caused due to which of the following activities?

(A) Volcanoes

(B) Smoke from factories

(C) Fossil burning

(D) All of these

(E) None of these

Answer: (D)

Explanation: All the activities given above are the caused of acid rain.

Global Warming

Global warming simply means increase in the average temperature of the Earth's atmosphere. The solar radiations falling on the Earth is partly absorbed and a part of it is reflected back into the space. The part of the rays reflected back is trapped by our atmosphere. This trapped radiation further warms the Earth, which is known as the greenhouse effect. This effect is however one of the major reason for life on this planet. The carbon dioxide present in the air is responsible for this greenhouse effect. Carbon dioxide is very essential for the life of the plants, but the excess amount of it is harmful. The amount of carbon dioxide is continuously on increase due to human activities and decreasing forest cover. The number of trees, which consume carbon dioxide is reducing, causing an increase in the carbon dioxide accumulation. Carbon dioxide traps heat and does not allow it to escape into the outer space.

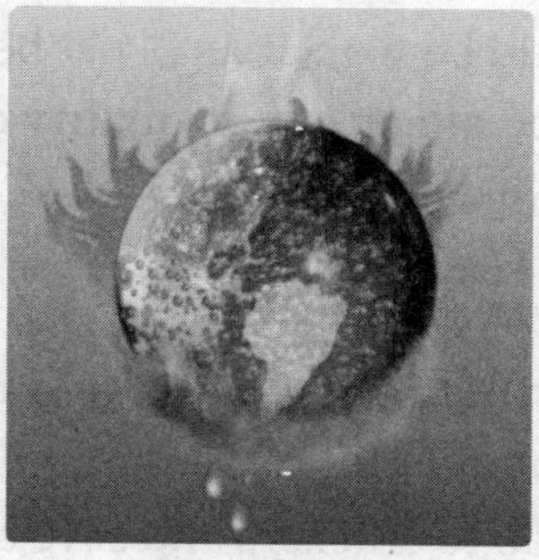

Global Warming

This results in an increase in the temperature of the Earth's atmosphere. The process of gradual increase in the Earth's temperature is called **global warming**. Global warming has become a major concern world wide. This is a serious issue and needs every one to work for this alarming cause. Rise in even 0.5° C can cause glacier to melt and sea levels to rise. It has a wide range of other effects like, on the pattern of rainfall, agriculture, forest, plants and animals.

Commonly Asked Question

1. **The gas responsible for green house effect:**

(A) Carbon dioxide (B) Methane

(C) Nitrous oxide (D) All of these

(E) None of these

Answer: (D)

Explanation: All the gases given above contribute in causing green house effect.

2. Global warming is known as:

(A) Average temperature of the Earth's atmosphere is gradually increasing

(B) Average temperature of the sun's atmosphere is gradually increasing

(C) Portion of the globe which faces the sun

(D) Both A and B

(E) None of the above

Answer: (A)

Explanation: Gradual increase in the average temperature of the Earth's atmosphere is known as global warning.

Remedies of Pollution

The fight against pollution should be won at any cost because the survival of our planet is in danger. Pollution has started affecting the quality of our daily lives. We all need to realize our responsibility and work accordingly.

Reduce Pollution

Burning of fossil fuels cause air pollution. We should reduce the use of such fuels and switch over to alternative fuels for our energy requirement like wind energy, solar energy, hydropower, etc. We should say no to crackers and save the environment from its harmful gases. The harmful chemicals that pollutes water should not be directly disposed of into the rivers and lakes. There should be proper treatment of water in every factories, before the water is released into the rivers and lakes. We should follow the **'3 R'** rule very strictly. That is **R**educe, **R**euse and **R**ecycle of natural resources. We should stop cutting of trees and should plant and nurture more trees and measures to conserve soil and wild life. Farmers should be encouraged to adopt safer ways of farming. They should use more of organic fertilizer. The use of chemicals pesticides and fertilizer should be discouraged. The plastic bags, one of the main cause of soil pollution, should be reduced or banned. As we all are responsible for the pollution and its effects, in the same way we all have a role to play in keeping our environment clean and healthy. We all should realize our responsibility in maintaining our natural resources in a healthy state.

Commonly Asked Question

1. **Pollution can be reduced by the use of which one of the following instead of petrol?**

   (A) CNG
   (B) LPG
   (C) Bio Gas
   (D) CFCs
   (E) A, B and C

   Answer: (E)

   Explanation: CNG, LPG and Bio gas can reduce the pollution that is why we can use them instead of petrol.

2. **What is meant by potable water?**

   (A) Water used for watering the pots
   (B) Water suitable for drinking
   (C) Water in a pot
   (D) Water which can be carried from one place to another
   (E) None of these

   Answer: (B)

   Explanation: The water which is drinkable is known as potable water.

DID YOU KNOW?

❖ To produce each week's Sunday newspapers, 500,000 trees is to be cut down.

❖ The amount of wood and paper we throw away each year is enough to heat 50,000,000 homes for 20 years.

❖ Americans use 2,500,000 plastic bottles every hour.

❖ Plastic bags and other plastic garbage thrown into the ocean kill as many as 1,000,000 sea creatures every year!.

❖ A modern glass bottle would take 4000 years or more to decompose — and even longer if it's in the landfill.

SUMMARY

- **Environment:** Environment is everything that make up the surrounding of living thing.
- **Types of pollution:** There are three major types of pollution, air, water and soil pollution.
- **Acid rain:** Coming down of the water droplet by mixing with harmful gases.
- **Global warming:** The gradual increase in the temperature of the Earth's atmosphere.

Self Evaluation Test–7

1. **Forests are called as the 'lungs of nature' why?**
   (A) Bring up the carbon dioxide level in the atmosphere.
   (B) Bring down the oxygen level in the atmosphere.
   (C) Maintain the balance of oxygen and carbon dioxide in the atmosphere.
   (D) All of these
   (E) None of these

2. **What is Sewage?**
   (A) Mining waste (B) Factory waste
   (C) Domestic waste (D) All of these
   (E) None of these

3. **Which one of the following is a biotic component of the environment?**
   (A) Water (B) Air
   (C) Land (D) Plant
   (E) None of these

4. **Non-biodegradable waste is one of the major cause of land pollution. Which one of the following is a better option to get rid of non-biodegradable waste?**
   (A) Burning (B) Burying
   (C) Recycling (D) Dumping
   (E) None of these

5. Under which one of the following groups, peels of vegetable should be kept?
(A) Biodegradable (B) Non-biodegradable
(C) Hazardous (D) Toxic
(E) None of these

6. We, human beings, depend on our ______ for all our needs.
(A) Ionosphere (B) Environment
(C) Lithosphere (D) Hydrosphere
(E) None of these

7. The process of gradual increase in the Earth's temperature is called___.
(A) Pollution (B) Green house effect
(C) Global warming (D) Acid rain
(E) None of these

8. Select the non-biodegradable waste from the following.

(A) 

(B) 

(C) 

(D) 

(E) None of these

9. Acid rain causes damage to__________.
(A) Animals life (B) Plants life
(C) Historical monuments (D) All of these
(E) None of these

10. Contamination of unwanted substances into water is called ________.
(A) Air pollution (B) Water pollution
(C) Land pollution (D) Soil pollution
(E) None of these

Chapter 8

Universe

Learning Objectives

- Stars and Planets
- Satellites
- Eclipses
- Galaxies
- Natural Phenomenon Related to Stars and Planets

Introduction

Universe is the collection of all the objects in space and the space itself. The universe includes everything that our eye can see and even those things which we can't see. When we look at the sky on a dark clear night, we see the entire sky dotted with countless stars, some bright and some are not so bright. On observing these dotted stars, we find that many of them twinkle and some do not twinkle. These objects, which do not twinkle are the planets. The stars, the planets, the moon and everything that we see in the sky are called **heavenly bodies**.

Heavenly Bodies in the Universe

The vast expanse of space that contains all the matters from the smallest particle to the planets, sun, moon, stars, asteroids and the biggest galaxy is called the **universe.** We do not exactly know how big our universe is. It is believed to be growing outward in every direction. Nobody really knows how the universe was formed. Most scientists believe that at first everything was solid heavy ball of matter. This ball exploded billions of years ago – and our universe was born. The explosion is called the **big bang.** How our universe was formed is still only a theory (an idea), astronomers continue to investigate the theory.

Stars and Planets

Stars

The heavenly bodies which appear to twinkle in the sky are called the **stars**. A star is a huge ball of hot burning gases. It gives out heat, light and energy. The stars that appear as twinkling points of light in the night sky are very far away from us. Hence they appear to be very small. The greatest characteristic of star is that they have light of their own. Sun is the nearest star to us. Hence the sun appears to be so big and glowing. Without the sun's heat and light our Earth would have been very cold. Life on Earth would have not been possible. Sun is the ultimate source of energy for us.

In a dark night sky we can see millions and millions of stars. To make it easy to identify stars, some have been grouped together to form shapes. These groups of stars are called **Constellation.** The shape of the constellation resemble familiar objects. To easily identify constellation, we should know what a particular constellation looks like and where to look for it in the night sky. Let us know about some constellations.

Ursa Major

It is one of the most famous constellations, which can be seen during summer time in the early part of the night. It is also known as big dipper or **great bear**.

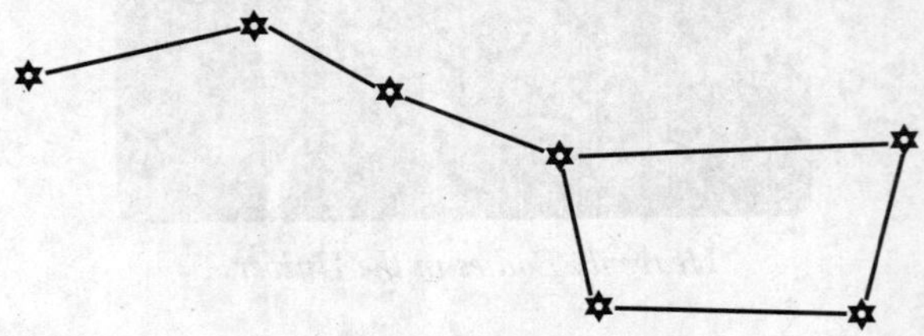

Ursa Major

Orion

Orion is another constellation that can be seen during winter in the late evenings. It is the most magnificent constellation. Orion is also known as **the hunter**.

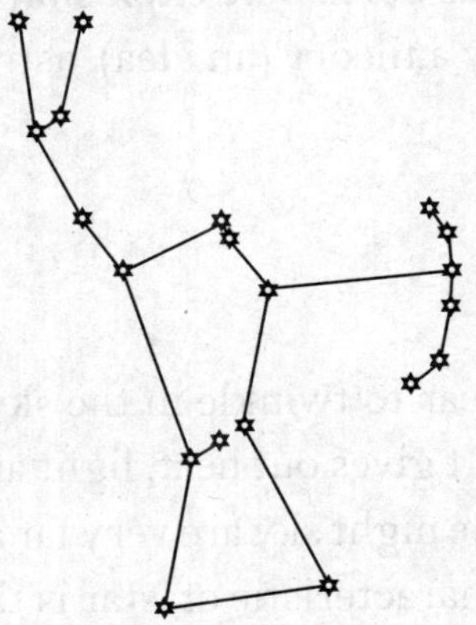

Orion

Planets

The heavenly bodies that do not have any light of their own and move around the stars are called planets. Planets reflect the light that fall on them from the star. Planets keep changing their positions with respect to the stars, as they move around a star in a certain orbit. Orbit is that definite path in which a planet moves around the star. In our solar system sun is situated at the centre and eight planets move around it in their orbits. Each planet rotates on its axis as well. The eight planets in the increasing order of distance from the sun are as follows. **Mercury, Venus, Earth, Mars, Jupiter, Saturn, Uranus and Neptune.**

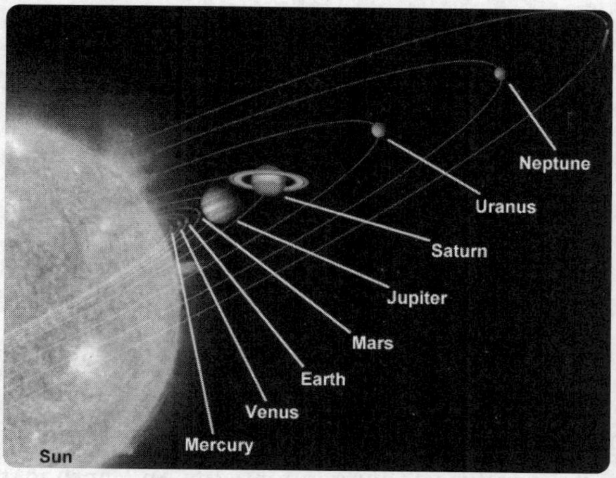

Our solar system

Mercury

It is the closest planet to the Sun. It is very hot during the day and very cold at night. It is also the smallest planet in our Solar System. Mercury can be observed just before sunrise or just after Sun set. Mercury rotates from west to east. It is made up of rocks and metals. Life does not exist as there is no air and the temperature is extreme. Mercury takes 88 days to go around the Sun.

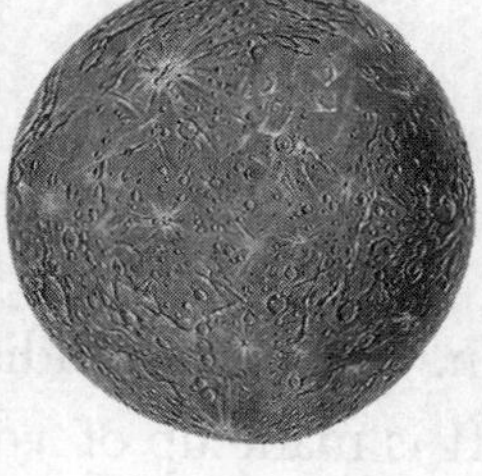

Mercury

Venus

Venus is the second planet from the Sun. It is the brightest planet in the night sky. It shines brightly some times in the western sky as the "evening star" and at other time in the eastern sky, before the Sun rise, as the "morning star". Venus is made up of rocks and metals. Rotation of venus on its axis is different from most of the planets. It rotates from east to west. Venus is the hottest planet of our Solar System.

Venus

Earth

Earth is the third planet in our Solar System. Earth appears bluish green from the space due to the presence of water and land mass. It is the only planet in our Solar System to have life on it. The special condition that supports life on Earth is its right distance from the Sun, as a result it has the right temperature range. Presence of water and suitable atmosphere are other conditions. Rotation of earth on its axis is from west to east. It takes 24 hours to rotate on its axis and 365 days to complete one revolution around the Sun.

Earth

Mars

It is the fourth planet from the Sun. It appears reddish in colour due to its red soil and rocks. It is also called red planet. It is made up of rocks and metals. Like most planets it also moves from west to east. It takes 24 hours and 37 minutes to move on its axis. Mars is about half the size of the Earth.

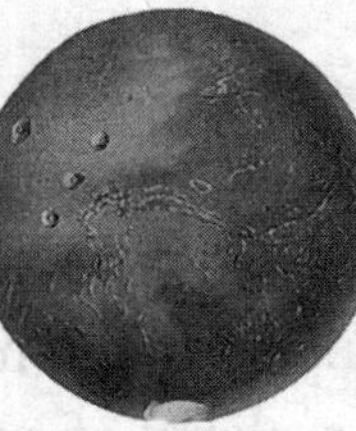

Mars

Jupiter

Jupiter is the largest planet of the Solar System. It is a giant ball of gases and is extremely hot. Jupiter has a big great red spot. This spot is actually a huge storm, which has been blowing on its surface for at least a few hundred years. Like most planets it moves from west to east. Jupiter spins very fast, pulling its clouds in to stripes. This is why jupiter shows striped pattern when we carefully look at it with telescope.

Jupiter

Saturn

Saturn is the most beautiful planet of our Solar System. Its spectacular rings distinguish it from all other planets. It is also a gas planet. The spectacular rings of the planet cannot be seen with the naked eye, we can observe them with a small telescope. It has shining rings around it. Another most amazing fact about the planet is that it is the least dense of all the planets in our Solar System (the planet is very light).

Saturn

Uranus

Uranus is the seventh planet from the Sun and is among the outermost planet. It is a large gas planet as it is far away from the Sun. Uranus takes 84 years to go around the sun. Like venus it also rotates from east to west. Most striking feature of uranus is that it has highly tilted rotational axis. This result in its orbital motion, which appears to roll on its side. The planet takes only 17 hours to spin on its axis.

Uranus

Neptune

Neptune is the farthest most planet of our Solar System. It is made up of mostly gases. When observed through a telescope two spots can be seen on its surface. These spots are actually big storms with very fast blowing winds. The day is shorter on neptune as it takes only 16 hours and 7 minutes to rotate around its axis. Neptune, being the outermost planet, takes the longest time to go around the Sun.

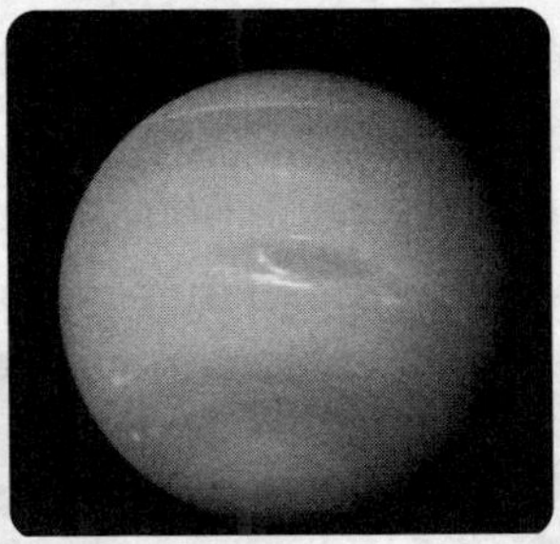

Neptune

Commonly Asked Question

1. **After Sun, the nearest star to the Earth is:**

(A) Sirius
(B) Moon
(C) Pole star
(D) Alpha centauri
(E) None of these

Answer: (D)

Explanation: Alpha centaury is 4.3 light years away from the Earth.

2. **Name a planet which can float on water.**

(A) Earth (B) Neptune

(C) Venus (D) Saturn

(E) Mars

Answer: (D)

Explanation: Saturn is the least dense of all other planets (is very light). Its density is less than water and so it can float in water.

Satellites

Satellites are free flying objects that move around a planet. There are mainly two types of satellites, **natural** and **artificial**. Natural satellites as the name suggests, are naturally present in the space. They are the heavenly bodies formed along with the planets and the stars of the galaxies. Artificial satellites or man made satellites are those free flying objects that are orbiting the Earth or planet and used for various purposes like communication, weather information, etc.

Most of the planets in our Solar System have their own natural satellites. The inner planets (planets close to the Sun) have less number of natural satellites when compared to the outer planets. Earth, the 3rd planet from the sun has only one satellite. We better know it as moon. The red planet mars has two satellites. The outer four planets of our Solar System is known for many satellites. Jupiter, the largest planet is said to have more than sixty (60) moons. Jupiter's moons are of different types. Some of them are much bigger than Earth's moon, whereas some are tiny, only a few miles across. The ringed planet, saturn is said to have sixty two (62) moons orbiting it. Titan is the largest moon of saturn. Uranus is known till date to have more than 20 moons. Neptune is the farthest planet having more than 10 moons. The number may be more.

Moon

Moon, which looks the brightest and biggest on a dark night is the only natural satellite of the Earth. There is no life on the moon due to lack of atmosphere. On the moon, as there is no atmosphere it becomes boiling hot during the day and freezing cold at night. Moon does not have light of its own. The bright moon as we see, is due to the reflection of sun's light from its surface.

Moon of the Earth

The surface of the moon is dusty and barren. There are many craters of different sizes on its surface. It also has large number of steep and high mountains. We can see mountains and craters on the moon from the earth with the help of a telescope. Most interesting fact about the moon is that its lighted or the bright part changes its shape everyday. This is because, as we already know that, moon doesn't have any light of its own. It reflects the light of the sun. When the moon moves in its orbit around the earth, different portion of the moon's surface reflects light from the sun. It is only that part of the moon, which reflects sunlight is seen by us and the rest of the moon is dark. This increasing and decreasing size of the lighted part of the moon is known as **phases of the moon.**

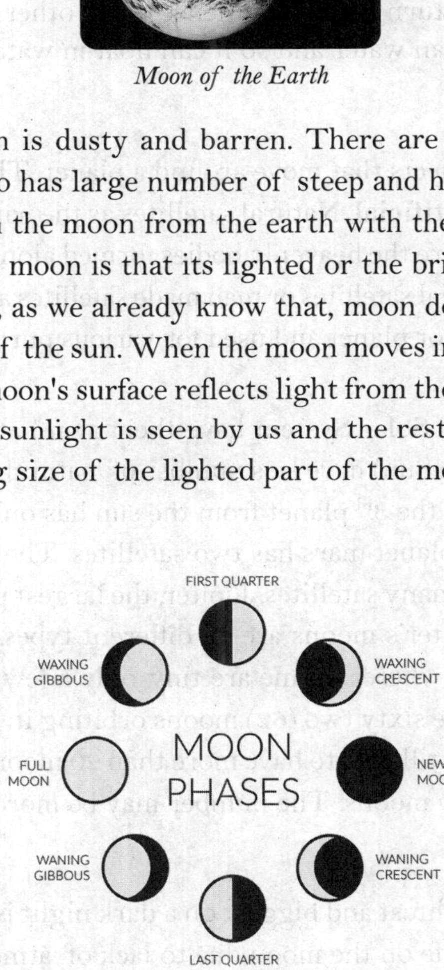

Phase of the Moon

Moon is always been an object of wonder for us. It was on 21st July 1969 **Neil Armstrong** the first man who landed on moon, and the spacecraft was **APOLLO 11.**

Neil Armstrong

Artificial Satellites

Artificial satellites or man made satellites are placed in the space orbiting the Earth and are used for various purposes like communication, weather prediction, etc. In the search of knowledge and better lifestyle, scientists have been successfully and continuously placing artificial satellites around the Earth. These artificial satellites are sent by rockets. They revolve around the Earth.

Weather satellite takes pictures of the clouds and wind systems. This helps to forecast the weather. Some satellites are used to photograph the Earth from above and give valuable information about our natural resources. Various scientific satellites are used to gather information about stars, planets, galaxies and our outer space. There are even spy satellites, which take picture for the military purposes. The worlds first artificial satellite was **SPUTNIK 1** launched on 4th October 1957 by the Russians.

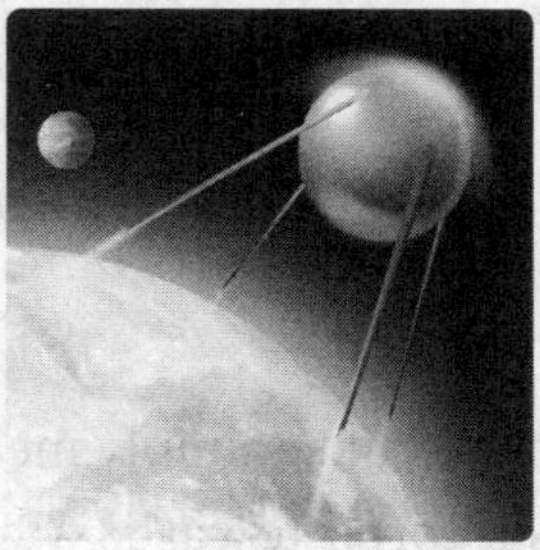

Sputnik 1

India has built and launched several artificial satellites. **ARYABHATTA** was the 1st Indian satellite. Other Indian satellites are INSAT, KALPANA-1, EDUSAT, 1RS etc.

First Indian Satellite: Aryabhatta

Commonly Asked Question

1. **Earth's closest neighbour in the space is_____.**
   (A) Sun (B) Venus
   (C) Mars (D) Moon
   (E) Alpha centauri

   Answer: (D)

   Explanation: Moon is our nearest neighbour.

2. **The first artificial satellite put into orbit was:**
   (A) Aryabhatta (B) Sputnik 1
   (C) Apollo 11 (D) INSAT –ID
   (E) INSAT –IC

   Answer: (B)

   Explanation: Sputnik 1 was launched in 1957.

Eclipses

Eclipse is a play of light and shadow. Eclipse simply means shielding away or hiding away something in ones shadow. Focus a torch towards a wall. Now put your hand between the wall and the lighted torch. Can you see the shadow of the hand on the wall? Yes, this is what happens during the eclipses. This process of shadow formation and shielding of one object's view happens in space too. The Earth and the Moon also cast shadow in space when sunlight falls on them. This causes solar and lunar eclipses. Simply we can say that depending on the shadow cast and the view of the heavenly body i.e. sun or the moon being blocked in the shadow from the Earths surface. It is either solar eclipse (sun's view blocked) or lunar eclipse (moon's view blocked).

Solar Eclipse

When the moon passes between the sun and the Earth. It then blocks the light of the Sun and cast a shadow on the Earth. People in the shadow area, can't see the Sun. Solar eclipse occurs only on a new Moon when the Sun, Moon and Earth are in a line.

There are two types of solar eclipse depending on the amount of shadow formed and the view of the sun blocked, **total solar** eclipse and **partial solar** eclipse.

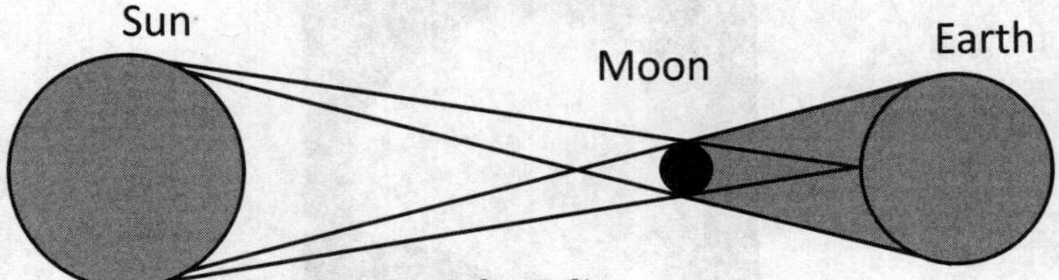

Solar Eclipse

Total Solar Eclipse

Total solar eclipse occurs when the dark shadow of the moon completely blocks the intense sun. Total solar eclipses are very rare celestial phenomenon. During a total solar eclipse, Sun seems to disappear during the day and the sky darkens in a few minutes. Total solar eclipse also depends on the position of moon and the Earth in its specific orbit. An eclipse that occurs when the moon is near its closest distance to the Earth and the Earth approaches its farthest distance from the sun, is a total solar eclipse. Because the moon will then appear to be large enough to cover completely the sun's bright side in its shadow. Total solar eclipses are beautiful celestial events, which can never be more than for a few minutes. In a year five to seven solar eclipses occur. Not more than two eclipses happen to be a total solar eclipse.

Total Solar Eclipse

Partial Solar Eclipse

The other type of eclipse is called the **partial solar eclipse.** Can you guess anything from the name? Yes, it is only a portion and not the complete thing itself. Partial solar eclipse occurs when a small or big portion, but never the complete, view of the sun is blocked by the moon's shadow. It simply means partial blocking of the sun's view by the moons shadow. Partial solar eclipse is usually seen from a large part of the Earth.

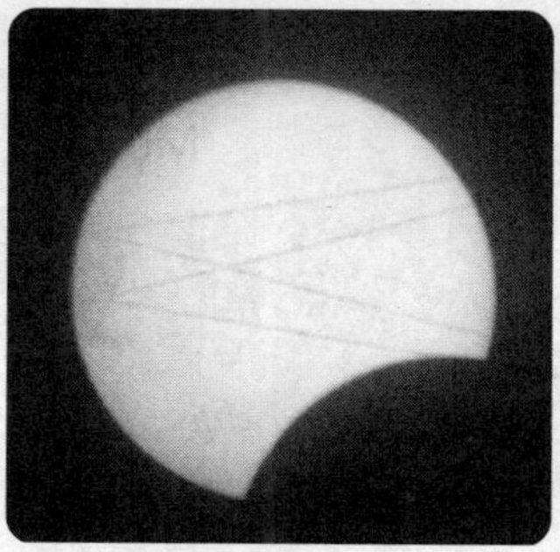

Partial Solar Eclipse

Looking directly at the sun, at any time can cause damage to our eyes. We don't feel like watching the bright and hot sun on any normal day. On the days of eclipse sun looks tempting and we all feel like watching it. But we should never watch a solar eclipse directly. Looking at the sun during an eclipse is dangerous. Looking at the sun, even for a few seconds, can cause permanent damage to our eyes. Viewing the sun through any kind of optical aid like a binoculars, telescopes or even an optical camera is extremely hazardous. Viewing a totally eclipsed sun is not as dangerous as partial eclipsed. Only certified, properly designed solar filters should be used for direct viewing of the sun, during an eclipse.

Lunar Eclipse

A lunar eclipse occurs when the Earth, the Sun and the Moon happens to come into a line and earth is between the sun and the moon. The earth casts a large shadow on the moon. Moon loses its brightness and becomes barely visible. Lunar eclipse always takes place on a full moon night. The type of eclipse and the length or duration of eclipse depends upon the moon location. Lunar eclipse may be viewed from anywhere on the night side of the earth. A lunar eclipse lasts for several hours. When the eclipse ends the moon returns to its natural brilliance. Duration of lunar eclipse is for a few hours, depending upon the portion of the moon in the earth's shadow. There are two types of lunar eclipse i.e. total lunar eclipse and the partial lunar eclipse.

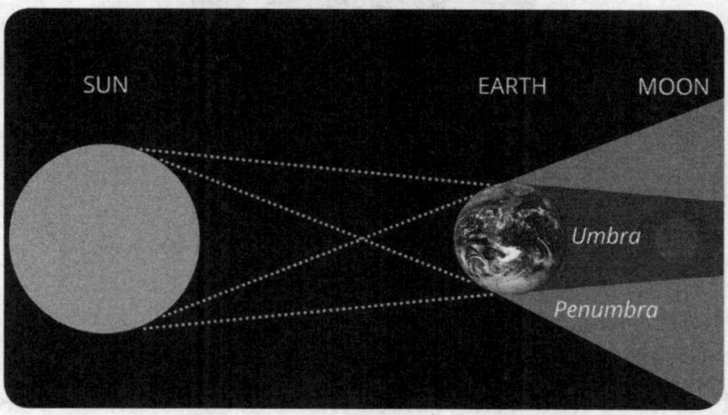

Lunar Eclipse

Partial Lunar Eclipse

Partial lunar eclipse occurs when little, some or most part of the moon but never the complete or full moon is in the Earths shadow. Eclipsed moon is no more bright as it use to be, instead it appears to be darkened on the place which is in the earths shadow.

Partial Lunar Eclipse

Total Lunar Eclipse

Total lunar eclipse occurs when the entire or the complete moon passes through the earth's shadow. These eclipses are spectacular to look at, due to the striking vibrant red colour of moon. A total lunar eclipse lasts for a few hours. The total time between the moons first and the last contact with the shadow is much longer and could last up to three to eight hours. Duration of total lunar eclipse at a given place on earth is only a few minutes. Eclipse duration is affected by the relative distance of the moon from the earth at the time of the eclipse.

Total Lunar Eclipse

The duration of the total lunar eclipse depends on the moon's speed through the earth's shadow. Number of eclipse in a year varies from zero to three. 1982 was a year when three total lunar eclipses occurred in a single calendar year. On 21st December this year we will be given a chance again by the earth, the moon and the sun to watch the spectacular total lunar eclipse.

Lunar eclipses are completely safe to watch. There is no need of any protective filters. We can use Binoculars to magnify the view.

Commonly Asked Question

1. Solar eclipse occurs when the sun, the earth and the _____ is in a straight line

(A) Mercury (B) Moon
(C) Venus (D) Titan
(E) None of the above

Answer: (B)

Explanation: It is the moon, which cast a shadow on the earth by blocking the sun. Moon comes between the sun and the earth.

2. The natural phenomenon, when Earth cast its shadow on Moon, is known as.

(A) Solar eclipse (B) Lunar eclipse
(C) Mars eclipse (D) All of these
(E) None of these

Answer: (B)

Explanation: The phenomenon, when Earth casts its shadow on Moon, is known as lunar eclipse.

Galaxies

Looking at a clear night sky, What do we see? We see thousands of stars that are shining very brightly, some are not. They look as if they have been scattered around the sky. But, actually, most stars are clustered together in huge groups. This huge group of stars is called **galaxies**.

Galaxy

The early universe was extremely hot. It took billion of years for the universe to cool down. Some pieces formed the basic elements like hydrogen and helium. Other pieces began to join together, and object began to be formed. According to the big bang theory, one billion years after the big bang explosion, matter began to come close to one another. Among these matters, there were great open spaces. These clumps of matter were the first galaxies. Billions of stars formed within these galaxies. Galaxies are formed in groups. A group may contain tens or even thousands of galaxies. Galaxies in a group are relatively close to one another. These galaxies are moving away from one another.

A typical galaxy contains hundreds of billions of stars and may be even more. Galaxy also contains planets, moons, comets, gases and dust. Today we know that universe contains billions of galaxies. It is believed that all the galaxies are in motion.

It is found that farther the galaxy is from our galaxy the greater the speed at which it is moving away from us. The greatest fact is that the entire universe is expanding. Hundreds of millions of galaxies have been found throughout the universe. These galaxies are so far away from the earth that even through the most modern, powerful and hi-tech telescope, most of the galaxies appear just as faint spots of light.

There are different types of galaxies with different shapes. According to the shape of the galaxies, they are classified into three major groups.

Elliptical Galaxy

Elliptical galaxy is elliptical in shape. These galaxies can look like a slightly flattened ball, or a dinner plate or an ostrich's egg. Elliptical galaxies generally do not contain new or young stars. About one third of the galaxies are elliptical in shape.

Elliptical Galaxy

Spiral Galaxies

Spiral galaxies are the most common type of galaxies. They look like a rotating pinwheel with arms flaring out of a central disc. Spiral galaxies are made up of young stars. The **Milky Way** is a spiral galaxy. The **Milky Way** galaxy spins like a top together with all its stars. Our sun and the trillions of stars present in our galaxy revolve around the centre of the galaxy.

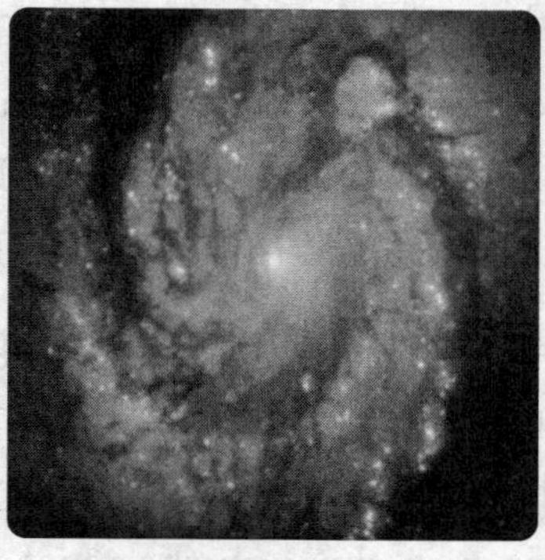

Spiral Galaxy

Irregular Galaxy

Galaxy which do not have any fixed or regular shape are called irregular galaxy. The shape of these galaxies resulted from a tremendous explosion that occurred in them long ago. In some other cases it is thought that the shape of the galaxy was affected by the gravitational pull of a neighboring galaxy. The strong pull caused stars from one galaxy to move to the other neighboring galaxy.

Irregular Galaxy

Commonly Asked Question

1. **Galaxies are a part of which one of the following?**

(A) Solar system (B) Constellation

(C) Universe (D) Satellites

(E) All the above

Answer: (C)

Explanation: Galaxy contains solar system, constellation and satellites. Galaxy is a small part of the vast universe.

2. **The galaxy called the milky way is a type of _____ .**

(A) Elliptical galaxy (B) Radio galaxy

(C) Irregular galaxy (D) Spiral galaxy

(E) None of the above

Answer: (D)

Explanation: Milk way is a spiral galaxy which looks like a rotating pinwheel with arms flaring out of the contract disc.

Natural Phenomenon Related To Planets and Stars

The natural phenomenon in the universe, which is associated with the heavenly bodies, like sun, earth, moon, etc., is spinning on their axis, an imagining line on which they spin.

Rotation of Heavenly Bodies

When the axis of rotation lies within the body of the object itself, the body is said to rotate upon itself or spin.

Most of the heavenly bodies in our galaxy like the planets, moon and the sun spin or rotate upon itself. This spin is better known as rotation. While rotating these bodies move around a central point called revolution. The process of revolution is not a property of planets alone. Moons also revolve with planet at its centre. Sun and the other stars revolve around the centre of our galaxy.

Our solar system has eight planets with their moons and the sun. The moons spin around itself while moving around their respective planets in their fixed orbit. All the planets in a similar manner spin on their axis while they revolve around the sun. Most of the planets in our solar system, including the earth spins in the same direction as they orbits the sun. The two exception to this are the planet venus and uranus.

Now let us look the effect of rotation and revolution on earth and its effect on us. The Earth spins around a line passing through its centre . Axis of earth is tilted at an angle of 23.5°. This titled imaginary line is called the axis of rotation. We all know that the rotation causes day and night. Earth completes one rotation in 24 hours. Thus our one day is 24 hours long.

When the earth rotates on its axis, half of the earth faces the sun and it is day time in that part. At the same time half of the earth which is away from the sun, are dark and so that part has night time. This is the reason for the difference in the time across the world. When it is active day time in our country, people of America has night.

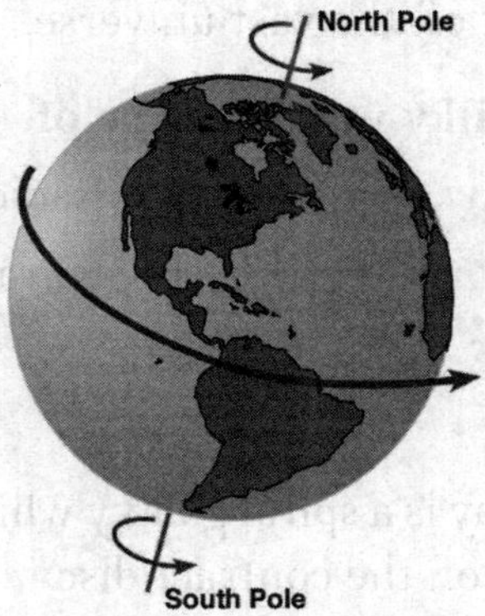

Rotation of the Earth Around Its Axis

Revolution of Heavenly Bodies

Revolution is the movement of the Earth around the Sun in its fixed orbit. The time taken by the Earth to complete one revolution is approximately 365.24 days. This is considered as 1 year. The revolution of the Earth around the sun causes change in season. The main reason for the different seasons is the tilted axis on which the Earth spins.

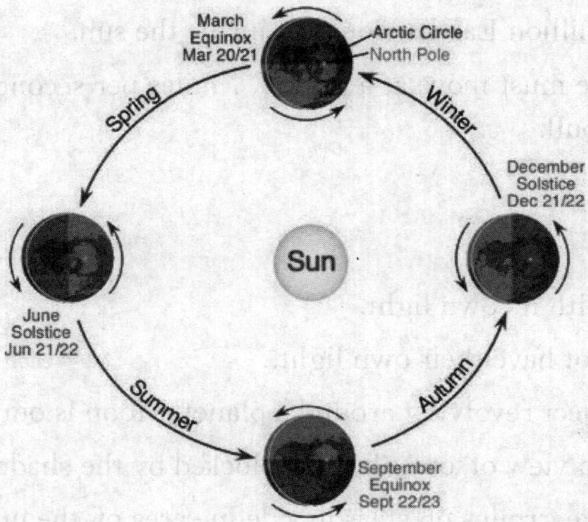

Showing the Revolution of the Earth

Depending upon which hemisphere of the Earth is closer to the sun and which one is farther we have summer and winter respectively.

The half of the Earth which gets more sunshine has summer while the other half has winter. This summer or winter lasts for six months and the situation reverses. There are situations when both the hemisphere are equidistant from the sun, then there is spring or autumn. Spring and autumn are pleasant time when it is neither very cold nor very hot. The path of the Earth around the sun during revolution is an ellipse (elliptical orbit) rather than a circle and this is the reason why Earth is closer to the sun sometimes and farther form it at other times. This is the cause of seasonal fluctuations.

DID YOU KNOW?

- The Earth spins at 1,000 mph but it travels through space at an incredible 67,000 mph.
- The moon weighs 81 billion tons.
- More than 1 million Earths would fit inside the sun.
- A space vehicle must move at a rate of 7 miles per second to escape the earth's gravitational pull.

SUMMARY

- **Star:** Shines with its own light.
- **Planets:** Do not have their own light.
- **Satellites:** Object revolving around a planet. Moon is our natural satellite.
- **Eclipse:** When view of one object is blocked by the shadow of the other.
- **Galaxies:** Huge groups of stars in a define area of the universe.
- **Phenomenon related to the planets and stars:** It is their movement around the central point and its axis.

Self Evaluation Test–8

1. **Find the star among the following.**

   (A) Moon (B) Titan
   (C) Alpha centauri (D) Europa
   (E) None of these

2. **Which one of the following planets is closest to the Sun?**

   (A) Mercury (B) Mars
   (C) Venus (D) Jupiter
   (E) None of these

3. **What name has been given to the path in which a planet moves around the sun?**

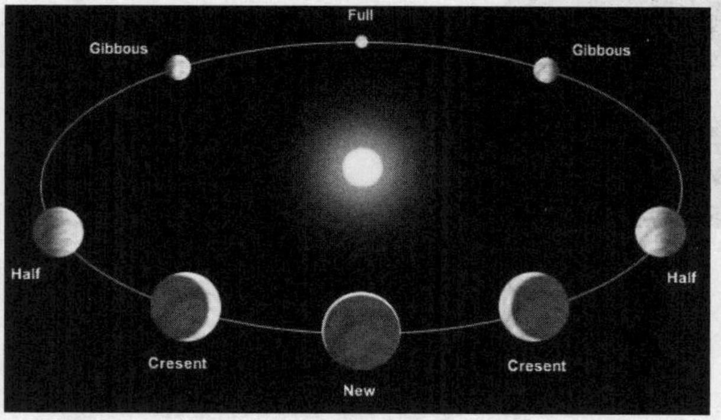

(A) Orbit (B) Axis
(C) Belt (D) All of these
(E) None of these

4. **A natural satellite that moves around the earth is______.**

(A) Moon (B) INSAT
(C) Aryabhatta (D) Apollo-9
(E) Apollo-11

5. **The first man to land on the moon's surface was_______.**

(A) Edwin Aldrin (B) Rakesh Sharma
(C) Yuri Gagarin (D) Kalpana Chawala
(E) Neil Armstrong

6. **Which phenomenon has been shown in the following figure?**

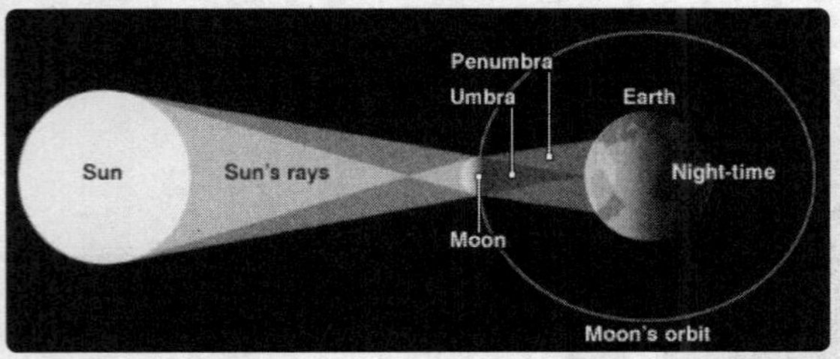

(A) Lunar eclipse (B) Solar eclipse
(C) Mars eclipse (D) Jupiter eclipse
(E) None of these

7. **Which one of the following is a gas planet?**
(A) Mars (B) Earth
(C) Venus (D) Jupiter
(E) None of these

8. **What name has been given to the galaxy which has been holding our solar system?**
(A) Milky Way (B) Androma
(C) M82 (D) M87
(E) All of these

9. **Name the planet that has been indicated by the letter X in the figure**

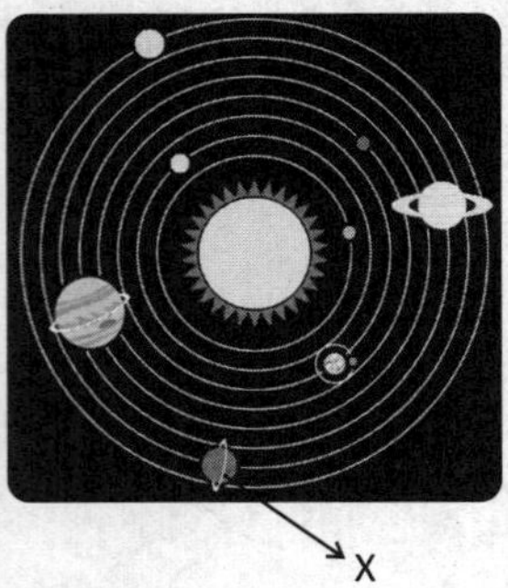

(A) Jupiter (B) Uranus
(C) Neptune (D) Pluto
(E) None of these

10. **The phenomenon of day and night occur because of:**
(A) Rotation of the Earth (B) Revolution of the Earth
(C) Rotation of the Moon (D) Rotation of the Mars
(E) None of these

Chapter 9

Reasoning and Aptitude

Learning Objectives

- Introduction
- Patterns
- Alphabet Test and Word Formation
- Coding and Decoding
- Direction Sense Test
- Ranking Test and Comparison
- Calendars and Possible Combinations
- Analogy
- Classification
- Figure Series
- Embedded Figures
- Figure Patterns
- Geometrical Shapes
- Mirror Images

Introduction

The process of thinking about something in a logical way in order to form a conclusion is called '**Logical Reasoning**'. It is the ability of mind to think and understand things in a logical way. In this chapter, we will learn what logical reasoning involves and how to integrate the application of Mathematics to problem solving.

Patterns

Pattern is a list of numbers or letters that follows a certain sequence or a certain rule. To find the missing term or next term in series to continue the given series, first we must have a rule. To solve them all, we have to do is figure out the pattern and come up with the next logical number or letter of the sequence.

Example:

What is the next number in the pattern given below?

4, 7, 13, 25, 49, ?

(A) 87 (B) 96 (C) 98 (D) 97
(E) 107

Answer (D)

Explanation: Here, pattern followed is:

4 → 7 → 13 → 25 → 49 → 97

+3, +6, +12, +24, +48

Also, 4 × 2 – 1 = 7, 7 × 2 – 1 = 13, 13 × 2 – 1 = 25, 25 × 2 – 1 = 49

Therefore, the missing number is 49 × 2 – 1 = 97

Example:

The values of A and B in the given number pattern are:

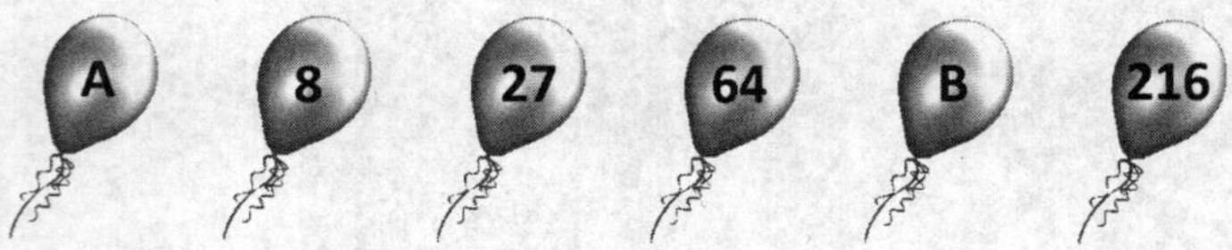

(A) 4, 125 (B) 1, 125 (C) 3, 243 (D) 1, 243
(E) None of these

Answer (B)

Explanation: Here, pattern followed is:

1 = 1 × 1 × 1, 8 = 2 × 2 × 2, 27 = 3 × 3 × 3, 64 = 4 × 4 × 4,

125 = 5 × 5 × 5, and 216 = 6 × 6 × 6

Therefore, the value of A and B is 1, 125

Example:

Find the missing number if a certain rule is followed in the given figure.

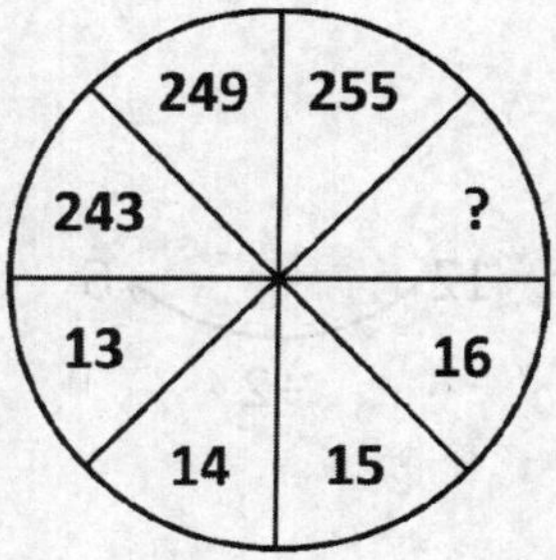

(A) 263 (B) 261 (C) 265 (D) 267
(E) 271

Answer (B)

Explanation: Here, pattern followed is:

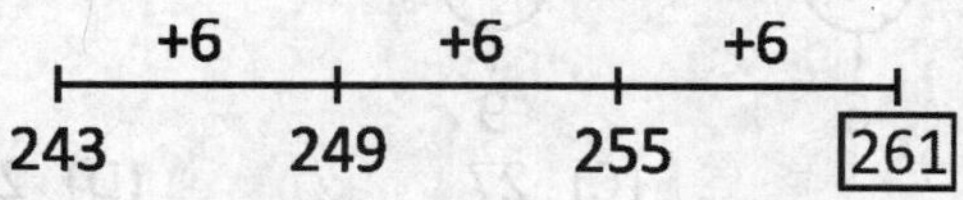

Therefore, the missing number is 261

Example:

Find the missing number if a certain rule is followed in the given figure.

5	3
11	9

7	5
8	6

20	7
25	12

18	7
?	12

(A) 23 (B) 21 (C) 25 (D) 27
(E) 29

Answer (A)

Explanation: Here, rule followed is:

5	3	5 + 9 – 3 = 11
11	9	

7	5	7 + 6 – 5 = 8
8	6	

20	7	20 + 12 – 7 = 25
25	12	

18	7	18 + 12 – 7 = 23
?	12	

Therefore, the missing number = 23.

Example:

If 24 is to 12 and 46 is to 23, then 12 is to:

(A) 4 (B) 6 (C) 8 (D) 12

(E) 24

Answer (B)

Explanation: Here, rule followed:

24 → 12 (÷2), 46 → 23 (÷2) and 12 → 6 (÷2)

Therefore, the required number = 6

Example:

Which number will replace the question mark(?) in the number pattern given below?

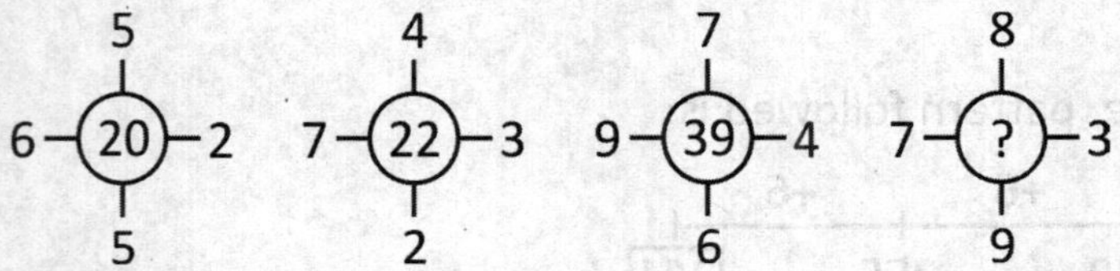

(A) 31 (B) 28 (C) 27 (D) 29

(E) 26

Answer (D)

Explanation: Here, rule followed is:

(6 × 5) – (5 × 2) = 20, (7 × 4) – (2 × 3) = 22, (9 × 7) – (6 × 4) = 39

and (7 × 8) – (9 × 3) = 29

Therefore, the missing number is 29

Example:

Find the missing term (?) in the given sequence.

Y2E	X3F	W4G	V5H	?

(A) U7L (B) U6I

(C) T6I (D) T7J

(E) None of these

Answer (B)

Explanation: Here, rule followed is:

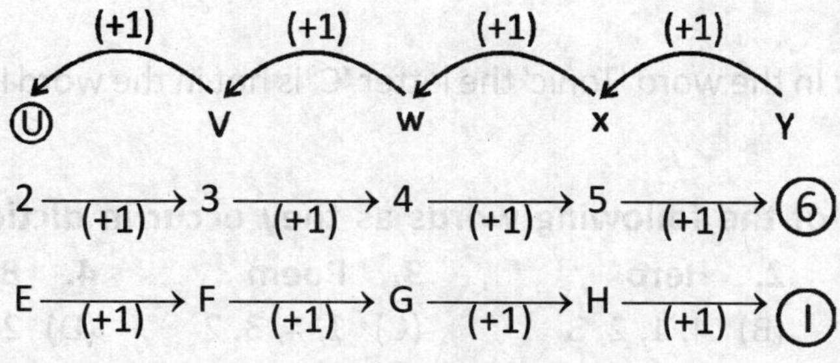

Therefore, the required missing term is U6I.

Alphabet Test and Word Formation

Alphabet test is one of the most common topic of verbal reasoning where we come across various types of questions as follows:

- Letter word problems
- Words arranging in alphabetical order
- Making the meaningful word
- Alphabet letter series

Example:

Find the category of the given word so formed by the combination of letters arranged according to form a meaningful word.

EHYAN

(A) Vegetable (B) Tree (C) Animal (D) River

(E) None of these

Answer (C)

Explanation: Word formed is HYENA and it is the name of an animal.

Example:

Find out the word which *cannot* be made from the letters of the given word.

IMAGINATION

(A) Giant (B) Mango

(C) Among (D) Tonic

(E) None of these

Answer (D)

Explanation: In the word 'Tonic' the letter 'C' is not in the word IMAGINATION.

Example:

Correct arrangement of the following words as they occur in dictionary is:

1. Cold **2. Hero** **3. Poem** **4. Boat**

(A) 3, 4, 1, 2 (B) 4, 1, 2, 3 (C) 1, 4, 3, 2 (D) 2, 3, 4, 1

(E) None of these

Answer (B)

Explanation: As in order, B comes first, then C, then H and then P.

Therefore, correct order is: Boat, Cold, Hero, Poem, or 4, 1, 2, 3.

Example:

Form a meaningful word by arranging the given numbers corresponding to the letter given below.

A	B	C	E	L
1	2	3	4	5

(A) 2, 4, 5, 3, 1 (B) 3, 4, 5, 2, 1 (C) 1, 3, 4, 2, 5 (D) 3, 1, 2, 5, 4

(E) None of these

Answer (D)

Explanation: The word formed by arranging the letters is CABLE, therefore arrangement of the numbers should be 3, 1, 2, 5, 4.

Example:

Choose one word which can be formed by using the letters of the given word.

RECTIFY

(A) Chief (B) Force (C) Trice (D) Recut

(E) None of these

Answer (C)

Explanation: All the letters of word 'Trice' are in the given word RECTIFY, but the letters H, O and U are not as they are given in the words 'Chief', 'Force' and 'Recut'.

Letter Series

Letter series usually consists of a series of letters which follow a certain pattern, or some letters are missing from the series. These missing letters are then given in a proper sequence as one of the alternatives.

Example:

Find the next letter in given series.

B Y C X D W E ?

(A) U (B) V (C) F (D) T

(E) None of these

Answer (B)

Explanation: The answer is 'V' because the pattern is to count first, one forward from A to Z and then the second, one backward from Z to A.

B (Y) C (X) D (W) E (V)

Example:

Find the next pair of letters in the given series.

KA JD IG HJ GM ?

(A) FN (B) FP

(C) EL (D) EQ

(E) None of these

Answer (B)

Explanation: The answer is FP, because the pattern is to count backward in ones for the first letter and count forward in three for the second letter.

K	J	I	H	G	F
A	D	G	J	M	P

Example:

Which of the following letters is 7th to the left of 6th letter from the right end?

ABCDEFGHIJKLMNOPQRSTUVWXYZ

(A) N (B) M (C) O (D) P

(E) None of these

Answer (A)

Explanation: 6th letter from the right end is U and 7th to the left of U is N.

Example:

Pick the odd one out.

(A) BFJ (B) AEI (C) HLP (D) KOR

(E) None of these

Answer (D)

In option (A): $B \xrightarrow{CDE} F \xrightarrow{GHI} J$, In option (B): $A \xrightarrow{BCD} E \xrightarrow{FGH} I$

In option (C): $H \xrightarrow{IJK} L \xrightarrow{MNO} P$, In option (D): $K \xrightarrow{LMN} O \xrightarrow{PQ} R$

Therefore, in option (D), KOR is different from the rest.

Example:

PL is to RO as TM is to:

(A) UN (B) VP

(C) VN (D) WP

(E) VM

Answer (B)

Explanation:

Here, $P \xrightarrow[(+2)]{Q} R$, and, $L \xrightarrow[(+3)]{MN} O$

Therefore, $T \xrightarrow[(+2)]{U} V$, and, $M \xrightarrow[(+3)]{NO} P$.

So, VP is the required term.

Example:

How many meaningful words could be formed from the letters T, A and C?

(A) Zero (B) Two (C) Three (D) Four

(E) None of these

Answer (B)

Explanation: Possible words are: ACT and CAT.

Example:

Which one letter occurs twice in MATHEMATICS, once in PATTIES but does *not* occur in SCIENTIST?

(A) T (B) M (C) A (D) E

(E) None of these

Answer (C)

Explanation:

The letters 'M', 'A' and 'T' occur twice in Ⓜ️ⒶⓉHEⓂⒶⓉICS but the only letter 'A' occurs once in PⒶTTIES and 'A' does not occur in SCIENTIST.

Example:

Find the letter which will end the first word and start the second word.

AG ? DGE

(A) O (B) A (C) U (D) E

(E) I

Answer (D)

Explanation: The answer is E, because it completes the first word AGⒺ and also begins the second word ⒺDGE.

Example:

Identify the one that does *not* belong to the group.

(A) CBD (B) QPR

(C) XWZ (D) MLN

(E) NMO

Answer (C)

Explanation: There are three consecutive letters in CBD, QPR and MLN but letters in XWZ are not consecutive.

Example:

Identify the one which is different from the rest.

(A) ML (B) JK (C) DC (D) SR

(E) QP

Answer (B)

Explanation:

Here, $M \xrightarrow{(-1)} L$, $J \xrightarrow{(+1)} K$, $D \xrightarrow{(-1)} C$, $S \xrightarrow{(-1)} R$, $Q \xrightarrow{(-1)} P$

Therefore, JK is different from others.

Odd One Out

'Odd one out' means a person, number or thing different from all other members of a particular group or set in some way. The object of 'odd one out' is to guess which one of the group of items does not belong and why it does not belong.

Example:

Which one of the following words is different from the rest?

(A) Bus (B) Truck (C) Car (D) Train
(E) Van

Answer (D)

Explanation: Bus, Truck, Car and Van move on road. Train moves on a railway track.

Example:

Find the 'odd one out'.

(A) 7533 (B) 9755 (C) 6422 (D) 8511
(E) 5311

Answer (D)

Explanation: $7 \xrightarrow{(-2)} 5 \xrightarrow{(-2)} 3(33)$, $9 \xrightarrow{(-2)} 7 \xrightarrow{(-2)} 5\ (55)$

$6 \xrightarrow{(-2)} 4 \xrightarrow{(-2)} 2(22)$, $8 \xrightarrow{(-3)} 5 \xrightarrow{(-4)} 1(11)$,

$5 \xrightarrow{(-2)} 3 \xrightarrow{(-2)} 1(11)$

Therefore, 8511 is 'odd one out'.

Example:

Identify the one that does *not* belong to the group.

(A) 29 (B) 37 (C) 35 (D) 31
(E) 41

Answer (C)

Explanation: 29, 37 and 31, 41 are prime numbers but 35 is a composite number.

Coding and Decoding

Coding is a method of expressing something in secret way and **decoding** is a process to understand a code language.

Word Coding/Substitution Coding

In word coding, some particular words are assigned certain substitute names. Then a question is asked that is to be answered in the substituted code language.

Example:

If 'India' is called 'Germany' 'Germany' is called 'Japan', and 'Japan' is called 'Britain', then 'Tokyo' is the capital of which country?

(A) India (B) Germany (C) Japan (D) Britain

(E) None of these

Answer (D)

Explanation: 'Tokyo' is the capital of 'Japan' and 'Japan' is called 'Britain'.

Example:

In a certain code language, BOOK is coded as 5@@* and PEN is coded as #$7, then how will BONE be coded in the same language?

(A) 5*7@ (B) 5@7$ (C) 5$@* (D) 7@5*

(E) None of these

Answer (B)

Explanation: Here,

B	O	O	K
5	@	@	*

and

P	E	N
#	$	7

Therefore,

B	O	N	E
5	@	7	$

Letter Coding

In letter coding, letters are used in forward or backward or in both directions for making some code language. In some questions, letters of a word are directly replaced by the other letters. For example:

Word	Code
PICTURE	FLXZDEM

Here P, I, C, T, U, R and E are replaced by F, L, X, Z, D, E and M, respectively. In this code, we can write the word PRICE as FELXM.

Example:

In a certain language, if the code for PEACOCK is KCOCAEP, then what is the code for ELEPHANT in that language?

(A) TAPLNHE (B) TANHPLEE
(C) TNAHPELE (D) TENLAEHP
(E) None of these

Answer (C)

Explanation: Letters of the word PEACOCK are written in reverse order as a code. Therefore, the code for ELEPHANT is TNAHPELE.

Example:

If in a certain code, TRIANGLE is written as AIRTELGN, then how will HEXAGONE be written in the same code?

(A) ENOGAXEH (B) ANXEEGHO
(C) AGHENEOX (D) AXEHENOG
(E) None of these

Answer (D)

Explanation: Here, TRIA | NGLE ⟹ AIRT | ELGN

Therefore, HEXA | GONE ⟹ AXEH | ENOG

Example:

If GOING is coded as IQKPI, then how is the word ALONG coded in that language?

(A) CNQPI (B) BMPOH
(C) DORQJ (D) GNOLA
(E) None of these

Answer (A)

Explanation: Here,

$G \xrightarrow[(+2)]{H} I$, $O \xrightarrow[(+2)]{P} Q$, $I \xrightarrow[(+2)]{J} K$, $N \xrightarrow[(+2)]{O} P$, $G \xrightarrow[(+2)]{H} I$

Therefore, $A \xrightarrow[(+2)]{B} C$, $L \xrightarrow[(+2)]{M} N$, $O \xrightarrow[(+2)]{P} Q$, $N \xrightarrow[(+2)]{O} P$,

$G \xrightarrow[(+2)]{H} I$. So, ALONG is coded as CNQPI.

Example:

Some letters and their codes have been given below:

A	C	E	D	G	B	H	F
d	5	J	s	l	8	y	p

The code for the word BEACH is:

(A) 8p5sJ (B) 8dJ5l (C) 5dJy8 (D) 8Jd5y

(E) None of these

Answer (D)

Explanation: We observe the given table and take the code for each letter and find the code for the word BEACH which is '8Jd5y'.

Number Coding

In number coding, numerals are assigned to words.

Example:

If FRANCE is coded as 539624 and EGYPT is coded as 47810, then how will CENTRE be coded?

(A) 420643 (B) 246034 (C) 240643 (D) 246304

(E) None of these

Answer (B)

Explanation:

F	R	A	N	C	E	E	G	Y	P	T
5	3	9	6	2	4	4	7	8	1	0

Therefore, CENTER will be coded as '246034'

Example:

In a certain code, 562401 is written as 784623, how will 152647 be written in the same code?

(A) 263758 (B) 458709

(C) 374869 (D) 347629

(E) None of these

Answer (C)

Explanation:

Here,

5	6	2	4	0	1
+2	+2	+2	+2	+2	+2
7	8	4	6	2	3

Therefore,

1	5	2	6	4	7
+2	+2	+2	+2	+2	+2
3	7	4	8	6	9

Example:

If 2 means 4, 4 means 6, 6 means 8 and 8 means 10, then which is the successor of 5?

(A) 4 (B) 6 (C) 8 (D) 10

(E) 2

Answer (A)

Explanation: Successor of 5 = 5 + 1 = 6 and 4 means 6.

Example:

If H = 8, HE = 13 and HEN = 27, then HUNT = ________?

(A) 64 (B) 61

(C) 63 (D) 65

(E) None of these

Answer (C)

Explanation: Clearly, in the given code, A = 1, B = 2, C = 3, ...,

so HUNT = 8 + 21 + 14 + 20 = 63

Symbol Coding

In symbol coding, symbols or figures are assigned to words.

Example:

If  **means** ,  **means** ,  **means**  **and**  **means** , **then which is *not* a polygone?**

(A) 

(B) 

(C) 

(D) 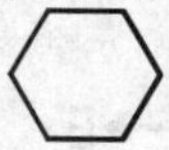

(E) None of these

Answer (D)

Explanation:  is not a polygone and 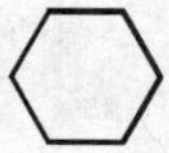 means .

Direction Sense Test

The concept behind the directions is same that we use in our daily life. To solve the direction sense test first we need to make a sketch of the data provided.

Four main Directions are: North (N), South (S), East (E), West (W).

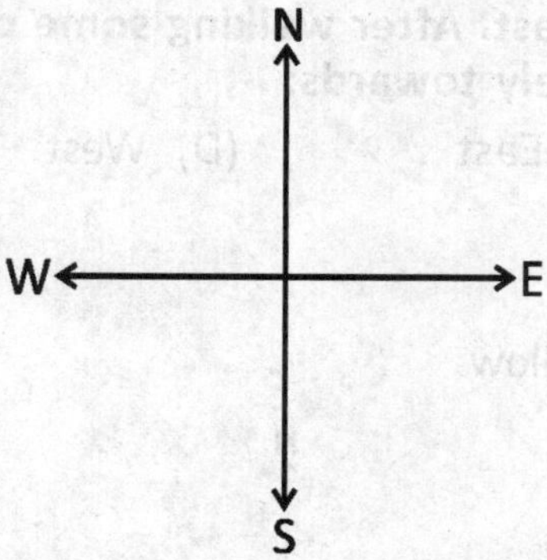

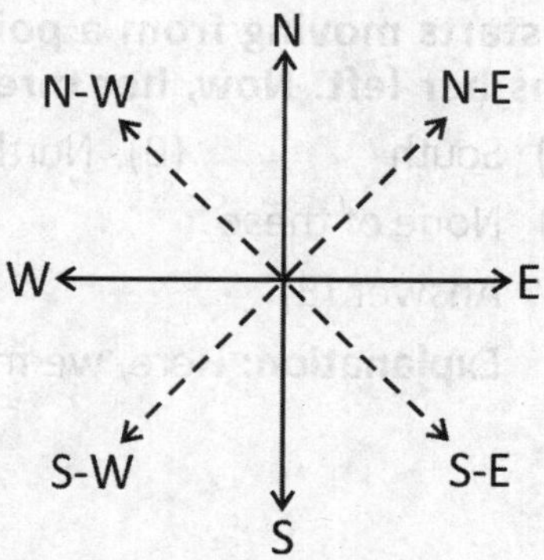

Four Cardinal Directions are: North–East (N-E), North–West (N-W), South–East (S-E), South–West (S-W).

Direction Facts:

- At the time of sunset, the shadow of an object (or a man facing East) is always in the East.
- At the time of sunrise, the shadow of an object is always in the West.
- If a man stands facing the North at the time of sunrise, his shadow will be towards his left and at the time of sunset, it will be towards his right.
- At 12: 00 noon, the rays of the sun are vertically downward, hence there will be no shadow.

Clockwise and Anticlockwise Turn

If you move in direction which is same as the moving direction of a clock hands, your movement is called **clockwise turn**.

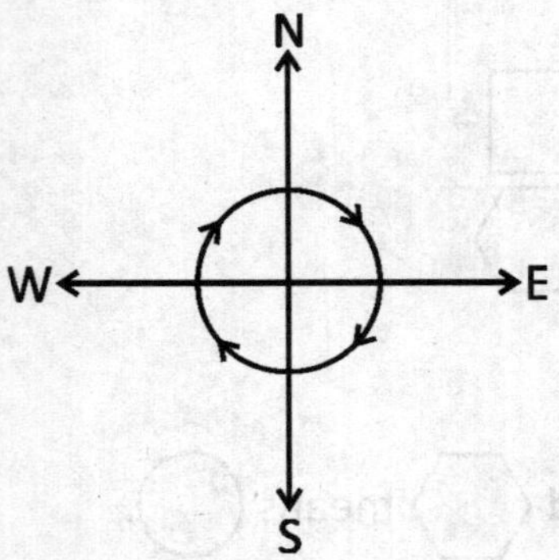

Clockwise Turn

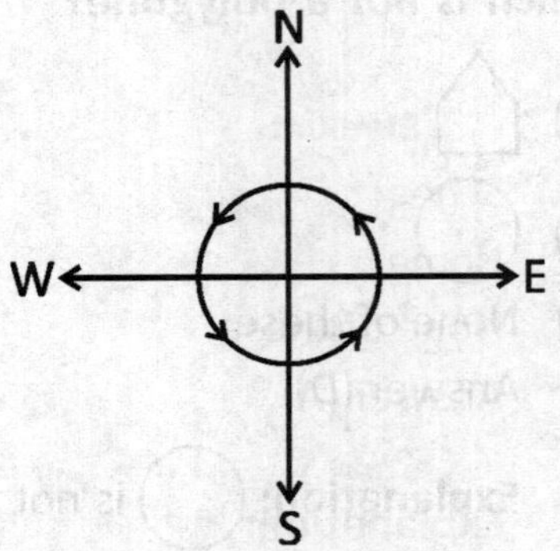

Anticlockwise Turn

If you move in the opposite direction of the clockwise direction, your movement is called **anticlockwise turn**.

Example:

Garima starts moving from a point P towards East. After walking some distance she turns her left. Now, her direction is definitely towards:

(A) South (B) North (C) East (D) West

(E) None of these

Answer (B)

Explanation: Here, we make sketch as follow:

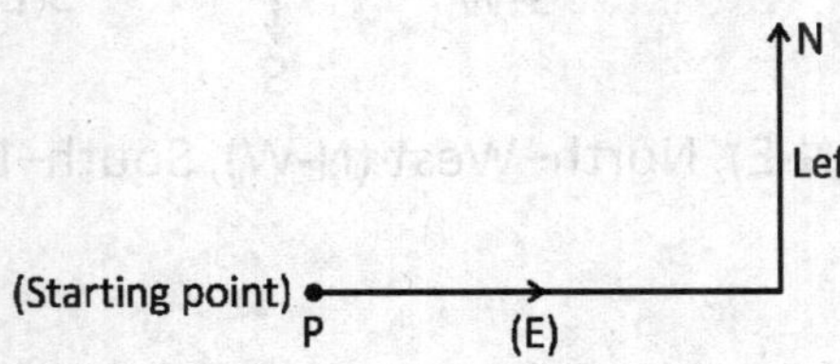

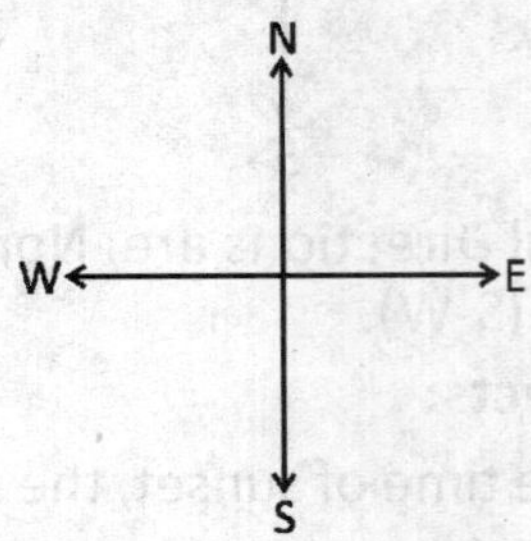

Example:

Joseph is facing the stadium. He makes a $\frac{3}{4}$ turn to the left. What will he be facing now?

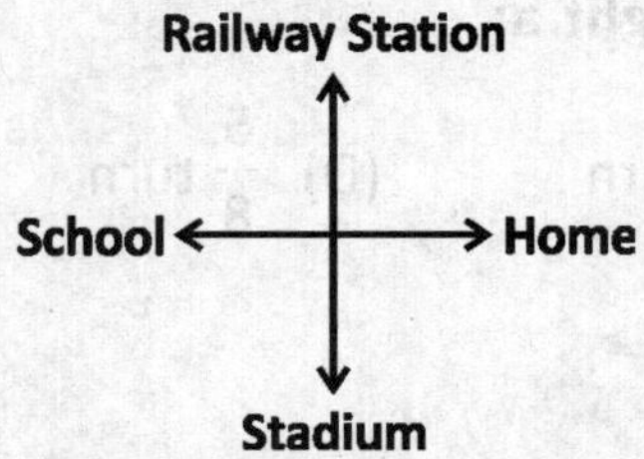

(A) School
(B) Railway Station
(C) Home
(D) Stadium
(E) None of these

Answer (A)

Explanation: In first $\frac{1}{4}$ turn, Joseph will face 'Home', in second $\frac{1}{4}$ turn, he will face 'Railway Station' and in third $\frac{1}{4}$ turn or in a complete $\frac{3}{4}$ turn, he will face 'School'.

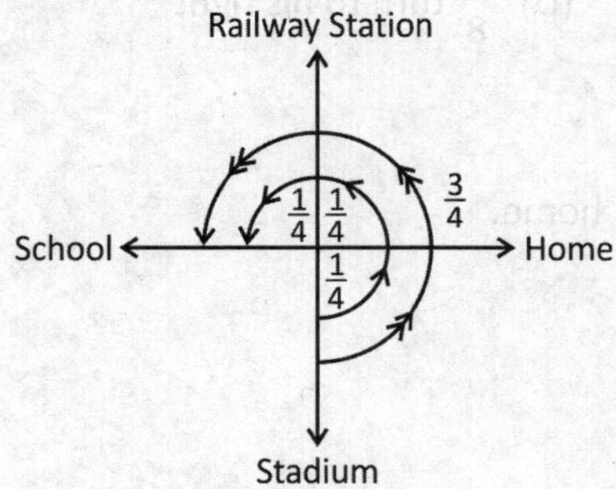

Example:

Rahul is facing his home.

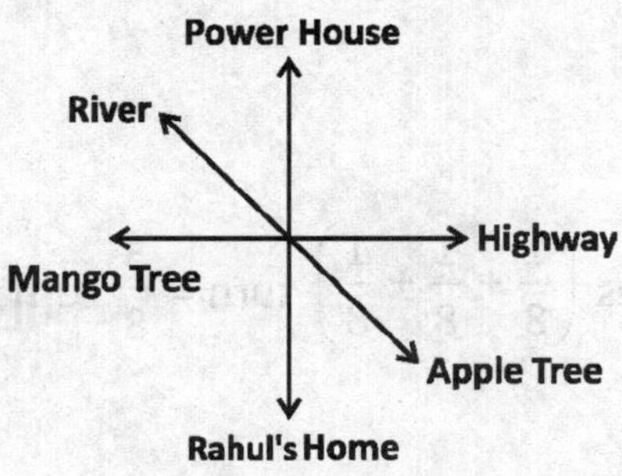

1. Rahul will face the 'River' if he makes to his right a:

(A) $\frac{1}{2}$ turn (B) $\frac{3}{4}$ turn (C) $\frac{3}{8}$ turn (D) $\frac{5}{8}$ turn

(E) None of these.

Answer (C)

2. If Rahul makes $\frac{5}{8}$ turn to his left, he will face:

(A) River (B) Power House (C) Highway (D) Apple Tree

(E) None of these

Answer (A)

3. To face Apple Tree, Rahul has to make:

(A) $\frac{3}{4}$ turn to his left (B) $\frac{3}{8}$ turn to his right

(C) $\frac{7}{8}$ turn to his right (D) $\frac{1}{8}$ turn to his right

(E) None of these

Answer (C)

Explanation: Rahul is facing his home.

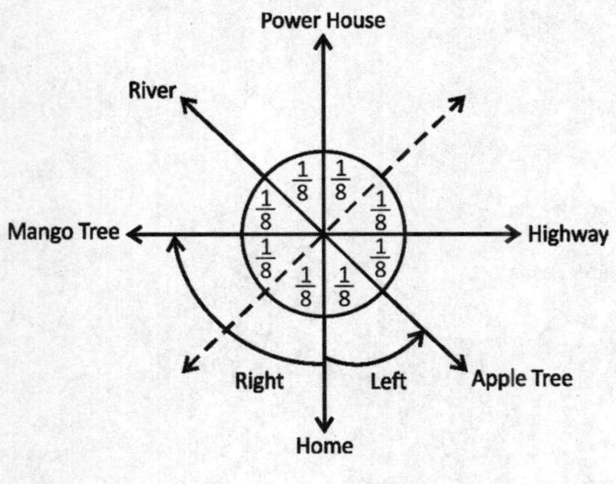

1. Rahul will face the 'River' if he makes $\left(\frac{1}{8}+\frac{1}{8}+\frac{1}{8}\right)$ turn = $\frac{3}{8}$ turn to his right.

2. If Rahul makes $\left(\frac{1}{8}+\frac{1}{8}+\frac{1}{8}+\frac{1}{8}+\frac{1}{8}\right)$ turn = $\frac{5}{8}$ turn to his left, he will face 'River'.

3. To face 'Apple Tree', Rahul has to make $\frac{1}{8}$ turn to his left, or,

$\left(\frac{1}{8}+\frac{1}{8}+\frac{1}{8}+\frac{1}{8}+\frac{1}{8}+\frac{1}{8}+\frac{1}{8}\right)$ turn = $\frac{7}{8}$ turn to his right.

Example:

Which one of the following is *incorrect* for the given diagram?

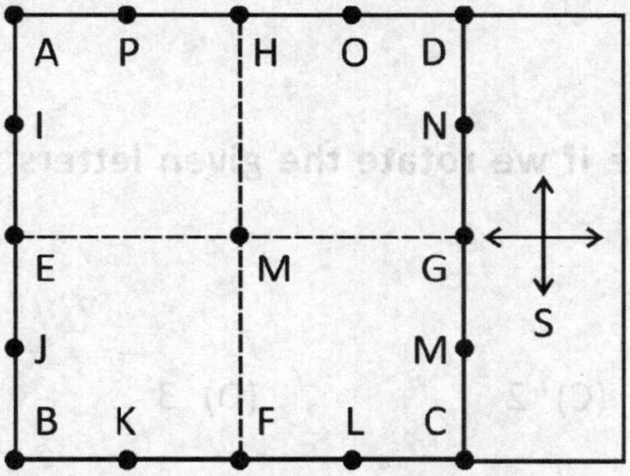

(A) Point A is in North–West of M.
(B) Point B is in South–East of M.
(C) Point E is in West of M.
(D) Point H is in North of M.
(E) None of these

Answer (B)

Explanation: Point A is in North–West of M. Point B is in **South–West** of M. Point E is in west of M. Point H is in north of M.

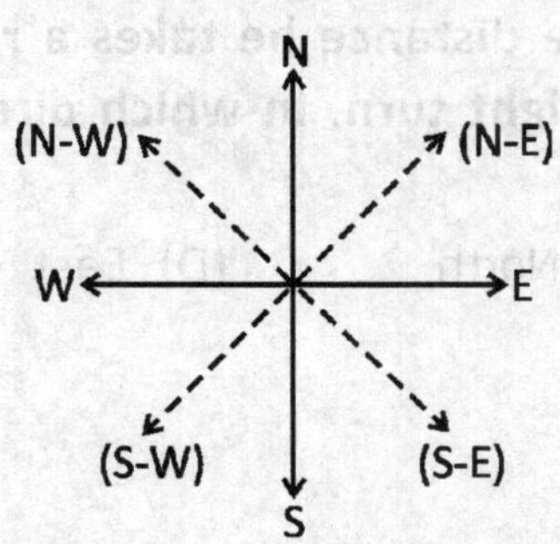

Therefore, the statement in option (B) is incorrect.

Example:

How many letters will appear the same if we rotate the given letters by $\frac{1}{2}$ turn?

UNISIZE

(A) 3 (B) 7 (C) 5 (D) 6

(E) None of these

Answer (C)

Explanation: The letters N, I, S, I and Z will appear the same if we rotate the given letters by $\frac{1}{2}$ turn?

Example:

How many letters will *not* appear the same if we rotate the given letters by $\frac{1}{2}$ turn?

OXAZINES

(A) 4 (B) 1 (C) 2 (D) 3

(E) None of these

Answer (C)

Explanation: All the letters except two letters A and E will appear the same if we rotate them by $\frac{1}{2}$ turn.

Example:

Amit walks towards West. After travelling some distance he takes a right turn and traveling some distance he again takes a right turn. In which direction he will be facing now?

(A) South (B) West (C) North (D) East

(E) None of these

Answer (D)

Explanation:

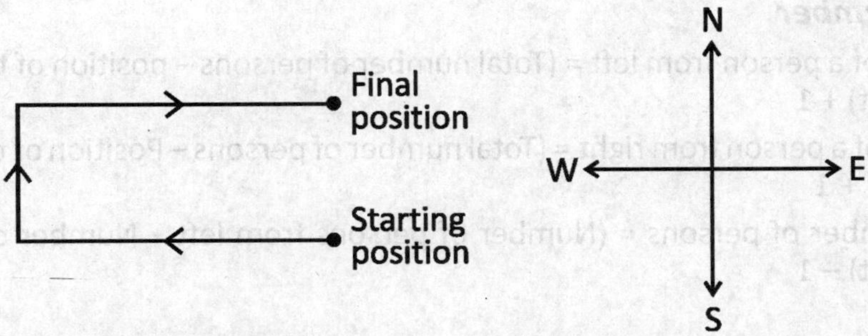

Here, Amit will be facing East direction.

Example:

One morning, Manoj and Lalit were walking towards each other face to face at a crossing. If Manoj's shadow was exactly to the left of Lalit, which direction was Lalit facing?

(A) East (B) West (C) North (D) South
(E) None of these

Answer (C)

Explanation: In morning, shadow will be towards West direction.

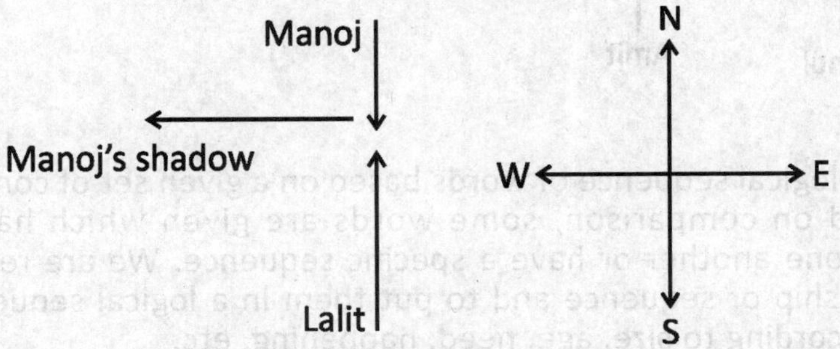

Therefore, Lalit was facing North direction.

Ranking Test and Comparison

Ranking Test

Rank means relative position and 'Ranking Test' in Reasoning deals with finding position in a group of persons or things in a certain arrangement. In the problems based on Ranking Test, generally the total number of persons and rank of a person from his left or right is given. We are required to find out the rank of a person from the other direction. If ranks of a person both from the top and the bottom are mentioned, we have to ask to comput either total number of persons or the rank of a particular person.

Points to Remember

- Position of a person from left = (Total number of persons – position of the person from right) + 1
- Position of a person from right = (Total number of persons – Position of the person from left) + 1
- Total number of persons = (Number of persons from left + Number of persons from right) – 1

Example:

I am ranked 13th from the left and 17th from the right in a line of people. How many people are there in the line?

Solution: Total number of people in the line = (My position number from left + My position number from right) – 1 = (13 + 17) – 1 = 30 – 1 = 29

Example:

If Rahul is 3rd from the left end and Amit is 5th from the right end. If 3 boys are in between them, then find the number of boys in the line.

Solution: Here, total boys in the line = 3 + 3 + 5 = 11

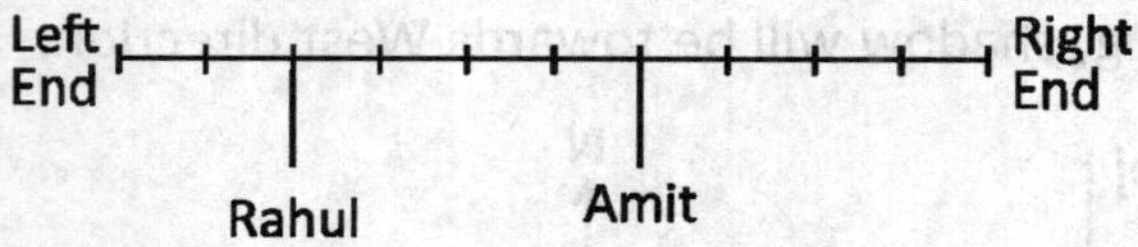

Comparison

It is logical puzzle or logical sequence of words based on a given set of condition. In the problems based on comparison, some words are given which have some relationship among one another or have a specific sequence. We are required to identify this relationship or sequence and to put them in a logical sequence. The sequence may be according to size, age, need, happening, etc.

Example:

"Rahul is older than Mohit. Mohit is older than Amit. Rekha is the youngest. Sanjay is the eldest".
If we arrange their ages in descending order, then who will be in the third place?

(A) Mohit (B) Amit (C) Rahul (D) Rekha
(E) None of these

Answer (A)

Explanation: Let us arrange group of children in descending order.

Rekha < Amit < Mohit < Rahul < Sanjay

Therefore, Mohit is in third place.

Example:

Read the statements given below:

- Pole A is higher than pole B but lower than pole C.
- Pole C is lower than pole D and pole E is the lowest.

If we arrange all five poles in ascending order on the basis of their height, which one will be in the middle?

(A) Pole D (B) Pole C (C) Pole B (D) Pole A

(E) None of these

Answer (D)

Explanation: Here, pole A is higher than pole B. Therefore, A > B > or, B < A

Pole A is lower than pole C. Therefore, A < C

Pole C is lower than pole D. Therefore, C < D

We have, B < A < C < D. Now, pole E is the lowest, therefore, E < B < A < C < D

Therefore, pole A will be in the middle.

Calendars and Possible Combinations

Birthdays, anniversaries, appointments and holidays, etc, all these have one thing in common, it is a day. It is difficult to remember dates so far that calendar comes to our rescue.

Possible Combinations

Consider the following example: How many possible combinations of one boy and one girl can be formed from 2 boys and 3 girls?

Let us see, if two boys are B_1 and B_2 and three girls are G_1, G_2 and G_3, the possible combinations are: B_1G_1, B_1G_2, B_1G_3, B_2G_1, B_2G_2, B_2G_3

Therefore, the number of possible combinations = 2 × 3 = 6. Now, we can say that the number of (1 - 1) possible combinations of (x - y) objects are (x × y).

Example:

If the day before yesterday was Monday, what will be day after tomorrow?

(A) Friday (B) Tuesday (C) Thursday (D) Saturday

(E) None of these

Answer (A)

Explanation: Here,

Day before yesterday	Monday
Yesterday	Tuesday
Today	Wednesday
Tomorrow	Thursday
Day after tomorrow	Friday

Example:

Rahul's birthday falls on the day just before 3rd Monday of April 20XX. The day on which Rahul celebrates his birthday will be:

April 20XX						
S	M	T	W	Th	F	S
1	2	3	4	5	6	7

(A) 14th (B) 15th
(C) 16th (D) 13th
(E) None of these

Answer (B)

Explanation: 3rd Monday of April 20XX is 16th. Hence, Rahul will celebrate his birthday on 15th April 20XX.

Example:

How many possible combinations of 1 Rat and 1 Hole can be made from 3 rats and 4 holes?

(A) 12 (B) 7 (C) 14 (D) 15
(E) None of these

Answer (A)

Explanation: Required number of possible combinations is 3 × 4 = 12

Example:

How many possible combinations of 1 Shirt and 2 Jeans can be formed using the given information?

Shirts	Jeans
Van Heusen	Levis
John Players	Lee
Peter England	Wrangler
Anvil	Diesel
	Numero Uno
	Spykar
	Flying Machine

(A) 36 (B) 24 (C) 28 (D) 32

(E) None of these

Answer (C)

Explanation: Number of brands of Shirts = 4

Number of brands of Jeans = 7

Hence, the required possible combinations = 4 × 7 = 28

Example:

If the given clock is 35 minutes fast, then the correct time before one and half an hour in the morning will be:

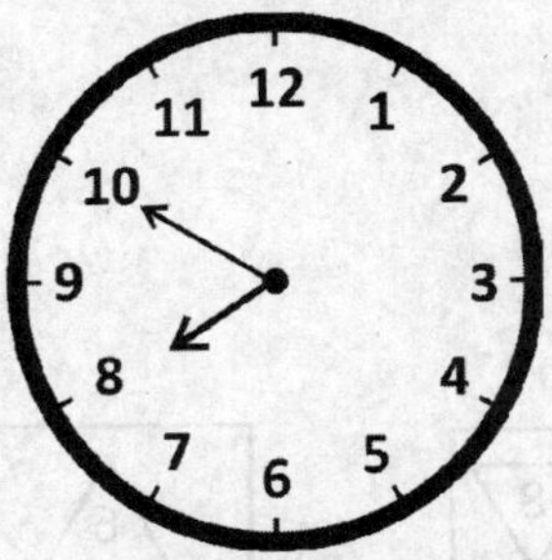

(A) 5:45 am (B) 5:55 am (C) 6:25 am (D) 6:50 am

(E) None of these

Answer (A)

Explanation: Current time showing by watch = 7:50 am

Correct time = 7:50 am – 35 minutes = 7:15 am

Time before one and half an hour = 7:15 am – 1 hour 30 minutes = 5:45 am

Analogy

Simple meaning of analogy is similarity. But, in terms of reasoning, the meaning of analogy is logical similarity in two or more things. In problems based on Analogy, we will usually be given one pair of images that are connected in a particular way and the first image of a second pair. We have to find the correct image to complete the second pair in the same way as the first pair.

Example:

Find the matching pair.

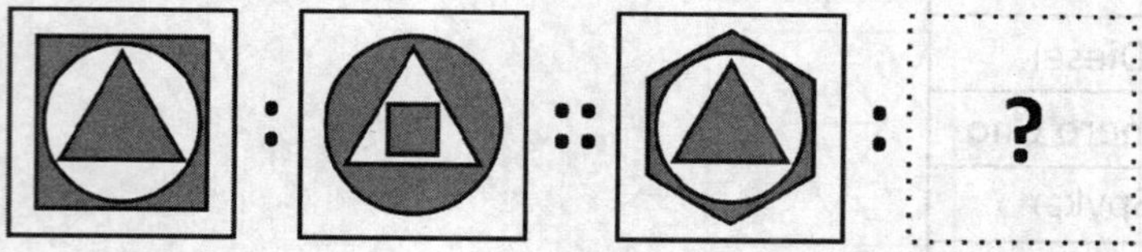

(A) 
(B) 
(C) 
(D) 

(E) None of these

Answer (B)

Explanation: In first figure of left pair, middle figure becomes the outer figure, outer figure becomes inner figure and inner figure becomes middle figure. In both figures of left pair, outer figures and inner figures are shaded, while middle figure is unshaded.

Example:

Find the missing pair.

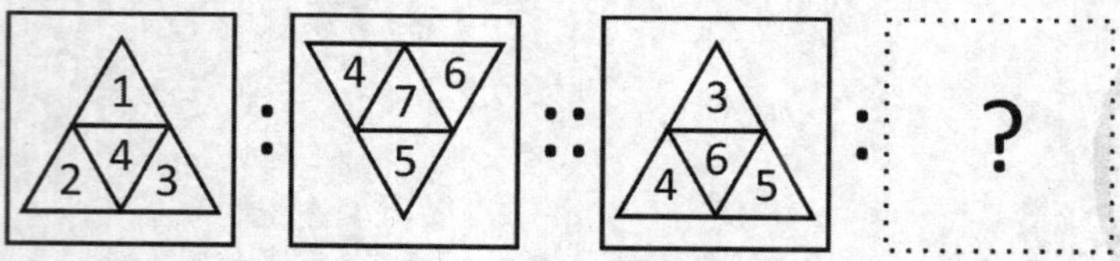

(A) 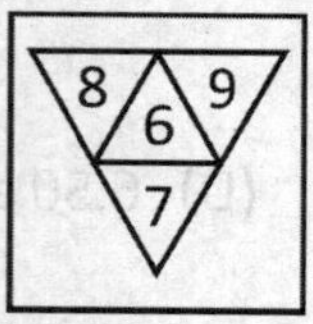

(B) 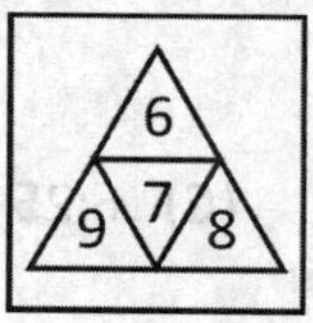

(C) 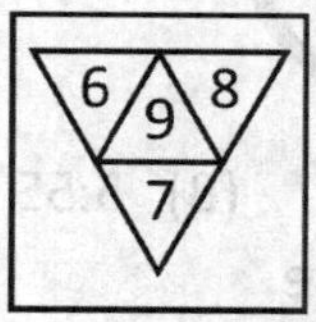

(D) 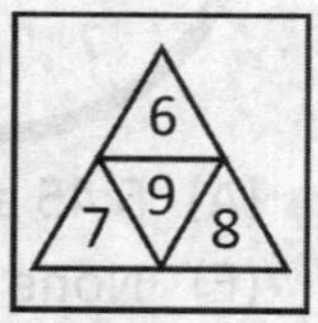

(E) 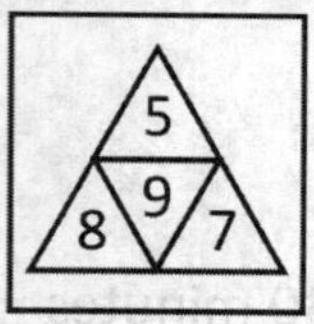

Answer (C)

Explanation: Here, pattern followed in left pair:

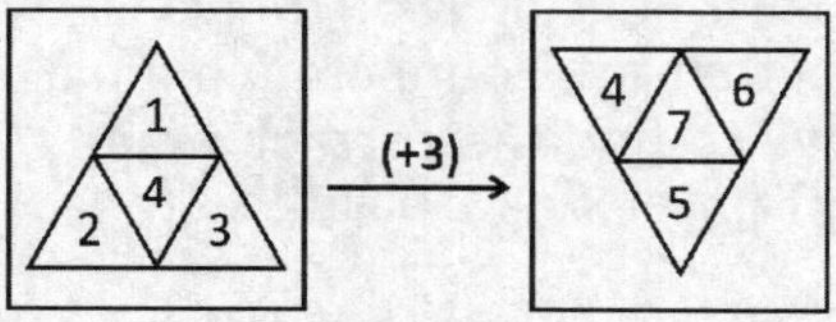

Therefore, pattern followed in right pair:

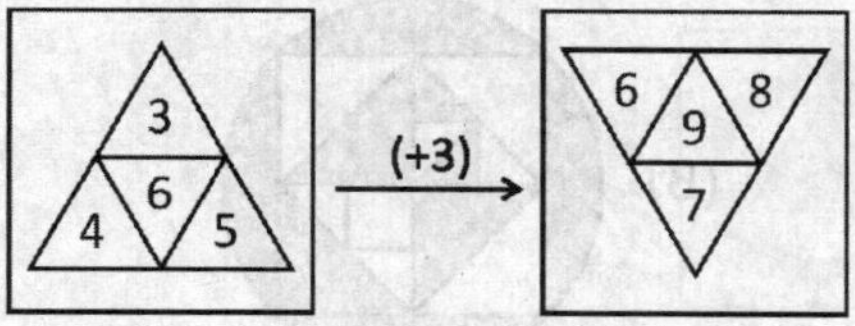

Classification

Classification of figures or shapes test our ability to work out, which shapes are similar and which are different in a given set of options. We need to use our observation skill to compare the given shapes, symbols and find the visual link or links.

Example:

Find the 'odd one out'?

(A) 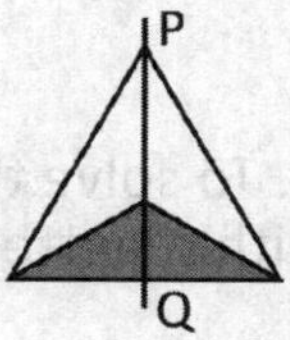

(B) 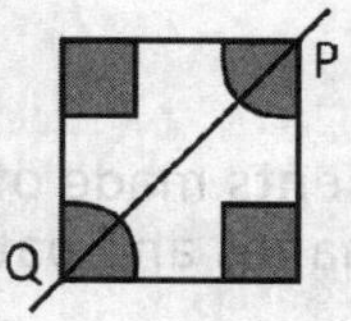

(C) 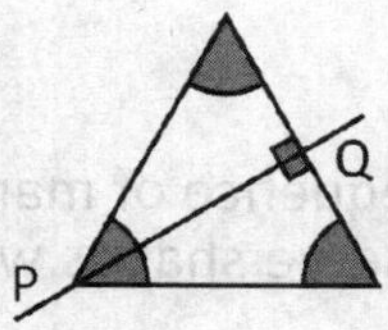

(D) 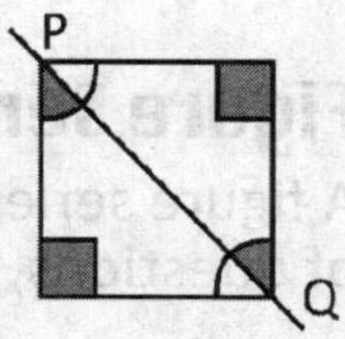

(E) 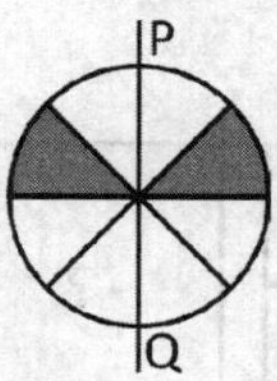

Answer (D)

Explanation: Figures in options (A), (B), (C) and (E) are symmetrical along PQ. But figure in option (D) is not symmetrical along PQ.

Example:

Which of the following figures is same as the given problem figure?

(A) 

(B) 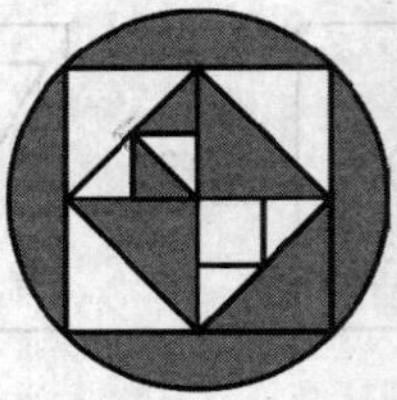

(C) 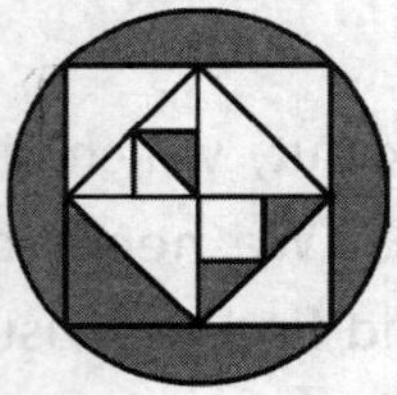

(D) 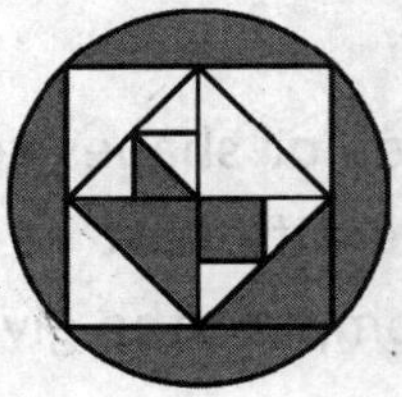

(E) None of these

Answer (B)

Explanation: By matching shaded parts of given circle, we find that figure in option (B) is same as the problem figure.

Figure Series

A figure series is a sequence of many elements made of figures. To solve these type of questions, we observe shapes within shapes and patterns within patterns.

Example:

What comes next?

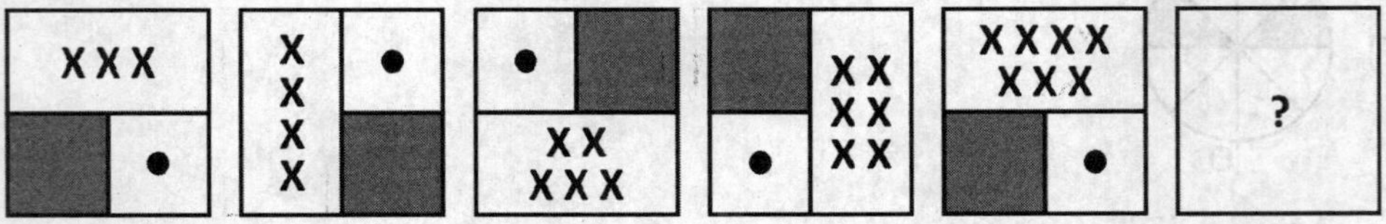

(A) 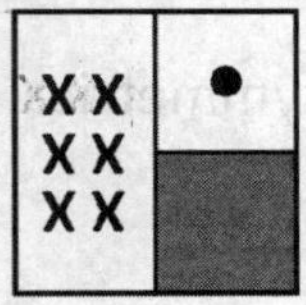

(B) 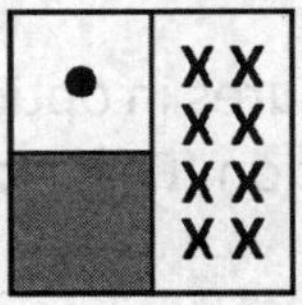

(C) 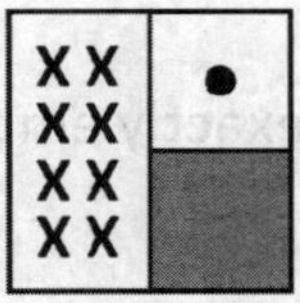 (D) 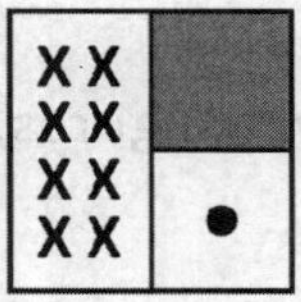

(E) None of these

Answer (C)

Explanation: Here, the square rotates one step anticlockwise in every next figure and one X is increasing in every next figure.

Hence, required figure is in option (C).

Embedded Figures

If a figure contains another figure as its parts, the figure part is called embedded figure. In such type of questions, a figure is given followed by four parts such that one of them is embedded in the given figure. We have to identify such part.

Example:

In which one of the following figures, the figure given below is exactly embedded as one of its part?

(A) 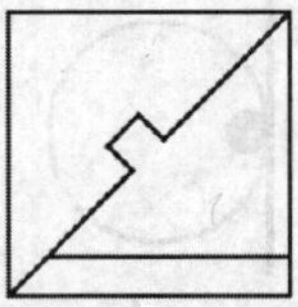 (B) 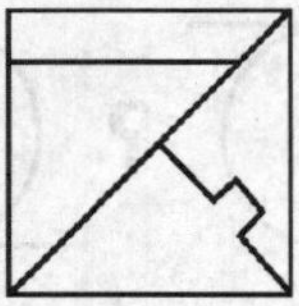 (C) 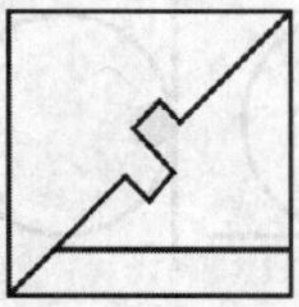 (D) 

(E) None of these

Answer (B)

Explanation: Figure given in question is the part of the figure given in option (B).

Example:

In which one of the following figures, the figure given below is exactly embedded as one of its part?

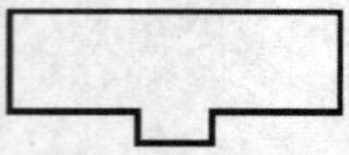

(A) 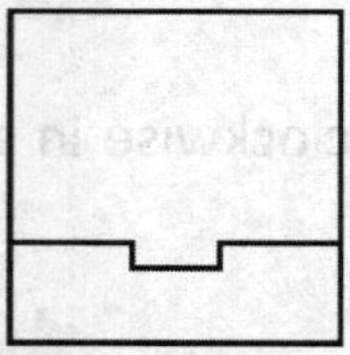

(B) 

(C) 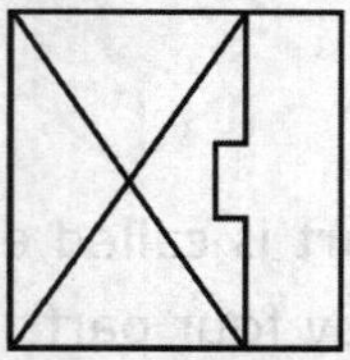

(D) 

(E) None of these

Answer (C)

Explanation: Figure given in question is a part of the figure given in option (C).

Figure Patterns

Figure pattern is a collection of figures that the follows a certain sequence or a certain rule.

Example:

Find the missing figure (?) in the given figure pattern.

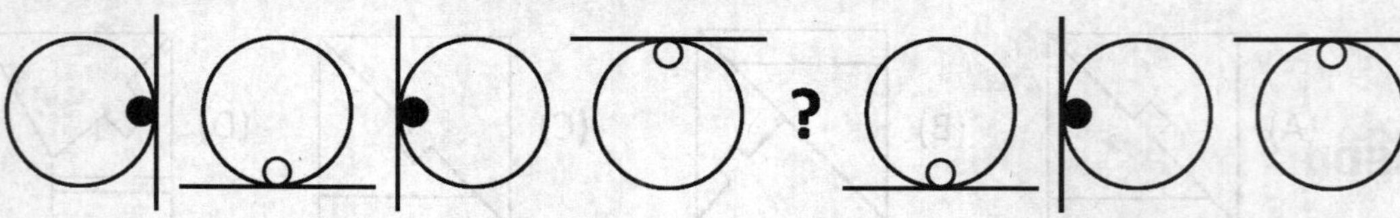

(A) 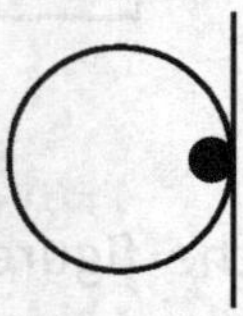

(B) 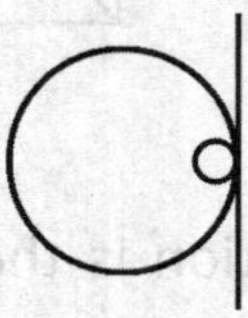

(C) 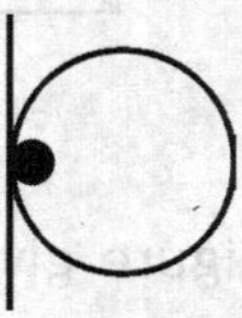

(D) 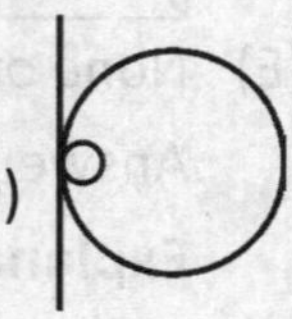

(E) None of these

Answer (A)

Explanation: Here, the figure rotates one step clockwise and in every next figure the inner small shaded circle is unshaded and in next step it is again shaded. Therefore, the required figure is given in option (A).

Example:

Which of the following figures will complete the figure given below?

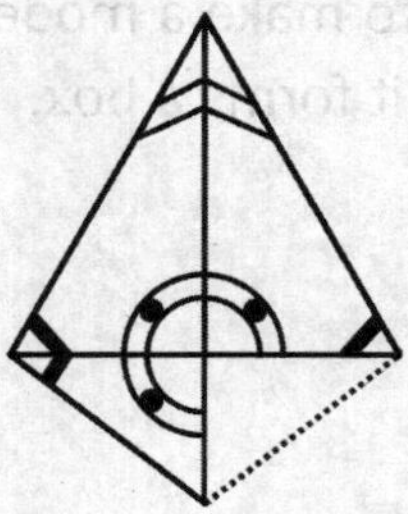

(A)  (B)  (C)  (D) 

(E) None of these

Answer (C)

Explanation: Here, the complete figure is:

Therefore, the required part of figure is in option (C).

Geometrical Shapes

Geometrical shapes come from geometry which is the maths of shapes made of points and lines. Some shapes are simple such as the triangle, square and circle, while other shapes are complex. While solving non verbal reasoning based on geometrical shapes, following points are important:

- **Largest Perimeter:** If the length of a figure does not change but width changes, then the figure having largest width have the largest perimeter.
- **Symmetrical Figure:** If a line divides a figure into two Identical parts, then the figure is symmetrical and the line is called **Line of Symmetry**.

- **Counting Geometrical Shapes**: In order to count the geometrical shapes, we identify the shapes and solids by their names and images.
- **Net of a Cube:** Net is a pattern that we can cut and fold to make a model of a solid shape. A net of a cube has 6 faces and when folded, it forms a box.

Example:

How many horizontal lines are there in the given figure?

(A) 4 (B) 6 (C) 12 (D) 8

(E) None of these

Answer (D)

Explanation: Here, given figure is symmetrical about the dotted line.

Now, number of horizontal lines on the left of dotted line is 4.

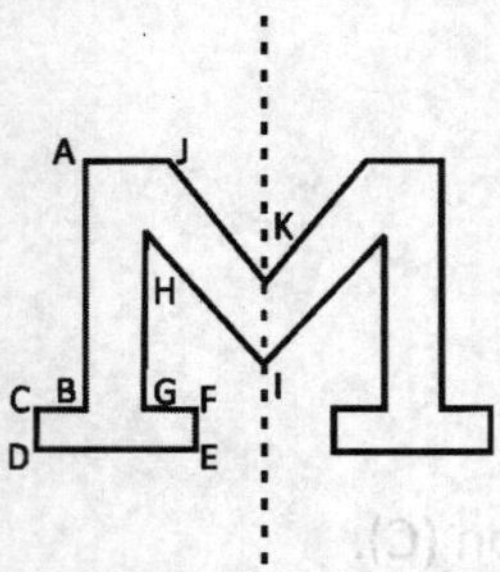

Hence, total number of horizontal lines is $4 \times 2 = 8$

Example:

Select the odd one out?

(A)  (B)  (C)  (D) 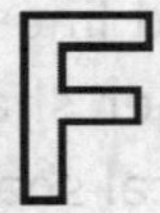

(E) 

Answer (D)

Explanation: Figure given in options (A), (B), (C) and (E) has exactly one line of symmetry. Figure given in option (D) has no line of symmetry.

Example:

Which of the following is a net cube?

(A) 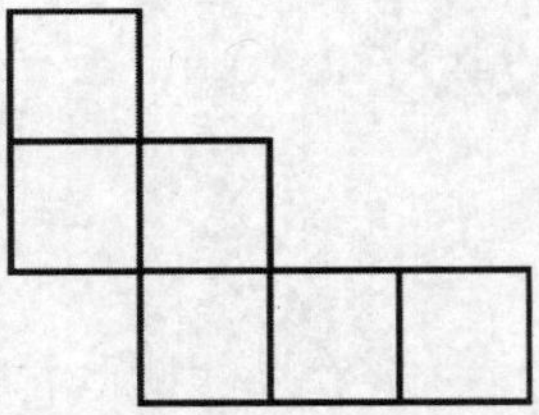

(B) 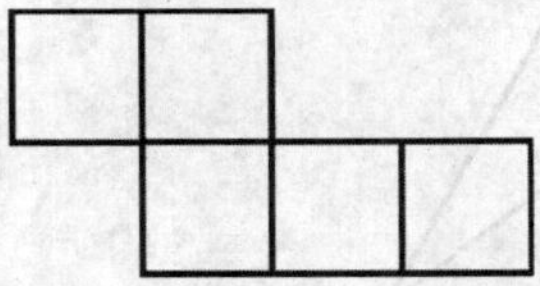

(C) 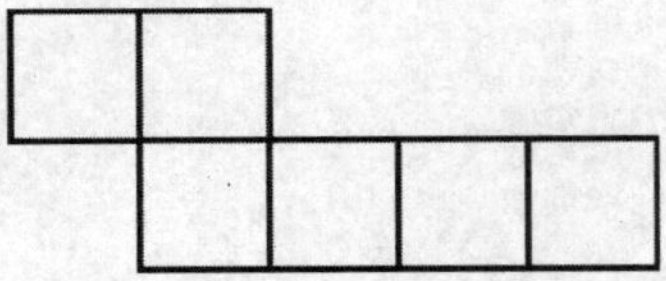

(D) 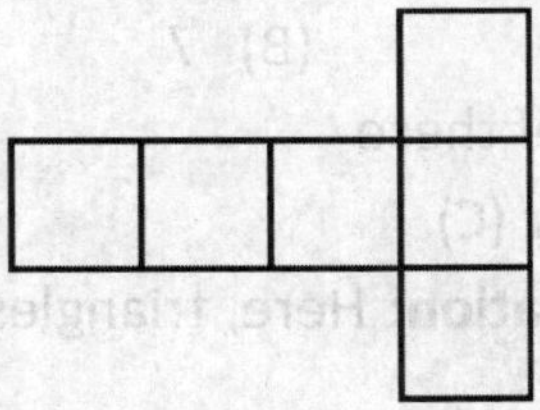

(E) None of these

Answer (D)

Explanation: Only figure given in option (D) can fold to make a model of solid shape.

Example:

Number of circles in the given figure is:

(A) 4 (B) 5 (C) 6 (D) 7

(E) None of these

Answer (B)

Explanation:

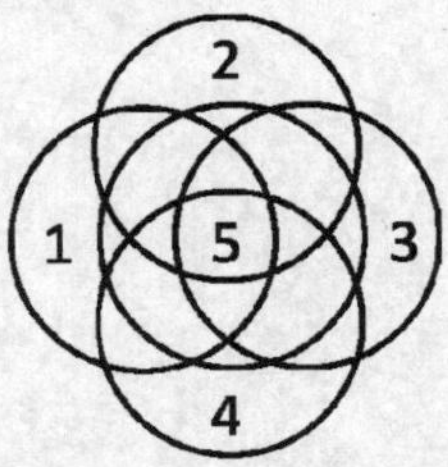

There are only 5 circles in the given figure.

Example:

Number of triangles in the given figure is:

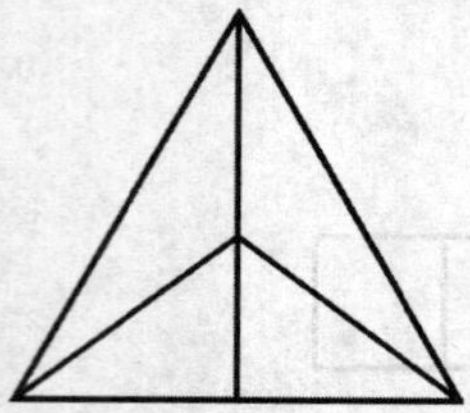

(A) 9 (B) 7 (C) 8 (D) 6

(E) None of these

Answer (C)

Explanation: Here, triangles are:

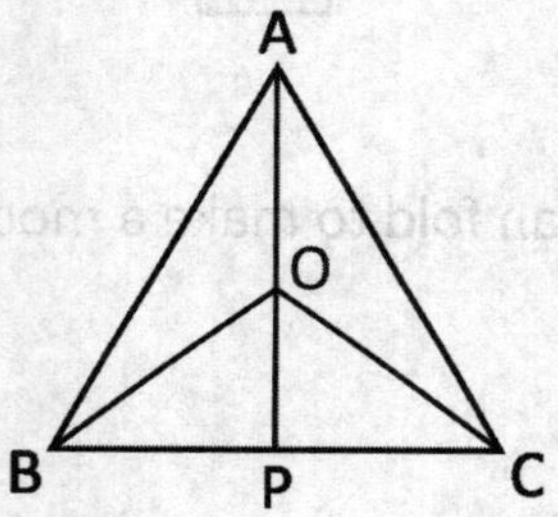

ABP, ACP, ABC, AOB, AOC, OBP, OCP and OBC

Therefore, the number of triangles is 8.

Example:

Which one of the following figures has a line of symmetry?

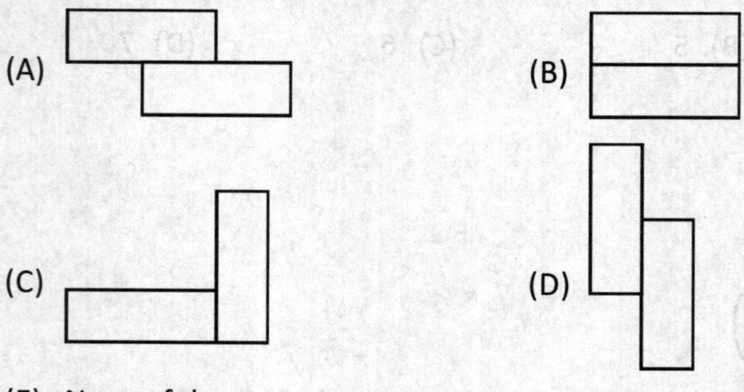

(E) None of these

Answer (B)

Explanation:

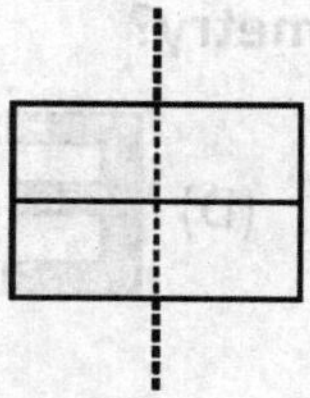

Only the figure given in option (B) has a line of symmetry.

Example:

How many lines of symmetry are there in the given figure?

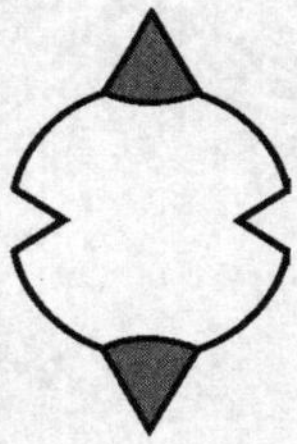

(A) Zero (B) One (C) Two (D) Four
(E) None of these

Answer (C)

Explanation:

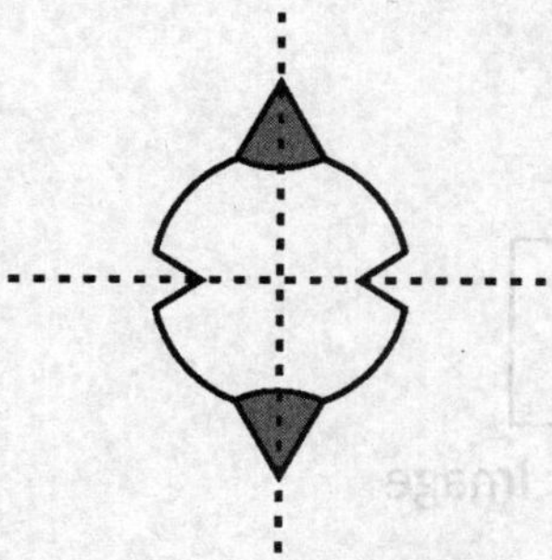

There are two lines of symmetry in the given figure.

Example:

Which one of the following has more than one line of symmetry?

(A) M (B) A (C) C (D) E

(E) None of these

Answer (E)

Explanation:

All the figures have exactly one line of symmetry.

Mirror Images

In a plane mirror, if we lift our right hand, the image in the mirror shows our left hand and if we lift our left hand, the image shows our right hand. Therefore, in a mirror image, the left part of an object becomes right part and the right part becomes left part.

Left Hand Side (LHS) $\rightleftarrows$ Right Hand Side (RHS)

For example,

Actual Image Mirror Image

Mirror Images of the Capital Letters and Numbers (1 to 9):

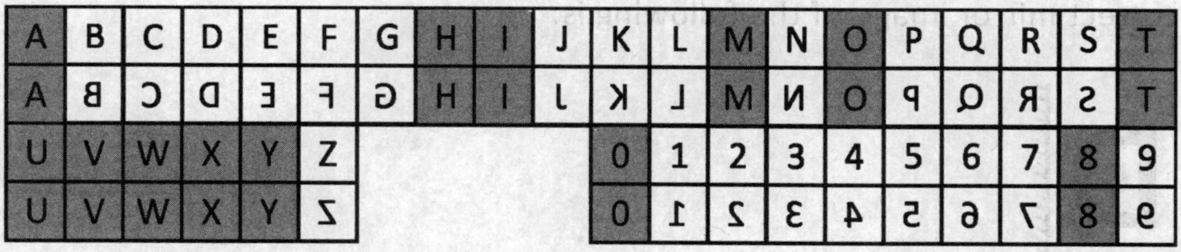

Example:

Find the mirror image of the combination of letters given below.

Mirror

(A) 

(B) 

(C) 

(D) 

(E) None of these

Answer (D)

Explanation:

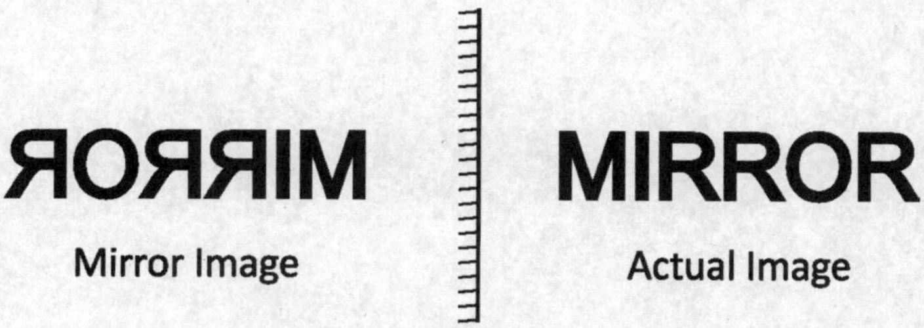

Mirror

Example:

The correct mirror image of the following is:

(A)  (B)  (C)  (D) 

(E) None of these

Answer (B)

Explanation:

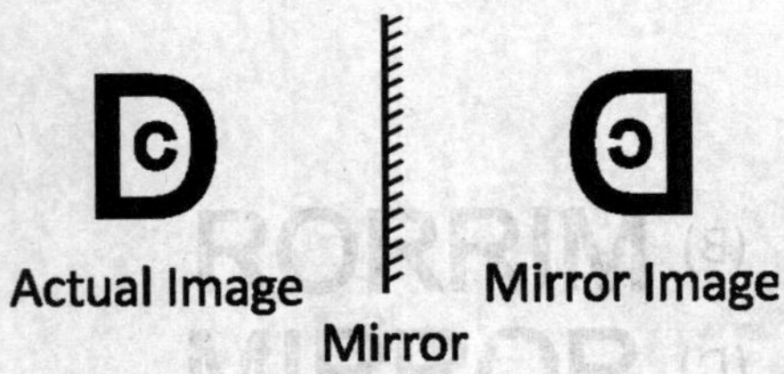

Summary

- The process of thinking about something in a logical way in order to form a conclusion is called **Logical reasoning**.
- Logical reasoning is the ability of the mind to think and understand things in a logical way.
- We do not use any general knowledge when answering logical reasoning questions. Everything we need to answer the question is included in the passage.
- While solving logical reasoning problems, we look at problems with different perspectives through observation, explanation and critical thinking.
- **Analogy** is a similarity between like features of two things on which comparison may be based.
- **Classification** of figures or shapes test our ability to work out, which shapes are similar and which are different in a given set of options.
- Logical reasoning based on grouping tests our understanding and recognition of shapes and patterns.
- The number of possible (1 - 1) combinations of (x - y) objects is x × y.
- If a line divides a figure into two identical parts, then the figure is symmetrical and the line is called **line of symmetry**.
- Net is a pattern that we can cut and fold to make a model of a solid shape. A net of a cube has 6 paces and when folded, it forms a box.
- In a mirror image, the left part of an object becomes right part and the right part becomes the left part.

Solved Problems

1. Find the value of P and Q in the given number pattern.

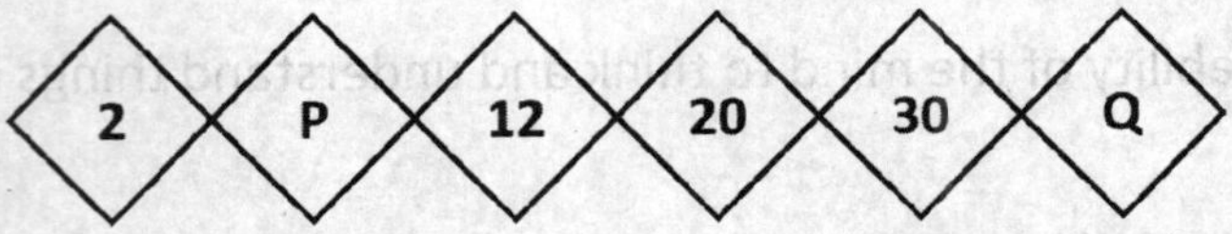

(A) 4, 24 (B) 6, 42

(C) 8, 56 (D) 10, 80

(E) None of these

Answer (B)

Explanation: Here, rule followed:

$2 \xrightarrow{(+4)} (6) \xrightarrow{(+6)} 12 \xrightarrow{(+8)} 20 \xrightarrow{(+10)} 30 \xrightarrow{(+12)} (42)$

Also, $1 \times 2 = 2$, $2 \times 3 = (6)$, $3 \times 4 = 12$, $4 \times 5 = 20$, $5 \times 6 = 30$, $6 \times 7 = (42)$.

Therefore, the values of P and Q are 6, 42.

2. If the given number table follows a certain rule row-wise or column-wise, the missing number will be:

13	**12**	**18**
5	**8**	**3**
61	**92**	**?**

(A) 50 (B) 52 (C) 54 (D) 60

(E) 47

Answer (A)

Explanation: Here, $13 \times 5 = 65 - 4 = 61$, $12 \times 8 = 96 - 4 = 92$

And, $18 \times 3 = 54 - 4 = (50)$.

3. Which one of the following words *cannot* be made from the letters of the given word?

UNIVERSITY

(A) Virtue (B) Insure (C) Unrest (D) Nestor

(E) None of these

Answer (D)

Explanation: The letter O in the word 'Nestor' is not given in the word UNIVERSITY.

4. Form a meaningful word by arranging the given numbers corresponding to the letter given below.

O	P	A	N	I
1	2	3	4	5

(A) 2, 4, 5, 3, 1 (B) 3, 2, 1, 4, 5

(C) 2, 5, 3, 4, 1 (D) 3, 1, 2, 4, 5

(E) None of these

Answer (C)

Explanation: The letters are arranged to form the meaningful word PIANO as follows:

P	I	A	N	O
2	5	3	4	1

Therefore, the combination of their numbers is 2, 5, 3, 4, 1.

5. If 'Sun' is called 'Blue', 'Blue' is called 'Moon', 'Moon' is called 'Voilet' and 'Voilet' is called 'Dark', then the colour of clear Sky is:

(A) Blue (B) Voilet (C) Dark (D) Moon

(E) Sun

Answer (D)

Explanation: The colour of clear Sky is 'Blue' and as given, 'Blue' is called 'Moon'. So, the colour of clear Sky is 'Moon'.

6. **In a certain code language, if PRINCIPAL is written as $#2*@2$75 and POLICE is written as $352@8, then how PEON is written in that code language?**

(A) $5#* (B) $83* (C) $23# (D) @8#7

(E) None of these

Answer (B)

Explanation: Here,

P	R	I	N	C	I	P	A	L
$	#	2	*	@	2	$	7	5

and,

P	O	L	I	C	E
$	3	5	2	@	8

Now,

P	E	O	N
$	8	3	*

. Therefore, code for PEON is $83*

7. **There are five tables, table A, table B, table C, table D and table E. Table A is taller than table D. Table B and table E are of the same height. Table C is shorter than table E. Table D is taller than table B. Which table is the tallest?**

(A) Table A (B) Table B

(C) Table D (D) Table E

(E) None of these

Answer (A)

Explanation: Here, table A is taller than Table D; therefore, (A > D)

Table C is shorter than Table E; therefore, (E > C)

Table D is taller than Table B; therefore (D > B)

Table B and Table E are of same height; therefore, (B = E)

Hence, A > D > B = E > C

So we have, Table A is the tallest one.

8. **Amit was facing North–East. He made an anticlockwise turn and ended up facing West. The turn Amit took is:**

(A) $\frac{1}{8}$ (B) $\frac{3}{8}$ (C) $\frac{5}{8}$ (D) $\frac{7}{8}$

(E) None of these

Answer (B)

Explanation: Here, first Amit was facing North–East.

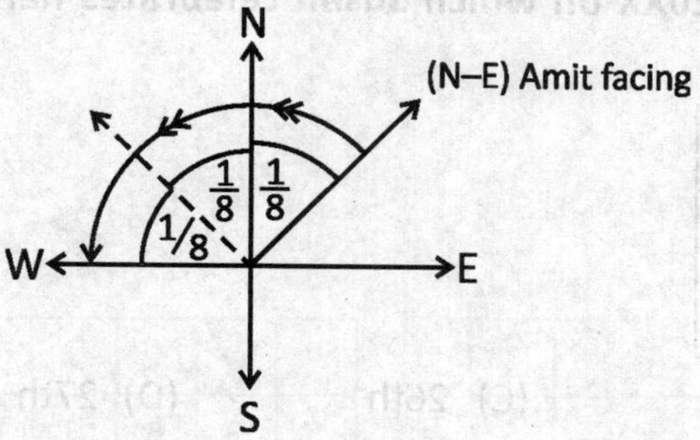

In first $\frac{1}{8}$ turn, Amit faced North. After second and third $\frac{1}{8}$ turn, Amit faced West.

Hence, the required anticlockwise turn = $\frac{1}{8}+\frac{1}{8}+\frac{1}{8}=\frac{3}{8}$

9. How many possible combinations of 1 Bike and 1 Car can be formed using the given information?

Bike	Car
TVS	Hyundai
Yamaha	Fiat
Kawasaki	Toyota
	Honda
	Suzuki

(A) 8 (B) 12 (C) 15 (D) 18

(E) None of these

Answer (C)

Explanation: Number of brands of Bikes = 3. Number of brands of Cars = 5

Therefore, the required number of possible combinations = 3 × 5 = 15

10. Susan's birthday falls on the day just before 4th Friday of the September 20XX. The day in September 20XX on which Susan celebrates her birthday is:

September 20XX						
S	**M**	**T**	**W**	**Th**	**F**	**S**
	1	**2**	**3**	**4**	**5**	**6**

(A) 24th (B) 25th (C) 26th (D) 27th

(E) None of these

Answer (B)

Explanation: Here, first Friday in September 20XX is 5th day

Therefore, 4th Friday is (5 + 7 × 3)th = (5 + 21)th = 26th day

Hence, the day in September 20XX on which Susan celebrates her birthday is (26 – 1)th = 25th day

11. There is a certain relationship between figure (i) and figure (ii). Establish a similar relationship between figure (iii) and figure (iv) by selecting a figure from the following options which will replace the question mark (?) in figure (iv).

(i) (ii) (iii) (iv)

(A) 

(B) 

(C) 

(D) 

(E) None of these

Answer (D)

Explanation: When first figure is rotated by $\frac{1}{2}$ turn, small circle inside the triangle becomes shaded and the shaded three strips become two unshaded strips. Therefore, missing figure (iv) is given in option (D).

12. Which of the following figure parts will complete the figure given below?

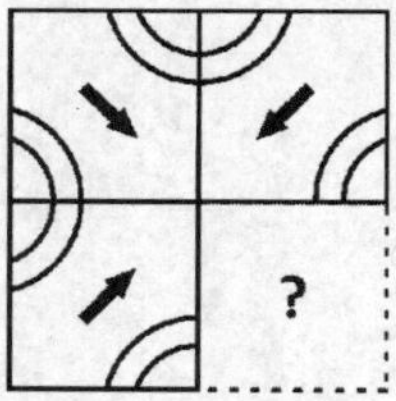

(A)  (B)  (C)  (D) 

(E) None of these

Answer (A)

Explanation: Let us complete the figure.

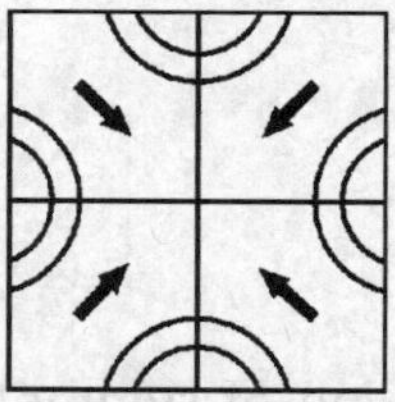

Figure given in option (A) is the required part of the figure.

13. What comes next in the given figure pattern?

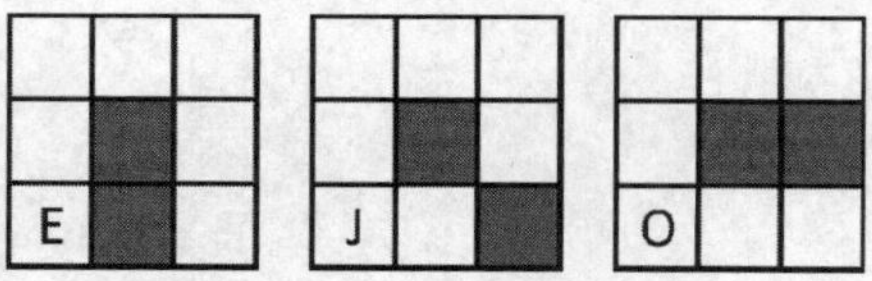

(A) 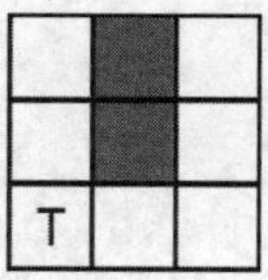

(B) 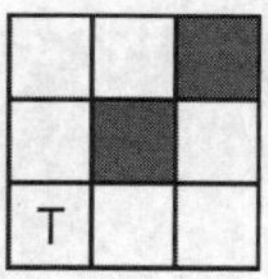

(C) 

(D) 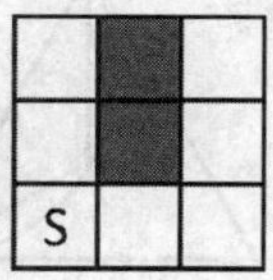

(E) None of these

Answer (B)

Explanation: Here, $E \xrightarrow[\text{FGHI}]{+5} J \xrightarrow[\text{KLMN}]{+5} O \xrightarrow[\text{PQRS}]{+5} T$ and the shaded unit squares turn anticlockwise by 45°. Therefore, the required figure is given in option (B).

14. Select the odd one out.

(A) 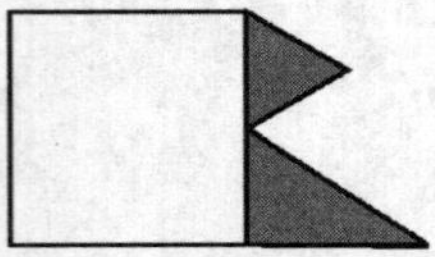

(B) 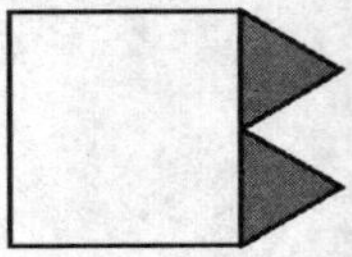

(C) 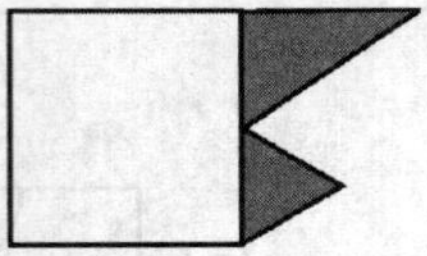

(D) 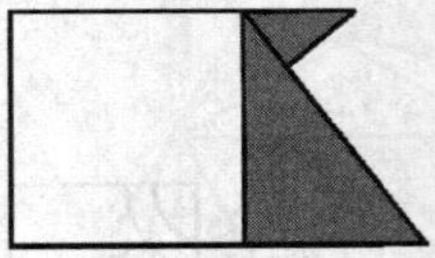

(E) 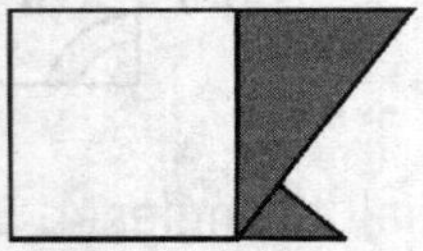

Answer (B)

Explanation:

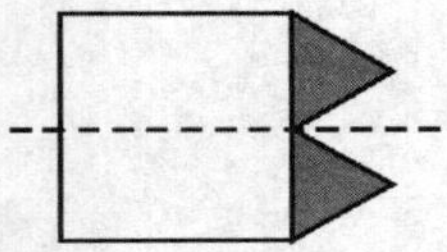

Figures given in options (A), (C) and (D) have no line of symmetry. Figure given in option (B) has one line of symmetry.

15. How many triangles are there in the figure?

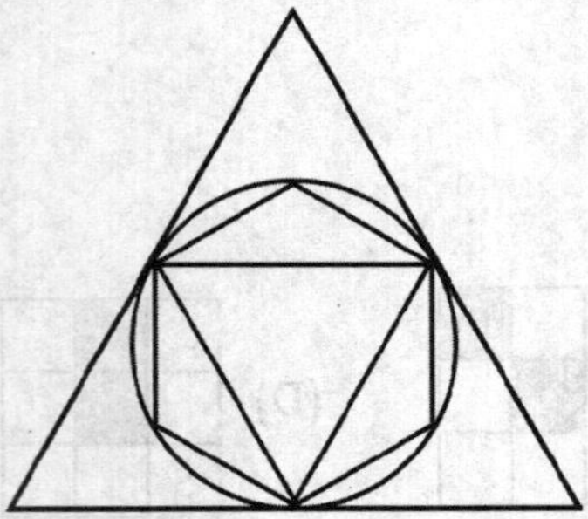

(A) 8
(B) 7
(C) 9
(D) 10
(E) None of these

Answer (A)

Explanation:

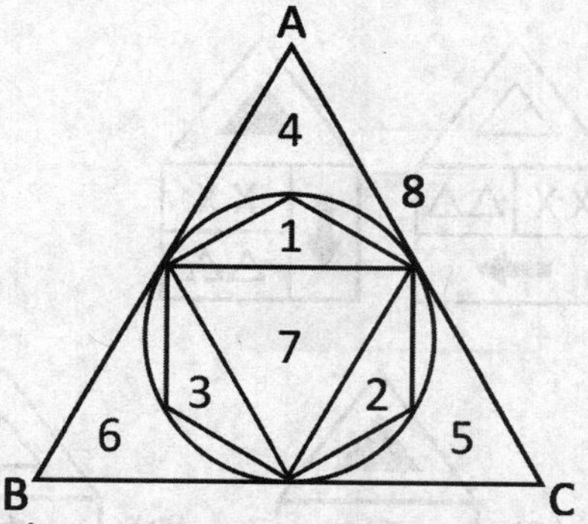

There are three small triangles 1, 2, 3 and four small triangles 4, 5, 6, 7 and one large triangle ABC. Therefore, the number of triangles in the given figure is 8.

16. Which of the following part is exactly embedded in given figure?

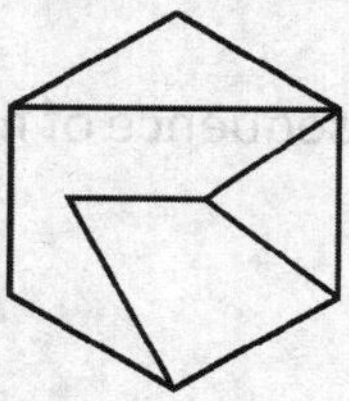

(A) 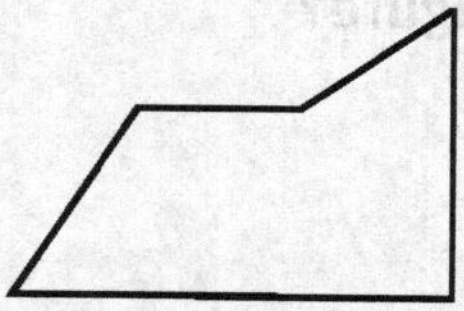

(B) 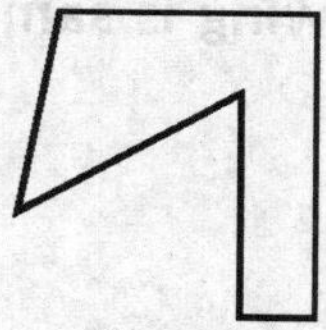

(C) 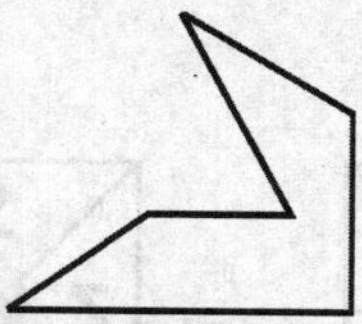

(D) 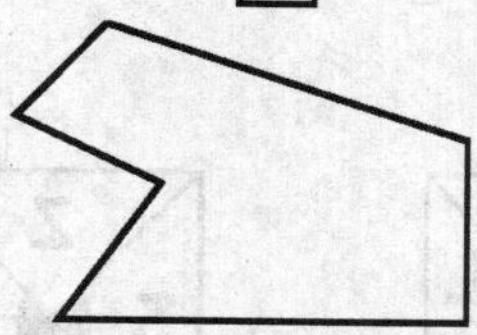

(E) None of these

Answer (C)

Explanation:

The required embedded part of the figure given in option (C) is shaded here:

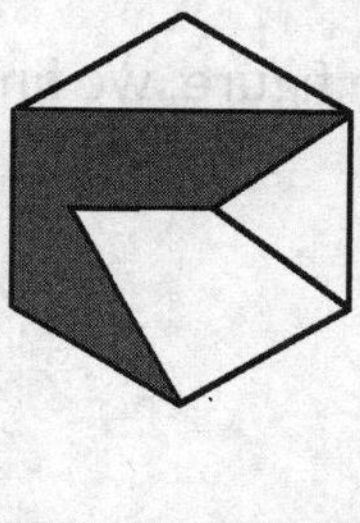

17. What comes next in the pattern given below?

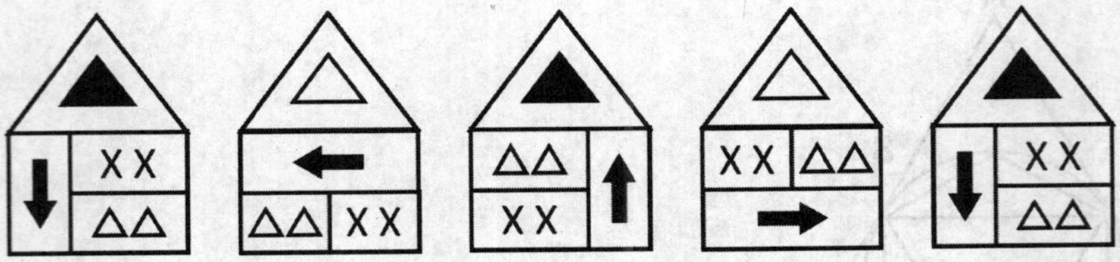

(A)  (B)  (C)  (D) 

(E) None of these

Answer (D)

Explanation: The required figure at sixth place in the given sequence of figures will be the same figure given at the second place.

Therefore, the required figure is in option (D).

18. Which of the following is same as the problem figure?

(A)  (B)  (C) 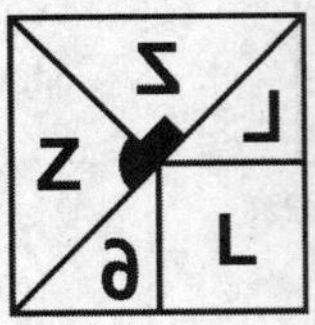 (D) 

(E) None of these

Answer (D)

Explanation: By matching the all parts of the problem figure, we find that the figure given in option (D) is same as problem figure.

19. Which one of the following figures is the mirror image of the given figure?

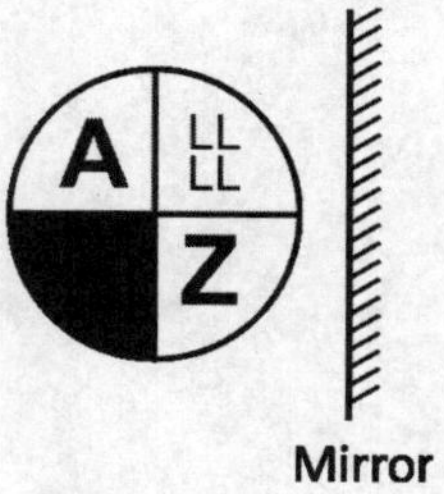

(A)  (B)  (C)  (D) 

(E) None of these

Answer (C)

Explanation:

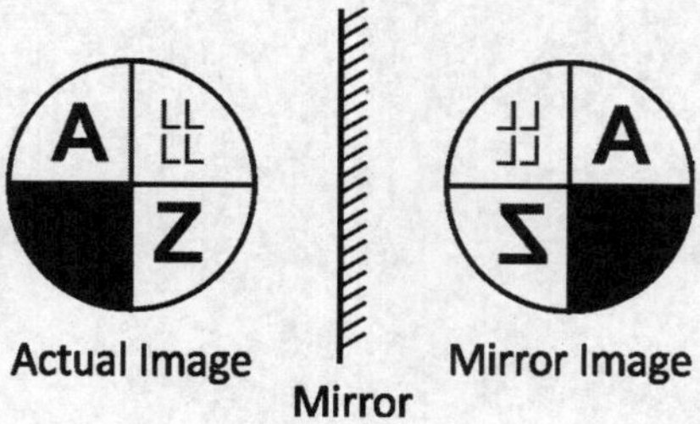

20. Which one of the following is mirror image of the given figure?

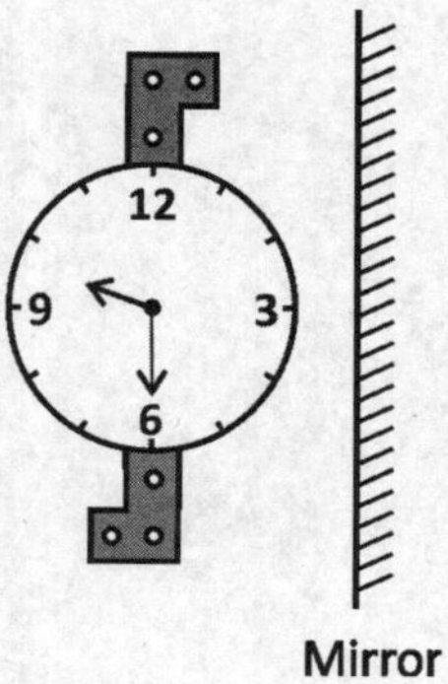

(A) 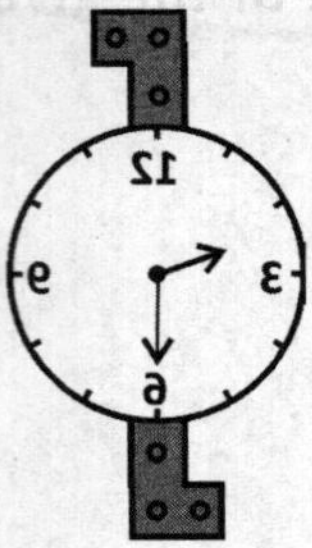

(B) 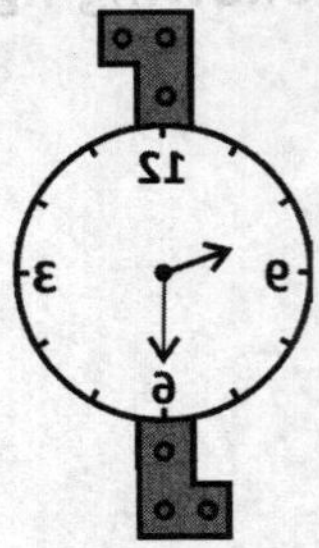

(C) 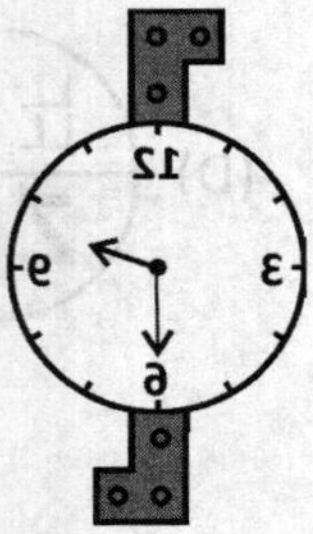

(D) 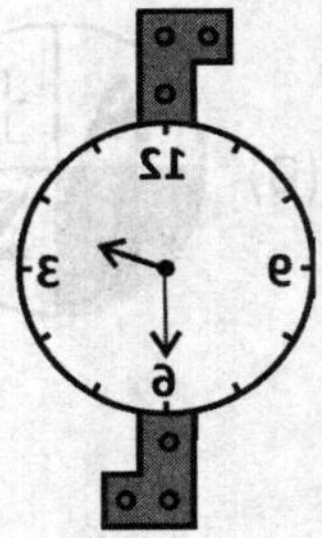

(E) None of these

Answer (B)

Explanation:

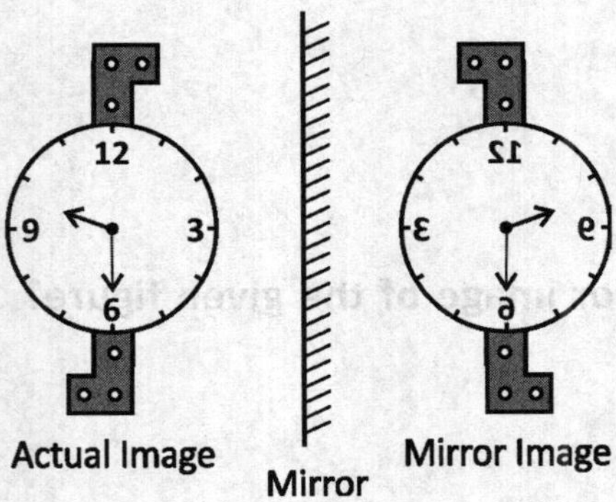

Practice Exercise 9

1. **Find the category of given word so formed by the combination of letters arranged accordingly to form a meaningful word.**

UPRTNI

(A) Cereal (B) Game (C) Animal (D) Vegetable
(E) None of these

2. **Correct arrangement of the following words as they occur in dictionary is:**

1. Cook **2. Rank** **3. Bank** **4. Book**

(A) 4, 3 , 1, 2 (B) 3, 4, 1, 2 (C) 3, 2, 4, 1 (D) 3, 2, 1, 4
(E) None of these

3. **Find the next letter in the given series:**

L	U	M	T	N	S	O	?

(A) Q (B) R (C) T (D) S
(E) None of these

4. **How many meaningful words could be formed from the letters U, B and T?**

(A) Zero (B) One
(C) Two (D) Three
(E) None of these

5. **If O = 15, OR = 33 and OUR = 54, then FOUR = ?**

(A) 58 (B) 59 (C) 60 (D) 64
(E) 142

6. **If UGLY is coded as SEJW, then how is the word NICE coded in that language?**

(A) LGAC (B) MHBD
(C) OJDF (D) LKEG
(E) None of these

7. **If** 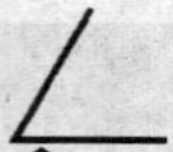 **means** 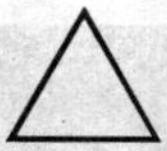,  **means** ,  **means**  **and**  **means** 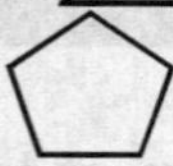**, then which figure has no line segment?**

(A)  (B)  (C)  (D) 

(E) 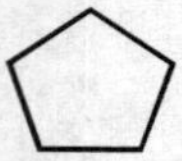

8. **How many letters will appear the same if we rotate the given letters by $\frac{1}{2}$ turn?**

BREATHING

(A) 5 (B) 4

(C) 2 (D) 3

(E) None of these

9. **A certain rule is followed in the given figure. Find the missing number.**

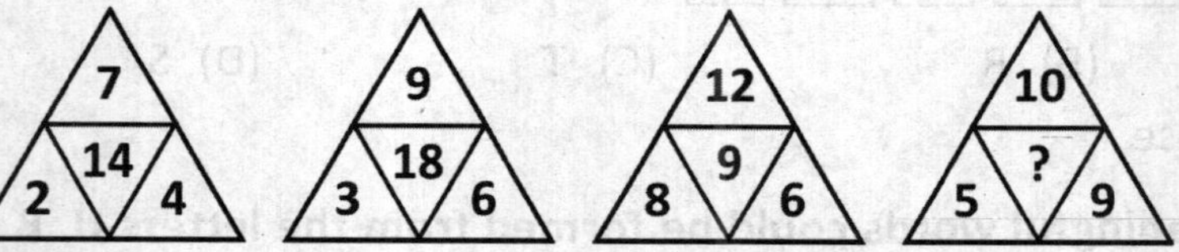

(A) 18 (B) 15

(C) 20 (D) 30

(E) 24

10. **Rahul starts moving from a point P towards North. After walking some distance he turns his right. Again after walking some distance he turns his right. Now his direction is definitely towards:**

(A) East (B) West

(C) North (D) South

(E) None of these

11. Find the matching pair.

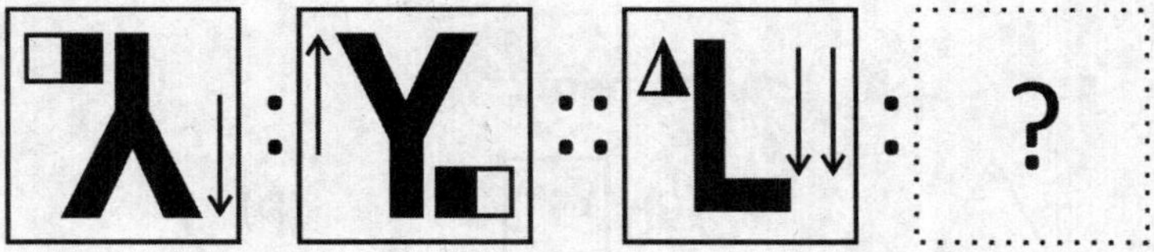

(A) 

(B) 

(C) 

(D) 

(E) None of these

12. Which one of the following figures is same as the given problem Figure (X)?

Figure (X)

(A) 

(B) 

(C) 

(D) 

(E) None of these

13. Which one of the following parts will complete the given Figure (X)?

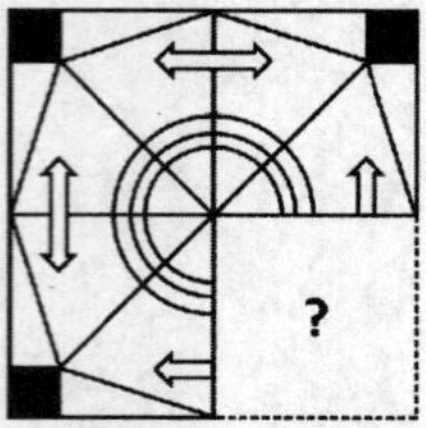

Figure (X)

(A) 

(B) 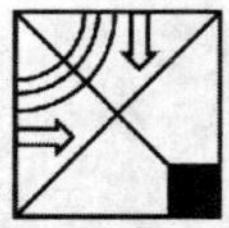

(C) 

(D) 

(E) None of these

14. How many triangles are there in the given figure?

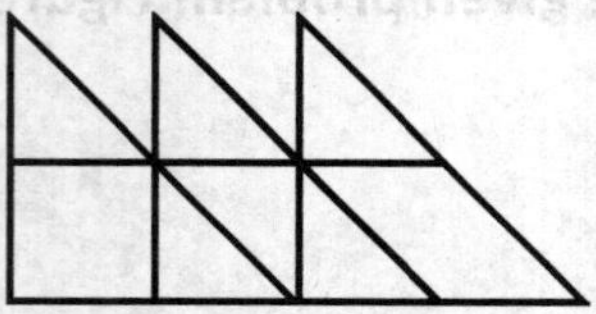

(A) 6

(B) 7

(C) 9

(D) 10

(E) None of these

15. Which of the following options is *not* embedded in the given figure?

(A) 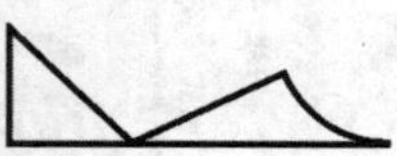

(B) 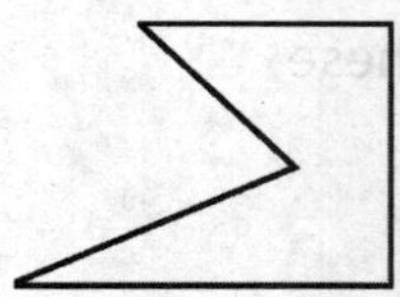

(C) 

(D) 

(E) None of these

16. Which one of the following is *not* a net cube?

(A) 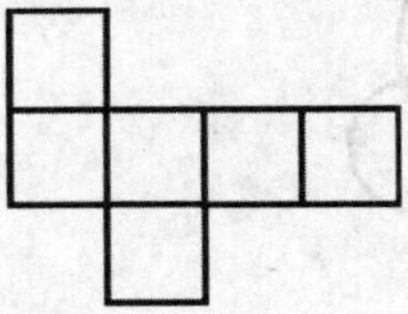

(B) 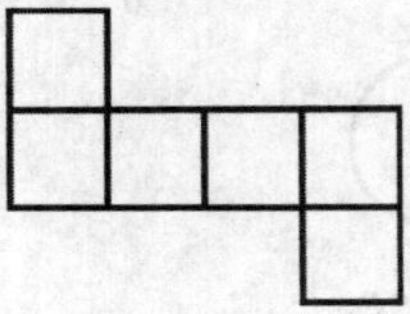

(C) 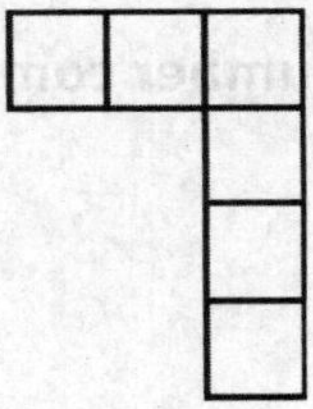

(D) 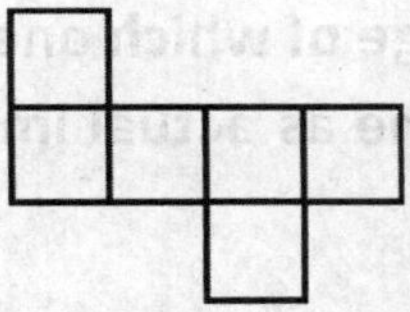

(E) None of these

17. How many letters of the given word have at least one line of symmetry?

CHEMISTRY

(A) 7
(B) 5
(C) 8
(D) 6
(E) None of these

18. Find the mirror image of the given figure, if mirror is placed vertically to the right.

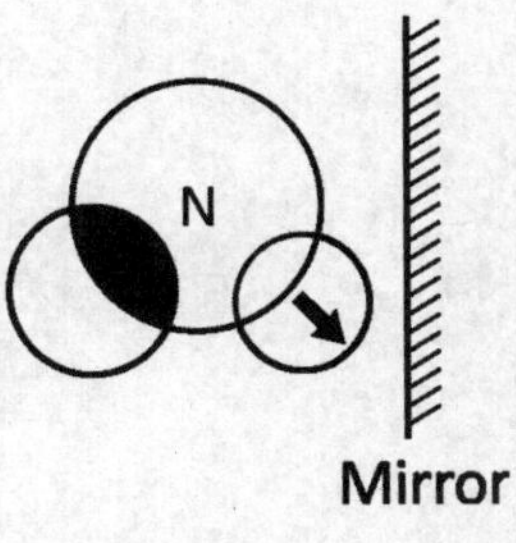

(A) 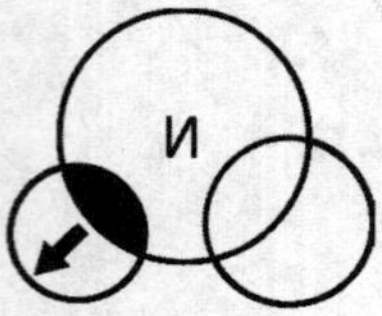

(B) 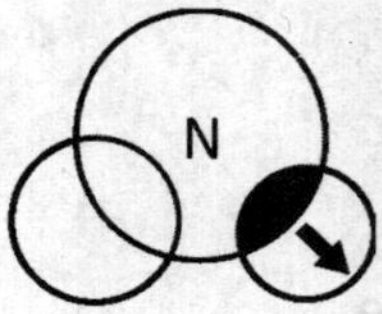

(C) 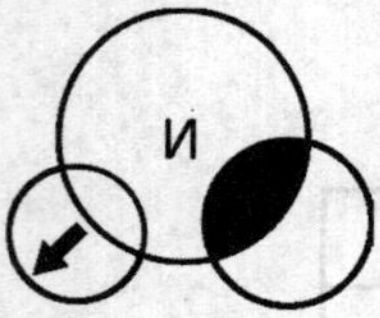

(D) 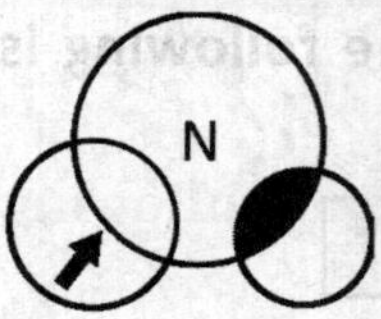

(E) None of these

19. The mirror image of which one of the following letter-number combinations will remain same as actual image?

(A) A7M4V

(B) A8RYZ

(C) A3XLU

(D) A8T0W

(E) None of these

20. Find the odd one out.

(A) 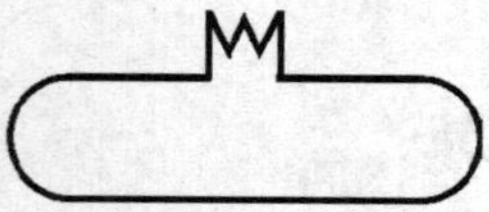

(B) 

(C) 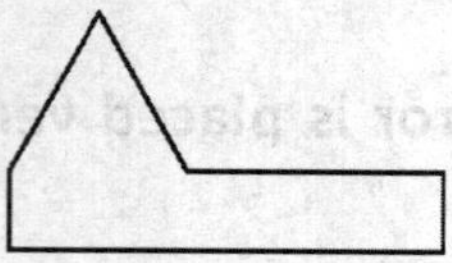

(D) 

(E) 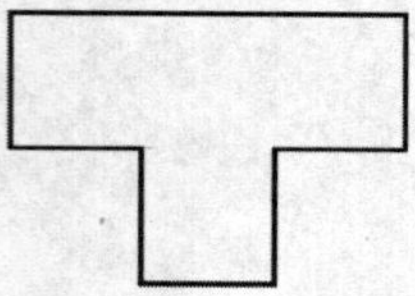

Practice Exercise-1

1. In which one of the following kind of habitats do microorganisms live?

(A) Aquatic
(B) Terrestrial
(C) Aerial
(D) All of these
(E) None of these

2. Which one of the following microorganisms can copy itself only when it enters into the body of a living organism?

(A) Algae
(B) Protozoa
(C) Viruses
(D) All of these
(E) None of these

3. Which one of the following organs is protected by skull?

(A) Lung
(B) Brain
(C) Kidney
(D) Heart
(E) None of these

4. In which one of the following organs of body the exchange of carbon dioxide and oxygen takes place?

(A) Brain
(B) Liver
(C) Lung
(D) Bladder
(E) None of these

5. The stomach is located in which part of the digestive system?

(A) The stomach is located between the esophagus and the large intestine
(B) The stomach is located between the esophagus and the small intestine
(C) The stomach is located between the small intestine and the large intestine
(D) The stomach is located between pharynx and esophagus and the small intestine
(E) None of these

6. Which one of the following parts of body filters extra water from the blood in the form of urine?

(A) Heart (B) Lung

(C) Kidney (D) Urinary bladder

(E) None of these

Questions 7 to 9 are based on the following figure:

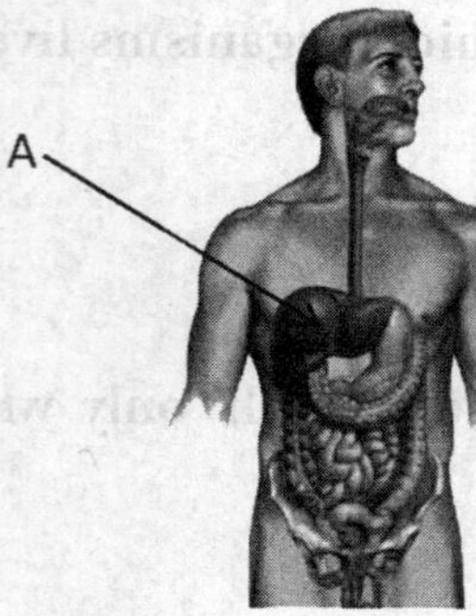

7. Name the organ which has been indicated by the letter A in the figure.

(A) Heart (B) Lung

(C) Liver (D) Stomach

(E) None of these

8. What function does A perform in the human body?

(A) It helps in digestion of food

(B) It pumps the blood throughout the body

(C) It helps in supplying oxygen from the air to body cells

(D) It filters the extra water from the blood

(E) None of these

9. Which one of the following is true about A?

(A) It is the smallest organ of the human body

(B) It is the largest gland of the human body

(C) It is the largest sense organ of the human body

(D) It is the largest system of the human body

(E) None of these

10. Which one of the following sense organs detects the sound?

(A) Tongue
(B) Skin
(C) Eye
(D) Ear
(E) None of these

11. Which one of the following sense organs is also the largest organ of human body?

(A) Tongue
(B) Skin
(C) Eye
(D) Nose
(E) None of these

12. Which one of the following parts of ear contains pinna?

(A) External ear
(B) Middle ear
(C) Internal ear
(D) All of these
(E) None of these

13. Which one of the following is a herbivorous animal?

(A) Hyena
(B) Crow
(C) Horse
(D) Lion
(E) None of these

14. Which one of the following gases is in largest amount in the atmosphere of Earth?

(A) Methane (B) Nitrogen
(C) Oxygen (D) Carbon dioxide
(E) None of these

15. Which of the following properties of carbon dioxide makes it an ideal gas for green house effect?

(A) It is a good absorber of heat

(B) It is poisonous in nature

(C) Increase in amount of carbon dioxide causes harm to the layer of ozone

(D) It is in the gaseous form in the atmosphere of the Earth

(E) None of these

16. Which one of the following is true about invertebrate animals?

(A) They are lacking of back bones

(B) They are lacking of sense organs

(C) They cannot reproduce their young ones

(D) They cannot survive in desert

(E) None of these

Questions 17 to 22 are based on the following figure:

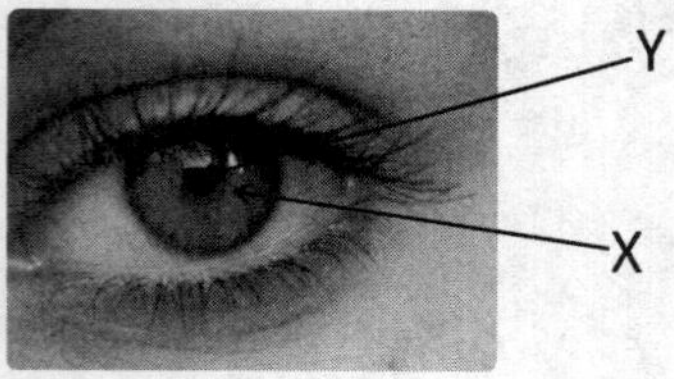

17. Name the part in the figure which has been indicated by X:

(A) Cornea (B) Pupil

(C) Iris (D) Eye lens

(E) None of these

18. What is the function of X in the human eye?

(A) It protects the pupil from dust and other materials

(B) It helps in cleaning the eye by releasing tear

(C) It controls the amount of light entering the eye

(D) It controls the contraction of eye lens

(E) None of these

19. Who of the following is correct?

Jack: Colour of X may be green, blue or brown.

Codi: X is a colourless pigment of eye.

(A) Jack
(B) Codi
(C) Both are correct
(D) Both are incorrect
(E) None of these

20. Name the eye part indicated by the letter Y in the figure.

(A) Iris
(B) Pupil
(C) Cornea
(D) Retina
(E) None of these

21. What happens to Y when we enters into a dark room from bright light ?

(A) It expands
(B) It shrinks
(C) It remains same
(D) First it shrinks then expands
(E) None of these

22. Why does the eye part indicated by Y in the figure look black?

(A) Because light can't enters into it
(B) Because its colour is black
(C) Because most of the light entering into Y is absorbed by the tissues inside the eye
(D) All of these
(E) None of these

23. When we go to moon our weight gets one-sixth as compared to the earth. Which one of the following forces is responsible for this?

(A) Frictional force
(B) Electrostatic force
(C) Magnetic force
(D) Gravitational force
(E) None of these

24. Two surfaces are in contact with each other. How can we reduce the friction between them?

(A) By increasing smoothness of the surfaces

(B) By decreasing the smoothness of the surfaces

(C) By increasing roughness of the surfaces

(D) All of these

(E) None of these

25. We find the kinetic energy using the formula *"kinetic Energy* $= \frac{1}{2} mv^2$ *. Here m stands for:*

(A) Mass

(B) Movement

(C) Magnetic pull

(D) Matter

(E) None of these

26. Galaxy is defined as the cluster of _____.

(A) Gases

(B) Planets

(C) Stars

(D) Satellites

(E) None of these

27. Distance between Earth and which one of the following is less than four million kilometers?

(A) Moon

(B) Mercury

(C) Sun

(D) Jupiter

(E) None of these

28. Which kind of teeth are used to tear the food?

(A) Molars

(B) Premolar

(C) Canines

(D) Incisors

(E) None of these

29. **Which one of the following is a layer of atmosphere?**
(A) Thermosphere
(B) Stratosphere
(C) Troposphere
(D) Mesosphere
(E) All of these

30. **One molecule of carbon dioxide is made up of ______.**
(A) Two carbon atoms and one oxygen atom
(B) Two carbon atoms and two oxygen atom
(C) One carbon atom and two oxygen atoms
(D) One carbon atom, one oxygen atom and one hydrogen atom
(E) None of these

31. **Name the atoms which are present in a molecule of ice?**
(A) Carbon and oxygen
(B) Oxygen and hydrogen
(C) Carbon and hydrogen
(D) Carbon, oxygen and hydrogen
(E) None of these

32. **Which kind of soil is found in the desert?**
(A) Sandy soil
(B) Loamy soil
(C) Clayey soil
(D) Chalky soil
(E) None of these

33. **Which one of the following kind of soil is considered ideal for agriculture and gardening?**
(A) Peaty soil (B) Loamy soil
(C) Clayey soil (D) Chalky soil
(E) None of these

34. Which one of the following is the heaviest heavenly body in our Solar System?

(A) Jupiter
(B) Saturn
(C) Mars
(D) Sun
(E) None of these

35. A bulb is an instrument which converts electrical energy into ______.

(A) Heat and light energy
(B) Light and sound energy
(C) Heat and sound energy
(D) Light and chemical energy
(E) None of these

36. A magnet has two poles, north pole and south pole. When the same pole come into contact with each other, the force of ______ is experienced.

(A) Attraction
(B) Repulsion
(C) Friction
(D) All of these
(E) None of these

37. Which one of the following spacecrafts was used in the mission "chandrayan 1" to put the satellite in the orbit of moon?

(A) PSLV - C11
(B) GSLV
(C) Aerian 5
(D) Atlantic
(E) None of these

Questions 38 to 40 are based on the following figure:

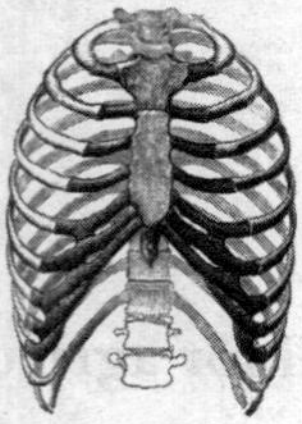

38. Name the structure which has been shown in the figure?

(A) Rib cage
(B) Backbone
(C) Limbs
(D) Skull
(E) None of these

39. What function does this structure serve?

(A) It protects brain

(B) It protects liver and kidney

(C) It protects heart and kidney

(D) It protects heart and lungs

(E) None of these

40. How many ribs are there in the structure?

(A) 12 (B) 18

(C) 24 (D) 30

(E) None of these

41. Which one of the following is used to see the microorganisms?

(A) Spectacles (B) Microscope

(C) Telescope (D) All of these

(E) None of these

42. Which one of the following gases is required as a raw material for the process of photosynthesis?

(A) Oxygen

(B) Carbon dioxide

(C) Hydrogen

(D) Hydrogen dioxide

(E) None of these

43. Reproduction is one of the most important characteristic features of animals.

Select the option that best describes the ways of reproduction in animals.

(A) Bird: lay eggs, mammals: lay eggs reptiles: give birth to young ones.

(B) Bird: lay eggs, mammals: give birth to young ones and reptiles: lay eggs.

(C) Bird: give birth to young ones, mammals: lay eggs and reptiles: lay eggs

(D) Bird: lay eggs and give birth to young ones, mammals: give birth to young ones and lay eggs and reptiles: lay eggs

(E) None of these

44. While walking on the road you step on an object and crush it. The shape of the object is changed. What kind of change takes place in the object?

(A) Chemical change
(B) Physical change
(C) Both chemical and physical change
(D) Partially physical and partially chemical
(E) None of these

45. Which one of the following statements is correct?

Statement 1: Whale cannot survive in desert.

Statement 2: Camel can survive in desert.

(A) Statement 1
(B) Statement 2
(C) Both statements are correct
(D) Both statements are incorrect
(E) None of these

46. While playing in the ground Steve strikes a football with greater force and the ball hits another ball in the way. What kind of energy is transferred by the ball kicked by Steve, to another ball?

(A) Potential
(B) Kinetic
(C) Light
(D) None of these
(E) None of these

47. If you keep an iron nail closer to the magnet, the nail gets attracted towards it. Which one of the following forces is responsible for this?

(A) Frictional force
(B) Gravitational force
(C) Static force
(D) Magnetic force
(E) None of these

48. **Which one of the following joints connects the fore arm to the upper arm?**
(A) Hinge joint (B) Ball and socket joint
(C) Pivot joint (D) All of these
(E) None of these

49. **Examine the following statements:**
Statement A: Fertilizers increase the fertility of the soil.
Statement B: Excessive use of fertilizers have adverse effect on soil and crops.
Which one of the following is correct with regard to the above statements?
(A) Only Statement A is correct
(B) Only Statement B is correct
(C) Both Statement A and Statement B are correct
(D) Both Statement A and Statement B are incorrect
(E) None of these

50. **Which one of the following is a non-renewable source of energy?**
(A) Tidal energy (B) Wind energy
(C) Solar energy (D) Fossil fuels
(E) None of these

Practice Exercise-2

1. **The microorganisms, which cause diseases are called_____.**
   (A) Pathogens (B) Pesticides
   (C) Microbes (D) Insecticides
   (E) None of these
2. **In which one of the following kind of habitats does the biggest mammal live?**
   (A) Aquatic (B) Terrestrial
   (C) Aerial (D) Aerobial
   (E) None of these
3. **Growing of canine teeth and strong claws in carnivores animals is a adaptation to_____.**
   (A) Easily suit the climatic condition
   (B) To catch and kill its prey
   (C) For chewing the flesh
   (D) To fight against the other competitor
   (E) (B) and (D)
4. **Name the biggest natural satellite of the planet saturn.**
   (A) Moon (B) Ganymede
   (C) Europa (D) Titan
   (E) None of these
5. **Who of the following is correct?**
   Jack: Biodegradable substances are the main cause of land pollution.
   Codi: Non-biodegradable substances are the main cause land pollution.
   (A) Jack (B) Codi
   (C) Both are correct (D) Both are incorrect
   (E) None of these

6. Hibernation is a process in which animals goes to winter sleep. What is the reason behind this?

(A) Due to tiredness
(B) Due to scarcity of food and extreme cold
(C) To compensate the consumed energy
(D) To digest the food
(E) None of these

7. Some animals have possessed flat grinding teeth to help in chewing the food. This type of adaptation is found in________.

(A) Producers
(B) Herbivores
(C) Carnivores
(D) Scavenger
(E) None of these

8. Some organisms go through several changes before being an adult, this process is called metamorphosis. In which one of the following options different stages of metamorphosis has been correctly arranged for a butterfly?

(A) Egg - pupa - caterpillar - adult butterfly
(B) Egg - caterpillar - pupa - adult butterfly
(C) Pupa - egg - caterpillar - adult butterfly
(D) Pupa - caterpillar - egg - adult butterfly
(E) None of these

9. Look at the following figure:

Which one of the following systems has been shown in the above figure?

(A) Digestive system
(B) Nervous system
(C) Respiratory system
(D) Circulatory system
(E) None of these

10. Identify the figure given below and name the system to which it belongs.

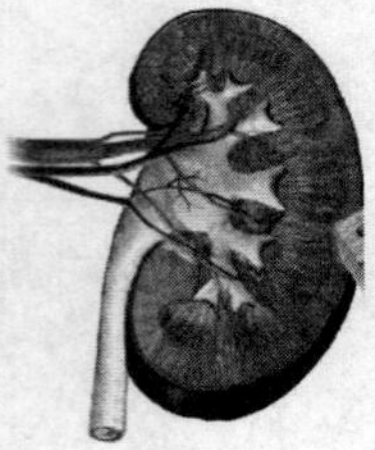

(A) Digestive system (B) Excretory system
(C) Respiratory system (D) Circulatory system
(E) None of these

11. In which one of the following parts of the digestive system saliva is mixed with food?

(A) Mouth (B) Oesophagus
(C) Stomach (D) Small intestine
(E) None of these

12. Which one of the following is called the centre of the nervous system?

(A) Liver (B) Skin
(C) Heart (D) Brain
(E) None of these

13. Environment is composed of both biotic and abiotic components. Find the biotic components from the following.

(A) Plants (B) Animals
(C) Microorganisms (D) All of these
(E) None of these

14. Ozone is a layer in the atmosphere of the Earth which prevents the attack of ultra violet rays coming from space. One molecule of ozone is made up of_______.

(A) 2 atoms of oxygen
(B) 3 atoms of oxygen
(C) 4 atoms of oxygen
(D) 2 atoms of oxygen and one atom of carbon
(E) None of these

15. Which one of the following reactions is responsible for generating heat and light energy in the core of the Sun?

(A) Nuclear fission
(B) Nuclear fusion
(C) Displacement reaction
(D) All of these
(E) None of these

16. Which one of the following is a source of energy?

(A) Petrol
(B) Coal
(C) Diesel
(D) All of these
(E) None of these

17. Name the planet which lies between the orbit of Jupiter and Uranus.

(A) Neptune
(B) Pluto
(C) Jupiter
(D) Saturn
(E) None of these

18. Galaxies have been classified into three groups according to their shape. Look at the shape of given galaxy carefully and identify it.

(A) Spiral
(B) Elliptical
(C) Irregular
(D) All of these
(E) None of these

19. Which one of the following gases is essential for the process of burning?

(A) Carbon dioxide

(B) Hydrogen

(C) Oxygen

(D) Methane

(E) None of these

20. When we put a piece of wood in the water, it floats and does not sink. Which one of the following forces is responsible for this?

(A) Frictional force

(B) Gravitational force

(C) Upthrust force

(D) Magnetic forces

(E) None of these

21. Sometimes in the sky we see a string of light for a very few moment. Actually these are meteors which burn on entering into the atmosphere of the earth. Which one of the following gives the required heat energy to the meteors to be burnt?

(A) Friction

(B) Gravitation

(C) Upthrust

(D) All of these

(E) None of these

22. We measures the potential energy of a body with the help of the formula "m × g × h". Here g stands for _____.

(A) Gravitational force

(B) Gravitational acceleration

(C) Gravitational constant

(D) All of these

(E) None of these

23. **Belt of asteroids lies between the orbit of the planets ______.**

(A) Earth and Mars

(B) Neptune and Jupiter

(C) Mars and Jupiter

(D) Jupiter and Saturn

(E) None of these

24. **When salt is dissolved in water, the salt particles get disappeared and taste of water gets salty. Name the solute particle of this solution.**

(A) Sand (B) Sugar

(C) Salt (D) Water

(E) None of these

25. **In which one of the following layers of atmosphere, the layer of ozone is present?**

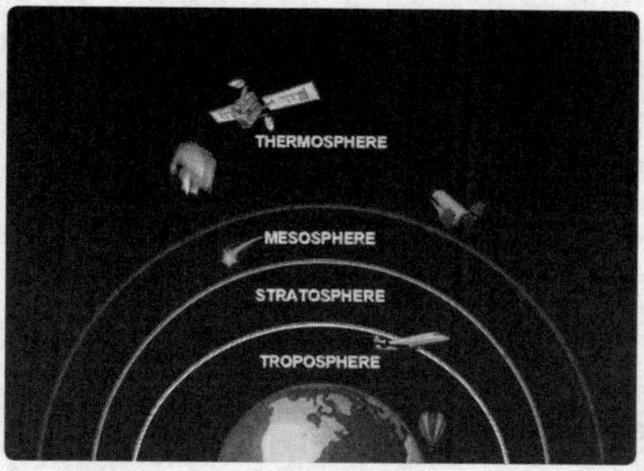

(A) Exosphere

(B) Stratosphere

(C) Mesosphere

(D) Thermosphere

(E) None of these

26. **Which one of the following food is rich in carbohydrate?**

(A) Egg (B) Rice

(C) Milk (D) Pulse

(E) None of these

27. When a substance is heated, distance between the molecules of the substance is______.

(A) Increased (B) Decreased

(C) Remains same (D) All of these

(E) None of these

28. In which one of the following states of matter, intermolecular force is least?

(A) Solid

(B) Liquid

(C) Gas

(D) In all states of matter, intermolecular force remains same

(E) None of these

29. Look at the following figure

The above mills have been set up to harvest the______.

(A) Wind energy

(B) Solar energy

(C) Hydrothermal energy

(D) Geothermal energy

(E) None of these

30. "Objects fall down towards the earth due to the force of________.

(A) Gravity (B) Friction

(C) Air (D) All of these

(E) None of these

Questions 31 and 32 are based on the following figure:

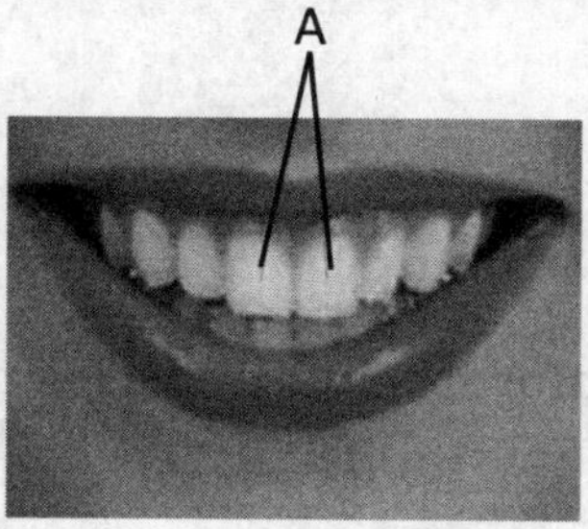

31. Name the teeth that the letter A indicates in the figure.

(A) Canine
(B) Molar
(C) Premolar
(D) Incisor
(E) None of these

32. What purpose does this teeth serve?

(A) It helps in chewing the food
(B) It helps in biting the food
(C) It help in grinding the food
(D) All of these
(E) None of these

33. Which one of the following systems is responsible for exchanging the information between body parts and the brain?

(A) Excretory system
(B) Respiratory system
(C) Nervous system
(D) Circulatory system
(E) None of these

34. Depletion of ozone layer is caused by __________.

(A) Land pollution
(B) Water pollution
(C) Soil pollution
(D) Air pollution
(E) None of these

35. Find the odd one from the following.

(A) Iris
(B) Sclera
(C) Pinna
(D) Pupil
(E) None of these

36. In which part of the digestive system the hydrochloric acid is released to kill the contaminated microorganisms and to digest the food?

(A) Small intestine
(B) Large intestine
(C) Stomach
(D) Liver
(E) None of these

37. The topmost layer of the Earth is called ____.

(A) Core
(B) Crust
(C) Mantle
(D) All of these
(E) None of these

38. At room temperature the camphor is found in ______ state.

(A) Solid
(B) Liquid
(C) Gas
(D) All of these
(E) None of these

39. Which one of the followings is a liquid?

(A) Cup
(B) Water
(C) Table
(D) Book
(E) None of these

40. Which of the following nutrients is also called body building material?

(A) Vitamins
(B) Minerals
(C) Carbohydrates
(D) Proteins
(E) None of these

41. Leaves of cactus plant are modified into spines. It is an adaptation to live in:

(A) Oceans
(B) Polar regions
(C) Desert
(D) All of these
(E) None of these

42. Consider the following two statements:-

Statement A: Energy is the ability to do work.

Statement B: Potential energy of the object is due to its motion.

Which of the following is correct with respect to the above statements?

(A) Statement A is correct
(B) Statement B is correct
(C) Both, Statement A and Statement B are correct
(D) Both, Statement A and Statement B are incorrect
(E) None of these

43. Which one of the following food items is a rich source of vitamins and minerals?

(A) Fruits
(B) Meat
(C) Eggs
(D) Pulses
(E) None of these

44. Which one of the following is located between stomach and large intestines?

(A) Mouth
(B) Food pipe
(C) Small intestine
(D) Anus
(E) None of these

45. The percentage of nitrogen in our atmosphere is about:

(A) 10% (B) 50%
(C) 68% (D) 78%
(E) All of these

46. Which one of the following has been excluded from the list of planets?

(A) Earth (B) Mars
(C) Jupiter (D) Pluto
(E) None of these

47. **Which one of the following statements is correct?**

Statement 1: Earth rotates on its axis.

Statement 2: Earth does not rotate on its axis.

(A) Statement 1
(B) Statement 2
(C) Both statements are correct
(D) Both statements are incorrect
(E) None of these

48. **Stratosphere is a layer of:**

(A) Earth crust
(B) Atmosphere
(C) Forest
(D) All of these
(E) None of these

49. **Which one of the following plants grow in water?**

(A) Neem
(B) Peepal
(C) Both (A) and (B)
(D) Hydrilla
(E) None of these

50. **Which one of the following organs is known as a control centre of our body?**

(A) Brain
(B) Heart
(C) Lungs
(D) Kidney
(E) All of the above

Practice Exercise-3

1. **In which one of the following organs smallest bone of the human body is present?**

(A) 

(B) 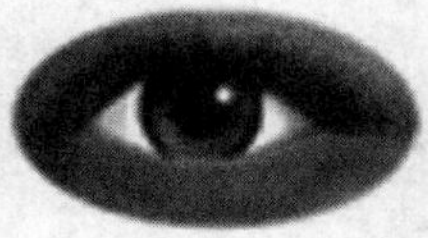

(C) 

(D) All of these

(E) None of these

2. **Which one of the following organs plays an important role in circulation of blood throughout the body?**

(A) 

(B) 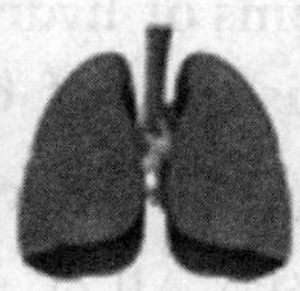

(C) 

(D) 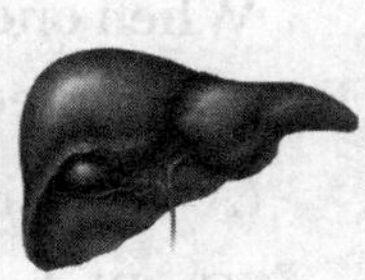

(E) None of these

3. **Which one of the following is a part of digestive system?**

(A) 

(B) 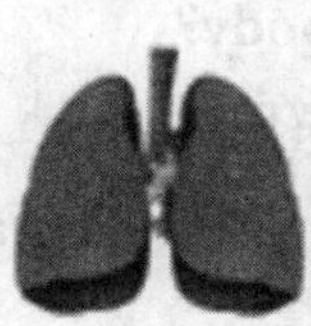

(C) 

(D) 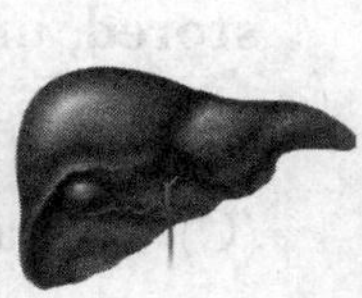

(E) None of these

4. Which one of the following is the products of "photosynthesis"?

(A) Carbon dioxide and sunlight

(B) Oxygen and sunlight

(C) Starch and glucose

(D) Glucose and oxygen

(E) None of these

5. Brain is protected by a bony structure called ________.

(A) Rib cage

(B) Skull

(C) Spinal chord

(D) Bladder

(E) None of these

6. If an object is placed at greater height, the potential energy of the object is _______.

(A) Increased

(B) Decreased

(C) Remains same

(D) All of these

(E) None of these

7. When one atom of oxygen and two atoms of hydrogen are combined together, one molecule of water is formed. This type of change is called ________.

(A) Physical change

(B) Chemical change

(C) Biological change

(D) All of these

(E) None of these

8. In which one of the following organs of the body waste material (urine) is stored, until it is passed out by the body?

(A) Kidney

(B) Lung

(C) Urinary bladder

(D) Gall bladder

(E) None of these

9. Which one of the following is a mammal?

(A) 

(B) 

(C) 

(D) 

(E) None of these

10. The force by which Earth attracts Moon is __________.

(A) Frictional force
(B) Mechanical force
(C) Gravitational force
(D) Magnetic force
(E) None of these

11. Which one of the following is a fossil fuel?

(A) Wind
(B) Water
(C) Sunlight
(D) Petroleum
(E) None of these

12. Which one of the following organs gives the sense of hearing?

(A) Nose
(B) Eye
(C) Skin
(D) Ear
(E) None of these

13. The outermost layer of the eye is known as__________.

(A) Lens
(B) Sclera
(C) Pupil
(D) Retina
(E) None of these

14. Name the system which has been shown in the following figure.

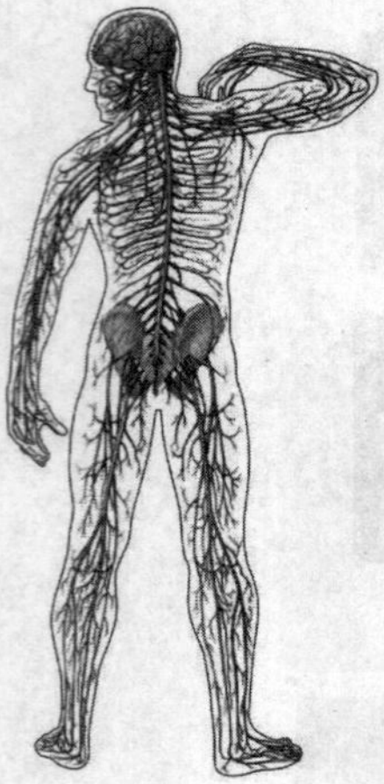

(A) Nervous system (B) Digestive system
(C) Excretory system (D) Respiratory system
(E) None of these

15. The atmosphere consists of mainly five layers. Mesosphere is present between______.

(A) The troposphere and the stratosphere
(B) The stratosphere and the thermosphere
(C) The thermosphere and the exosphere
(D) All of these
(E) None of these

16. Gaseous form of water is called ________.

(A) Water (B) Ice
(C) Water vapour (D) All of these
(E) None of these

17. When a solid substance is changed into gas without coming into liquid, the process is called ________.

(A) Evaporation (B) Vaporization
(C) Sublimation (D) Condensation
(E) None of these

18. Which one of the followings living things does not have backbone?

(A) Scorpion
(B) Crocodile
(C) Fish
(D) Horse
(E) None of these

19. Which one of the following is an arboreal animal?

(A) 

(B) 

(C) 

(D) 

(E) None of these

20. A group of stars seen as forming a figure or design is called_____.

(A) Galaxy
(B) Constellation
(C) Cluster
(D) Satellite
(E) None of these

21. On which one of the following planets do we live?

(A) Jupiter
(B) Neptune
(C) Uranus
(D) Earth
(E) None of these

Questions 22 to 25 are based on the following figure:

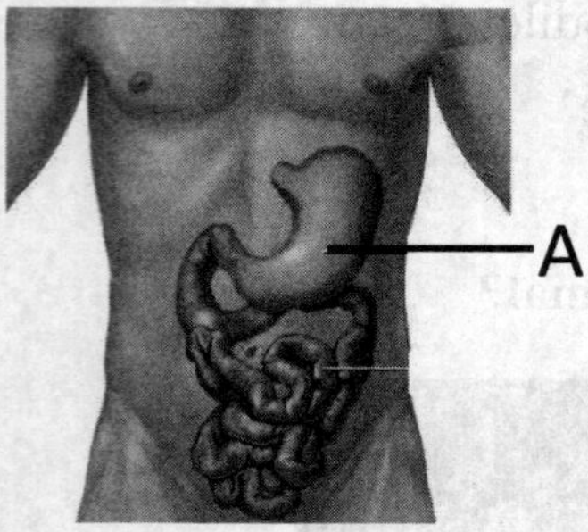

22. Name the organ which has been indicated by the letter A.

(A) Oesophagus
(B) Stomach
(C) Small intestine
(D) Large intestine
(E) None of these

23. 'A' belongs to which one of the followings organ systems?

(A) Nervous system
(B) Respiratory system
(C) Circulatory system
(D) Digestive system
(E) None of these

24. Which one of the following organs takes the food to A from mouth?

(A) Wind pipe
(B) Small intestine
(C) Oesophagus
(D) Gall bladder
(E) None of these

25. After reaching the food into A, some activities take place, then the food is further supplied to______.

(A) Large intestine (B) Small intestine
(C) Oesophagus (D) Liver
(E) None of these

26. **In the following figure melted magma has been shown.**

Which one of the following kind of rocks is formed when it cools down?

(A) Igneous rock
(B) Sedimentary rock
(C) Metamorphic rock
(D) All of these
(E) None of these

27. **Which one of the following is one of the major cause of soil erosion?**

(A) Afforestation
(B) Deforestation
(C) Building of dams
(D) Over use of fossils fuels
(E) None of these

28. **Terrace farming or step farming helps in ______ soil erosion.**

(A) Reducing (B) Increasing
(C) Removing (D) All of these
(E) None of these

29. **Which one of the following layers of soil is made up of unweathered, non porous and impervious parent rocks ?**

(A) A horizon (B) B horizon
(C) C horizon (D) D horizon
(E) None of these

30. **Which one of the following layers of soil is rich in humus?**

(A) A horizon (B) B horizon
(C) C horizon (D) D horizon
(E) None of these

31. Which one of the following is a scavenger?

(A) 

(B) 

(C) 

(D) 

(E) None of these

32. Which one of the following is the largest Moon of our solar system?

(A) Titan
(B) Europa
(C) Ganymede
(D) Leda
(E) None of these

33. The planet Mars is also known as ________.

(A) Red planet
(B) Blue planet
(C) White planet
(D) Black planet
(E) None of these

34. The animals, which have no back bones are called ________.

(A) Vertebrates
(B) Invertebrates
(C) Mammals
(D) Reptiles
(E) None of these

35. Which one of the following animals undergoes aestivation?

(A) Man
(B) Cat
(C) Lion
(D) Snake
(E) Both (B) and (D)

36. Which one of the following is called as producers?

(A) Plants
(B) Animals
(C) Microorganisms
(D) Birds
(E) None of these

37. An atom is made up of three fundamental particles. Name them.

(A) Alpha, Beta, Gamma
(B) Electron, Proton, Neutron
(C) Hydrogen, helium, oxygen
(D) All of these
(E) None of these

38. Which one of the followings foods is/are rich source(s) of protein?

(A) Pulses
(B) Egg
(C) Fish
(D) All of these
(E) None of these

39. Which one of the following kinds of teeth are responsible for grinding the food?

(A) Incisors
(B) Canines
(C) Molars
(D) All of these
(E) None of these

40. Which one of the following instruments converts electrical energy into heat energy?

(A) 

(B) 

(C) 

(D) 

(E) None of these

41. In the given figure which type of organ system has been shown?

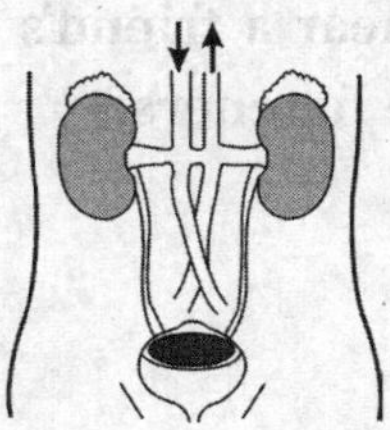

(A) Circulatory System
(B) Nervous System
(C) Respiratory System
(D) Digestive System
(E) Excretory System

42. Which one of the following is the largest terrestrial planet in our Solar System?

(A) Earth (B) Mars

(C) Venus (D) Mercury

(E) All of these

43. Which type of joints permits maximum movements?

(A) Ball-and-Socket Joints

(B) Hinge Joints

(C) Gliding Joints

(D) Saddle Joints

(E) None of these

44. The given picture shows water rushing downstream during a flood. The water is said to possess which type of energy since it is moving?

(A) Kinetic energy (B) Potential energy

(C) Statical energy (D) All of these

(E) None of these

45. You know that speakers come in all shapes and sizes, enabling you to listen to music on your I Pod, enjoy a film at the cinema or hear a friend's voice over the phone. What types of work speakers do for the listeners?

(A) Convert sound into an electrical signal

(B) Convert electrical signals into audible sound

(C) Convert sound into a mechanical signal

(D) All of these

(E) None of these

46. Which one of the following is an amphibian?

(A) Mouse
(B) Salamander
(C) Fish
(D) Parrot
(E) None of these

47. Find the odd one out:

(A) Retina
(B) Pupil
(C) Lens
(D) Ribs
(E) None of these

48. Which one of the following facts is/are correct?

(A) Earth revolves around the Sun.
(B) Mars revolves around the Sun.
(C) Jupiter revolves around the Sun.
(D) All of these
(E) None of these

49. Which one of the following is an example of gaseous state of matter?

(A) Air
(B) Ice
(C) Milk
(D) Coal
(E) None of these

50. Neem is a:

(A) Herb
(B) Shrub
(C) Tree
(D) Climber
(E) None of these

Practice Exercise-4

1. **Digestion of food is a ______.**
   (A) Physical change
   (B) Chemical change
   (C) Nuclear change
   (D) Atomic change
   (E) None of these

2. **Which one of the following instruments is used to measure the atmospheric pressure?**
   (A) 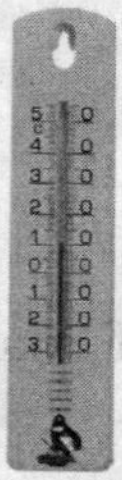
   (B) 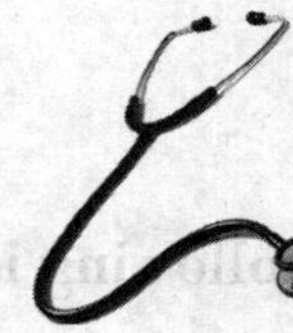
   (C) 
   (D) 
   (E) None of these

3. **Thermometer is used to measure ______.**
   (A) Temperature
   (B) Pressure
   (C) Speed
   (D) Mass
   (E) None of these

4. **Statement: Take a glass of water and pour a teaspoon of salt into it. After some time you will notice that salt has disappeared.**
   Which one of the following terms is correct for disappearing of salt into water?
   (A) Condensation of salt
   (B) Evaporation of salt
   (C) Vaporization of salt
   (D) Dissolution of salt
   (E) None of these

Question 5 to 8 are based on the following figure:

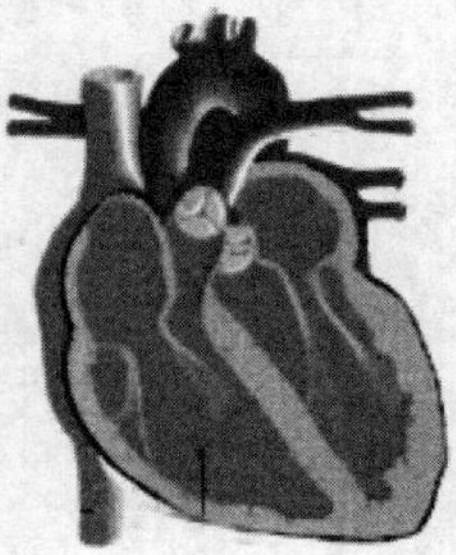

5. Identify the organ shown in the figure and point out the function that it serves in our body.

(A) It pumps the blood throughout the body
(B) It purifies the blood
(C) It filters the water from blood
(D) It maintains the water level in the blood
(E) None of these

6. To which one of the following organ systems does it belongs?

(A) Respiratory system
(B) Circulatory system
(C) Digestive system
(D) Excretory system
(E) None of these

7. This organ shows a special movement to perform its function. Choose the option which is correct about its movement.

(A) It moves back and forth
(B) It moves up and down
(C) It expands and contract
(D) It moves left to right
(E) None of these

8. Its movement is known by which one of the following terms?

(A) Heart beating
(B) Heart attack
(C) Osmosis
(D) Circulation
(E) None of these

9. Which one of the following is not a sense organ?

(A) Skin
(B) Tongue
(C) Hair
(D) Ear
(E) None of these

10. Which one of the following animals lives in water?

(A) Camel
(B) Elephant
(C) Whale
(D) Horse
(E) None of these

11. Who of the following is correct?

Jack: Gases like oxygen, carbon dioxide, nitrogen, are also dissolved in ocean water.

Codi: Only solid substances like salt are dissolved in the ocean water.

(A) Jack
(B) Codi
(C) Both are correct
(D) Both are incorrect
(E) None of these

12. When water starts boiling, bubbles are formed. Which one of the following reason is responsible for this?

(A) These bubbles are actually dissolved gases which separate from water on heating.
(B) These bubbles are nothing just water droplets which keep on changing into gas.
(C) These bubbles are water vapours which formed due to boiling of water.
(D) All of these
(E) None of these

13. Change in the states of matter is a _______.

(A) Physical change
(B) Chemical change
(C) Biological change
(D) All of these
(E) None of these

14. In which one of the following states of matter intermolecular force is negligible?

(A) Solid (B) Liquid
(C) Gas (D) All of these
(E) None of these

15. A substance is in solid state. If we heat the substance, the force between the molecules gets ________.

(A) Strengthen
(B) Weakened
(C) Remained same
(D) Inter molecular force is independent of heat
(E) None of these

16. Which one of the following organs is specialized for filtering water from blood?

(A) Heart (B) Lung
(C) Liver (D) Kidney
(E) None of these

17. Observe the following figure carefully.

will it help in reducing the rate of soil erosion?

(A) Yes
(B) No
(C) It has nothing to do with the soil erosion
(D) All of these
(E) None of these

18. Which kind of habitat has been represented in the given figure?

(A) Terrestrial
(B) Aquatic
(C) Aerial
(D) Aerobial
(E) None of these

19. Which one of the following is an igneous rock?

(A) Granite
(B) Limestone
(C) Slate
(D) Marble
(E) None of these

20. Which one of the following is a sedimentary rock?

(A) Granite
(B) Limestone
(C) Slate
(D) Marble
(E) None of these

21. Look at the following figure carefully

What has been shown in the given figure?

(A) Wind mill
(B) Nuclear power plant
(C) Dam
(D) All of these
(E) None of these

22. In the following figure, molecular structure of a substance has been shown. The substance is in ________ state

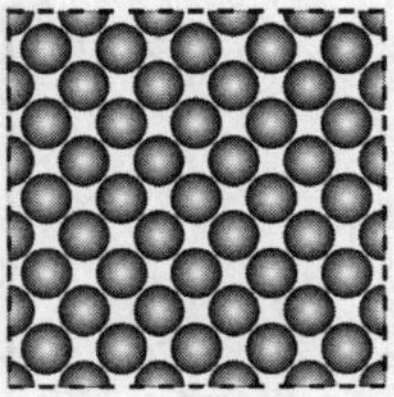

(A) Solid (B) Liquid
(C) Gaseous (D) All of these
(E) None of these

23. Which one of the following is a biotic component of the environment?

(A) Water (B) Plant
(C) Air (D) Sunlight
(E) None of these

24. Which one of a following is a carnivorous animal?

(A)  (B) 

(C)  (D) 

(E) None of these

25. Which one of the following is a chemical change?

(A) Bursting of tyre
(B) Turning milk sour
(C) Breaking up of stones
(D) Falling of an object from a height
(E) None of these

26. We find the potential energy of an object by the formula "mgh". Here m stands for __________.

(A) Movement (B) Mass

(C) Matter (D) Motion

(E) None of these

27. Which one of the following is a metamorphic rock?

(A) Slate (B) Limestone

(C) Shale (D) Granite

(E) None of these

28. Which one of the following natural phenomenon has been shown by the given picture?

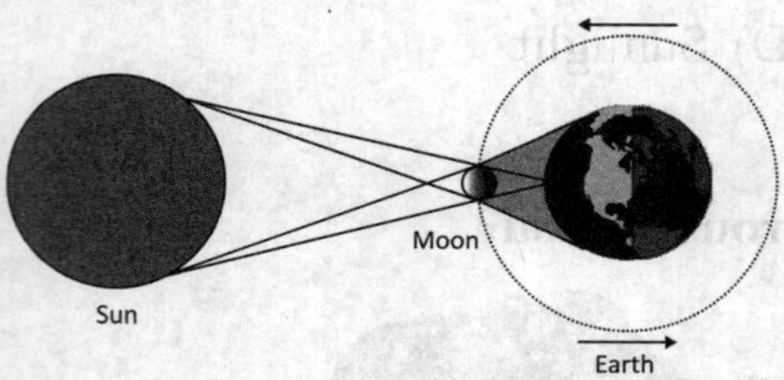

(A) Solar eclipse (B) Lunar eclipse

(C) Formation of day and night (D) Change in season

(E) None of these

29. Which one of the following animals produces their off springs by laying egg?

(A) 

(B) 

(C) 

(D) 

(E) None of these

30. What name has been given to the animals that feed on dead and decaying organic matter?

(A) Parasite

(B) Carnivorous

(C) Scavengers

(D) Omnivorous

(E) None of these

31. Which one of the following systems is responsible for controlling sense organs?

(A) Respiratory system

(B) Digestive system

(C) Excretory system

(D) Nervous system

(E) None of these

32. Which one of the following helps in maintaining temperature of the body?

(A) Blood (B) Insulin

(C) Sugar (D) Capillaries

(E) None of these

Questions 33 to 35 are based on the following figure:

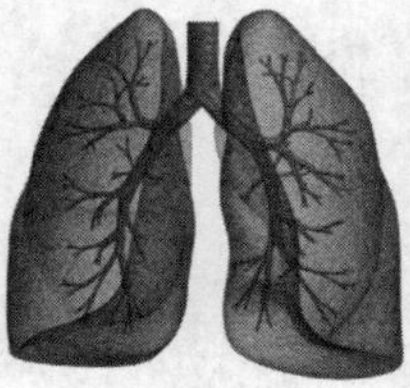

33. Identify the organ shown in the above figure:

(A) Lungs

(B) Liver

(C) Kidney

(D) Gall bladder

(E) None of these

34. Which one of the following functions it serves?

(A) It helps in filtering water from the blood

(B) It helps in oxygenating the blood

(C) It helps in circulating the blood

(D) All of these

(E) None of these

35. To which one of the following systems does it belong?

(A) Respiratory system

(B) Circulatory system

(C) Nervous system

(D) Digestive system

(E) None of these

36. Which one of the following is a non-renewable source of energy?

(A) Solar energy (B) Wind energy

(C) Hydropower energy (D) Fossil fuel energy

(E) None of these

Questions 37 to 38 are based on the following figure:

37. The leaves of the given tree is falling to the ground because of:

(A) Frictional force

(B) Gravitational force

(C) Magnetic force

(D) Electrostatic force

(E) None of these

38. The leaves are just coming down instead of going up or in any other direction. This phenomenon gives the conclusion that_____.

(A) Leaves automatically falls down

(B) Leaves do not want to go up in the air

(C) Something pulling the leaves down

(D) Leaves are dead so they fall down

(E) None of these

39. Which one of the followings statements is correct?

Statement 1 : Insects are invertebrates.

Statement 2 : Fishes are vertebrates.

(A) Statement 1

(B) Statement 2

(C) Both statements are correct

(D) Both statements are incorrect

(E) None of these

40. Look at the following figure carefully.

The above plant has been set up to harness_____.

(A) Solar energy (B) Wind energy

(C) Water energy (D) Geothermal energy

(E) None of these

41. Which one of the following has no role in the digestion of food?

(A) Liver (B) Small intestine

(C) Stomach (D) Kidney

(E) None of these

42. Choose the incorrect option about the given figure.

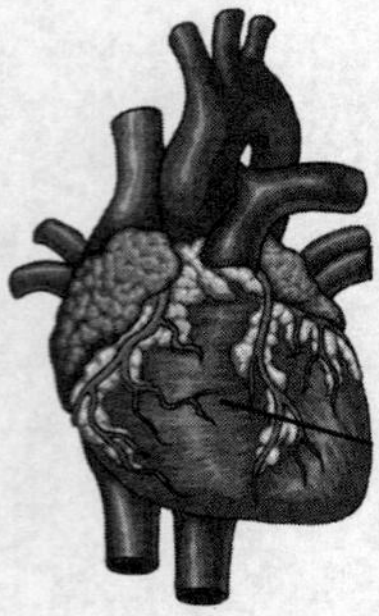

(A) It is heart
(B) It is an internal organ
(C) It is a part of circulatory system
(D) It is protected by skull
(E) None of these

43. Which one of the following joints allows movement in all directions?

(A) Ball and socket joint
(B) Pivot joint
(C) Hinge joint
(D) Gliding joint
(E) None of these

44. I am the part of eye. I can be of different colours. I have a small opening in the center. Who am I ?

(A) Pupil
(B) Iris
(C) Sclera
(D) Choroid
(E) None of these

45. When something delicious is cooked in our kitchen we smell it and can imagine its taste. How is it possible?

(A) Sense of smell and taste are linked
(B) Nose and tongue are close to each other
(C) Smell itself shows taste
(D) All of these
(E) None of these

46. What kind of energy does the stretched rubber band possess?

(A) Kinetic energy
(B) Potential energy
(C) Magnetic energy
(D) All of these
(E) None of these

47. Which one of the following is an invertebrate?

(A) Whale
(B) Dolphin
(C) Cat
(D) Spider
(E) None of these

48. Which one of the following is a gas planet?

(A) Saturn
(B) Venus
(C) Mars
(D) All of these
(E) None of these

49. What part of Earth is covered with water?

(A) One-fourth
(B) Two-fourth
(C) Three-fourth
(D) All of these
(E) None of these

50. Which one of the following is correct for atmosphere?

(A) Blanket of water around Earth
(B) Blanket of air around Earth
(C) Blanket of soil around Earth
(D) Blanket of fire around Earth
(E) None of these

Practice Exercise-5

1. **Look at the following figure carefully.**

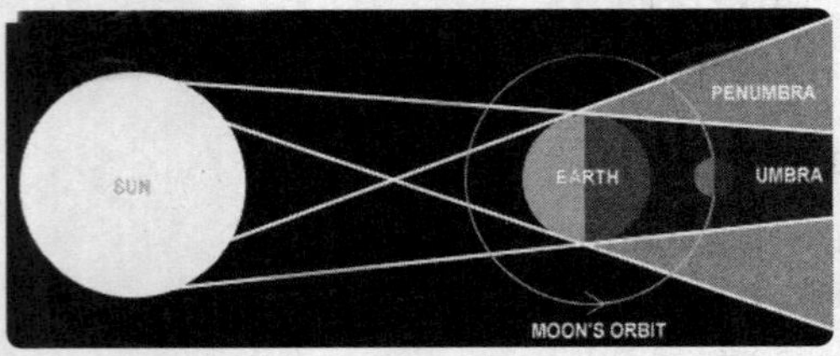

Which one of the following natural phenomenon has been shown in the above figure?

(A) Solar eclipse
(B) Lunar eclipse
(C) Formation of day and night
(D) Changing of season
(E) None of these

2. **Look at the following figure.**

The above picture is showing ________ pollution.

(A) Water (B) Soil
(C) Noise (D) Air
(E) None of these

Questions 3 and 4 are based on the following figure

3. Name the teeth that has been indicated by the letter A?

(A) Incisor
(B) Canine
(C) Premolar
(D) Molar
(E) None of these

4. What function these teeth serve?

(A) It helps in cutting the flesh of its prey
(B) It helps in grinding the flesh of its prey
(C) It helps in swallowing the flesh of its prey
(D) It helps in killing its prey and in tearing the flesh
(E) None of these

5. How many canine teeth a lion has?

(A) 2
(B) 4
(C) 6
(D) 8
(E) None of these

6. Green plants make their own food by the process of photosynthesis. In which part of the plant the process of photosynthesis occurs?

(A) Leaves
(B) Flowers
(C) Root
(D) All of these
(E) None of these

7. What are the essential raw materials that plants required for the process of photosynthesis?

(A) Water, sunlight, glucose and carbon dioxide
(B) Water, glucose, and carbon dioxide
(C) Water, sunlight and carbon dioxide
(D) Water, sunlight, oxygen and carbon dioxide
(E) None of these

8. **Which one of the following is a mammal?**

(A) 

(B) 

(C) 

(D) 

(E) None of these

Questions 9 to 11 are based on the following figure:

9. **What has been shown with the help of the given figure?**

(A) Environment
(B) Habitat
(C) Food chain
(D) Ecosystem
(E) None of these

10. **Which one of the following is an autotroph in the figure?**

(A) Green plant
(B) Frog
(C) Snake
(D) Eagle
(E) None of these

11. **What information does the above figure give?**

(A) The figure gives information that how the animals live together in a same environment.
(B) The figure gives information that they all are terrestrial animals.
(C) The figure gives the information that every living things are ultimately converted into non-living thing.
(D) The figure gives the information that how the living organisms are dependent on one another for their food.
(E) None of these

12. The animals which eat both plants and animals are called:

(A) Herbivores (B) Carnivores

(C) Omnivores (D) All of these

(E) None of these

13. Malaria is a disease caused by_______.

(A) Virus (B) Bacteria

(C) Ring worm (D) Protozoa

(E) None of these

14. Influenza is a disease caused by________.

(A) Virus (B) Bacteria

(C) Ring worm (D) Protozoa

(E) None of these

15. Observe the following figure carefully:

Burning of candle is which one of the following kind of change?

(A) Physical change (B) Chemical change

(C) Biological change (D) All of these

(E) None of these

16. Which one of the following is not a matter?

(A) Flower (B) Water

(C) Air (D) Happiness

(E) None of these

17. What kind of pollution has been shown in the given figure?

(A) Soil pollution (B) Water pollution
(C) Air pollution (D) All of these
(E) None of these

18. Contamination of unwanted substances in the air is called_____.
(A) Soil pollution (B) Water pollution
(C) Air pollution (D) All of these
(E) None of these

19. Which one of the following is an igneous rock?
(A) Sandstone (B) Lime stone
(C) Slate (D) Pumice
(E) None of these

20. The following animal belongs to the group of:

(A) Herbivores (B) Carnivores
(C) Omnivores (D) All of these
(E) None of these

21. Which one of the following sense organs gives the sense of touch?
(A) Eye (B) Ear
(C) Nose (D) Skin
(E) Tongue

22. Which one of the following planets is the second largest planet of our Solar System?
(A) Jupiter (B) Saturn
(C) Mars (D) Neptune
(E) None of these

23. Which one of the following is not a part of our Solar System?

(A) Neptune (B) Asteroids
(C) Proxima centauri (D) Sun
(E) None of these

24. Which one of the following is a biodegradable substance?

(A) Wood (B) Dead plants
(C) Dead animals (D) All of these
(E) None of these

25. In which kind of habitat does the camel live?

(A) Terrestrial (B) Aquatic
(C) Aerial (D) Arboreal
(E) None of these

26. Which one of the following is an invertebrate animal?

(A) Lion (B) Fish
(C) Rat (D) Earthworm
(E) None of these

27. The animals which mostly live in the air are called _______ animals

(A) Terrestrial (B) Aquatic
(C) Aerial (D) Arboreal
(E) None of these

28. The ______ allows movement at the wrist and ankle.

(A) Gliding joint (B) Pivot joint
(C) Hinge joint (D) Ball and socket joint
(E) None of these

29. Which one of the following is a junk food?

(A) Patties (B) Mango
(C) Banana (D) Milk
(E) None of these

30. The two objects of same mass are moving with different speed. The object which has greater speed has possessed _____ amount of kinetic energy.

(A) Greater (B) Smaller
(C) Same (D) All of these
(E) None of these

31. Air is an example of ______ state of matter.

(A) Solid (B) Liquid
(C) Gaseous (D) All of these
(E) None of these

32. In our Solar System, there is a single heavenly body that produce its own light. Name it.

(A) Earth (B) Moon
(C) Sun (D) Comet
(E) None of these

Questions 33 to 35 are based on the following figure:

33. The mills, shown in the figure, has been set up to convert ______.

(A) Wind energy into chemical energy
(B) Wind energy into electrical energy
(C) Wind energy into solar energy
(D) Wind energy into fossil fuel energy
(E) None of these

34. The source of energy, which the mills harvest to produce electrical energy, is a ________ source of energy

(A) Renewable (B) Nonrenewable
(C) Exhaustible (D) All of these
(E) None of these

35. Who of the following is correct?

Jack: This method of harvesting natural resources pollutes the environment. So we should stop it immediately.

Codi: This is a renewable source of energy and does not pollute the environment.

(A) Jack (B) Codi
(C) Both are correct (D) Both are incorrect
(E) None of these

36. Observe the following figure carefully. Is it helpful for the environment?

(A) It is polluting the environment therefore it is not good.
(B) It is cleaning the environment therefore it is good.
(C) It has nothing to do with the environment.
(D) All of these
(E) None of these

37. Which one of the following is an example of solid state of matter?

(A) Milk (B) Air
(C) Kerosene (D) Book
(E) None of these

38. Which kind of food is not good for our health?

(A) Green vegetables (B) Fruits
(C) Milk (D) Junk food
(E) None of these

39. Which one of the following forces works only when objects are in contact with each other?

(A) Magnetic force (B) Gravitational force

(C) Frictional force (D) Electrostatic force
(E) None of thee

40. In which one of the following states of matter, the force between the molecules of the matter is greatest?

(A) Solid (B) Liquid
(C) Gas (D) All of these
(E) None of these

41. Which one of the following is the outermost layer of atmosphere?

(A) Troposphere (B) Stratosphere
(C) Mesosphere (D) Exosphere
(E) None of these

42. Which one of the following is a breathing organ of a mammal?

(A) Stomata (B) Gills
(C) Lungs (D) Skin
(E) None of these

43. Plants cannot prepare its food during the night because:

(A) Sunlight is not available during the night
(B) Carbon dioxide is not available during the night
(C) Water vapour is not available during the night
(D) Oxygen is not available during the night
(E) None of these

44. Name the green pigment which traps the solar energy for the process of photosynthesis.

(A) Stomata (B) Chlorophyll
(C) Lenticels (D) All of these
(E) None of these

45. You must have noticed that during extremely hot or cold season mosquitoes and other insects vanishes all of a sudden. What force them to disappear?

(A) Excess of food (B) Excess of oxygen
(C) Harsh climate (D) All of these
(E) None of these

46. **Examine the following statements:**

Statement A: Polar ice is melting slowly. This activity increases the sea level.

Statement B: Global warming causes the melting of polar ice.

Which one of the following is correct with regard to the above statements?

(A) Only Statement A is correct

(B) Only Statement B is correct

(C) Both Statement A and Statement B are correct

(D) Both Statement A and Statement B are incorrect

(E) Both Statement A and Statement B are partly correct

47. **Various human activities, such as burning of coal, create more greenhouse gases in the atmosphere which contributes in increasing global warming. Which one of the following gases is a greenhouse gas?**

(A) Nitrous oxide (B) Ozone

(C) Water vapour (D) All of these

(E) None of these

48. **Energy resources come from nature. An energy supply that is replaced as quickly as it is used, such as wind, is called ________.**

(A) Non-renewable source of energy (B) Fossil fuels

(C) Renewable source of energy (D) Natural gas

(E) None of these

49. **Non-renewable energy supply cannot be replaced as quickly as it is used. The main disadvantages of nonrenewable energy is:**

(A) It disturbs wildlife.

(B) It contributes to the formation of acid rain.

(C) It contributes to global warming.

(D) All of these

(E) None of these

50. **The flat part of a leaf is called:**

(A) Leaf blade (B) Stomata

(C) Petiole (D) All of these

(E) None of these

Model Test Paper

Section-A (Science)

1. Identify the stomach from the following.

(A) 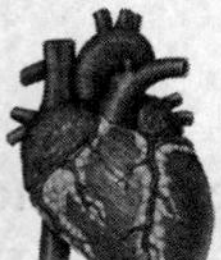

(B) 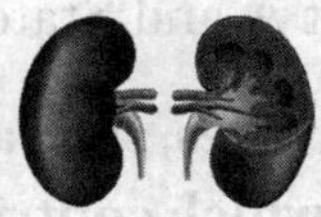

(C) 

(D) 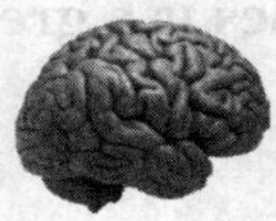

(E) None of these

2. What does the following symbol represent?

(A) No entry
(B) No parking
(C) No U turn
(D) No horn
(E) None of these

3. Which of the following gives birth to young ones?

(A) 

(B) 

(C) 

(D) 

(E) None of these

4. Which one of the following is a creeper plant?

(A) Pitcher plant (B) Lotus plant

(C) Mango tree (D) Strawberry plant

(E) None of these

5. Mushrooms are:

(A) Algae (B) Fungi

(C) Bacteria (D) Virus

(E) None of these

6. Which one of the following animals belongs to the group of amphibians?

(A)  (B) 

(C)  (D) 

(E) None of these

7. The push or pull applied on an object is known as:

(A) Force (B) Pressure

(C) Area (D) Surface

(E) None of these

8. Which of the following is an arboreal animal?

(A)  (B) 

(C)  (D) 

(E) None of these

9. **How many teeth does a fully grown adult human have?**
   (A) 32 (B) 34 (C) 36 (D) 28
   (E) None of these

10. **Which one of the following is a solid substance?**
    (A) Oxygen (B) Carbon dioxide
    (C) Water (D) Brick
    (E) None of these

11. **Which one of the following is an aquatic plant?**
    (A) Hydrilla (B) Lemon plant (C) Rose plant (D) Peepal tree
    (E) None of these

12. **Object A is heavier than object B means:**
    (A) the length of object A is more than object B.
    (B) the length of object A is less than object B.
    (C) the mass of object A is more than object B.
    (D) the mass of object A is less than object B.
    (E) None of these

13. **Air contains which one of the following gases?**
    (A) Nitrogen (B) Oxygen
    (C) Carbon dioxide (D) All of these
    (E) None of these

14. **Which one of the following food is not good for our health?**
    (A) Eggs (B) Vegetables (C) Fruits (D) Junk food
    (E) None of these

15. **Consider the following two statements:**

    Statement A: We should plant trees in order to reduce air pollution.

    Statement B: Acid rain keeps the building clean.

    Which of the following is correct with respect to the above statements?
    (A) Statement A (B) Statement B
    (C) Both the statements are true (D) Both the statements are false
    (E) None of these

16. Match the following:

1.	Larva of housefly	a.	Tadpole
2.	Larva of butterfly	b.	Nymph
3.	Young one of grasshopper	c.	Caterpillar
4.	Young one of frog	d.	Maggot

(A) 1 → d, 2 → c, 3 → b, 4 → a (B) 1→ c, 2 → d, 3 → b, 4 → a

(C) 1 → b, 2 → c, 3 → d, 4 → a (D) 1 → a, 2 → c, 3 → b, 4 → d

(E) None of these

17. Which of the following is the abiotic factor of the environment?

(A) Air (B) Water

(C) Temperature (D) All of these

(E) None of these

18. Which one of the following is a cold blooded animal?

(A)  (B) 

(C)  (D) 

(E) None of these

19. Pick the odd one out.

(A) Kilometre (B) Centimetre

(C) Millimetre (D) Barometre

(E) None of these

20. Consider the following two statements:

Statement A: Micro-organisms are very small in size and cannot be seen with naked eye.

Statement B: Some micro-organisms are useful for us.

Which of the following is correct with respect to the above statements?

(A) Statement A (B) Statement B

(C) Both the statements are correct. (D) Both the statements are incorrect.

(E) None of these

21. Which one of the following plants eats insects?

(A) Venus flytrap (B) Lotus
(C) Mango tree (D) Cactus
(E) None of these

22. Which of the following statements is true about force?

(A) Force can change the direction of a moving ball.
(B) Force can increase the speed of a moving ball.
(C) Force can decrease the speed of a moving ball.
(D) All of these
(E) None of these

23. A car travels 12 km in 15 minutes. Find the speed of the car.

(A) 40 km/h (B) 44 km/h
(C) 48 km/h (D) 52 km/h
(E) None of these

24. Which of these is an example of chemical change?

(A) Cooking of food (B) Breaking of glass
(C) Cutting a cloth into four pieces (D) Melting of ice
(E) None of these

25. In which of the following conditions magnets will repel each other?

(A) 

(B) 

(C) 

(D) All of these
(E) None of these

26. Which of the following is correct about the given picture?

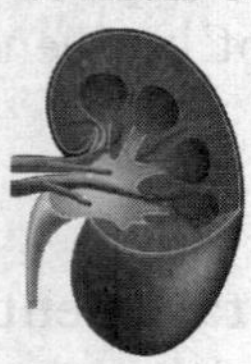

(A) It is a part of the nervous system. (B) It is a part of the digestive system.
(C) It is a part of the skeletal system. (D) It is a part of the excretory system.
(E) None of the these

27. Which layer of soil contains rich amount of humus ?

(A) A Horizon (B) B Horizon
(C) C Horizon (D) D Horizon
(E) None of these

28. What special term is used to represent the amount of water vapor present in air?

(A) Moisturiser (B) Humus
(C) Humidity (D) Fog
(E) None of these

29. Choose the non-renewable source of energy from the following.

(A) Wind Energy (B) Solar Energy
(C) Geothermal Energy (D) Fossil fuel
(E) None of these

30. X is a bird which hunts prey in darkness and has big eyes and a good sense of hearing. What is the name of X ?

(A) Bat (B) Owl
(C) Eagle (D) Vulture
(E) None of these

Section-B (Mental Ability and Reasoning)

31. Replace the question mark.

AB : BA	BC : CB	CD : DC	DE : ?

(A) EF (B) ED (C) DE (D) HG
(E) None of these

32. There are 3 white dogs and 5 black dogs. Weight of each of the white dog is 5 kg and that of each of the black dog is 3 kg. How much do all the dogs weigh together?

(A) 15 kg (B) 45 kg
(C) 30 kg (D) 14 years
(E) None of these

33. Find the mirror image of the letter 'B'.

(A) 

(B) 

(C) B

(D) 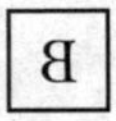

(E) None of these

34. If day before yesterday was Saturday what day will be the day after tomorrow?

(A) Wednesday (B) Friday

(C) Sunday (D) Monday

(E) None of these

35. Complete the following series.

37, 27, 18, 10, ______

(A) 9 (B) 3

(C) 8 (D) 15

(E) None of these

36. Fill in the gap with correct option

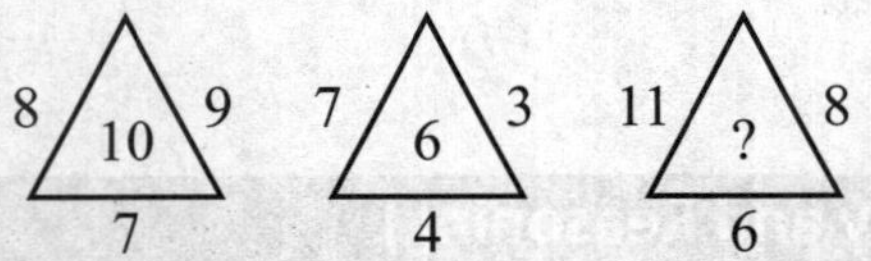

(A) 13 (B) 10

(C) 11 (D) 12

(E) None of these

37. If M + N = 9, L + N = 8 and L + L = 6, then find the value of M.

(A) 3 (B) 4

(C) 7 (D) 5

(E) None of these

38. Find the odd one out.

(A) Onion (B) Carrot

(C) Radish (D) Green pea

(E) None of these

39. Find the number of triangles in the figure.

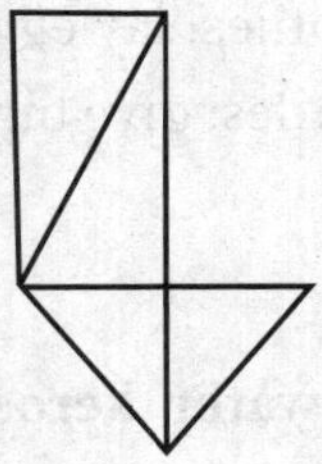

(A) 6 (B) 3 (C) 4 (D) 7

(E) None of these

40. In a row, Meera is 13th from the either sides. How many persons are there in the row?

(A) 26 (B) 16 (C) 25 (D) 21

(E) None of these

Section-C (Scholar's Zone)

41. Which of the following is/are the biotic components of the environment?

(1) Plants (2) Water

(3) Humidity (4) Insects

(A) Only (2) and (3) (B) (2), (3) and (4)

(C) (1), (2) and (3) (D) Only (1) and (4)

(E) None of these

42. Obsidian is a/an:

(A) Igneous rock (B) Sedimentary rock

(C) Metamorphic rock (D) Another name of quartzite

(E) None of these

43. Reproduction is one of the most important characteristic feature of animals. Select the option that best describes the ways of reproduction in animals.

(A) Birds: lay eggs, mammals: give birth to young ones and reptiles: give birth to young ones.

(B) Birds: lay eggs, mammals: give birth to young ones and reptiles: lay eggs.

(C) Birds: give birth to young ones, mammals: lay eggs and reptiles: lay eggs

(D) Birds: give birth to young ones, mammals: lay eggs and reptiles: give birth to young ones

(E) None of these

44. Classify the following substances as solid, liquid and gas: water, kerosene, coal, hydrogen, petrol.

(A) Solid - coal; Liquid - water, kerosene, petrol; Gas - hydrogen.

(B) Solid - coal; Liquid - water, petrol; Gas - hydrogen, kerosene.

(C) Solid - coal, petrol; Liquid - water, kerosene; Gas - hydrogen.

(D) All of these

(E) None of these

45. Which of the following statements is true about molar teeth?

1. Molar teeth are used for grinding food.
2. Molar teeth are broader than premolar.
3. There are six molar teeth in each jaw.
4. The front three teeth in the middle of each jaw are molar teeth.

(A) 1 and 4 (B) 2, 3 and 4

(C) 1, 2 and 3 (D) 2 and 3

(E) None of these

46. Which of the following statements is true?

(A) The eggs of a bird have a hard and protective shell.

(B) The yolk of the egg provides nutrition to the chick growing inside it.

(C) Insects also reproduce by laying eggs.

(D) All of these

(E) None of these

47. Consider the statements given below:

Alex: The process of digestion begins in the mouth.

Lizzie: From the mouth food passes to stomach through the food pipe.

Chelsy: From the stomach where some of the food is digested, the food passes into small intestine.

Who is correct?

(A) Lizzie (B) Chelsy

(C) Alex (D) All of these

(E) None of these

48. Consider the following statements:

Alex: The motion of merry-go-round is an example of circular motion.

Brian: A body covering unequal distance in equal intervals of time is said to be in non-uniform motion.

Lara: Air transport is the fastest means of transport.

Who is correct?

(A) Brian (B) Alex

(C) Lara (D) All of these

(E) None of these

49. Consider the following two statements.

Statement A: Oxygen gas is not present in the atmosphere.

Statement B: Ozone layer is responsible for absorbing the ultraviolet radiations from the Sun.

Which of the following is correct with respect to the above statements?

(A) Statement A

(B) Statement B

(C) Both the statements are correct.

(D) Both the statements are incorrect.

(E) None of these

50. Match the following.

1. Length	a. Litre
2. Volume	b. Second
3. Time	c. Metre
4. Mass	d. Kilogram

(A) 1→c, 2→a, 3→b, 4→d (B) 1→a, 2→b, 3→d, 4→c

(C) 1→b, 2→d, 3→a, 4→c (D) 1→a, 2→d, 3→c, 4→b

(E) None of these

Answer Keys

Self Evaluation Test

Chapter - 1 Plant Kingdom

1.	(A)	2.	(D)	3.	(B)	4.	(A)	5.	(D)
6.	(D)	7.	(B)	8.	(A)	9.	(B)	10.	(B)

Chapter - 2 Animal Kingdom

1.	(D)	2.	(E)	3.	(B)	4.	(D)	5.	(A)
6.	(B)	7.	(C)	8.	(A)	9.	(B)	10.	(B)

Chapter - 3 Functioning of Human Body

1.	(B)	2.	(E)	3.	(C)	4.	(B)	5.	(D)
6.	(D)	7.	(E)	8.	(C)	9.	(B)	10.	(C)

Chapter - 4 Matter

1.	(D)	2.	(A)	3.	(D)	4.	(C)	5.	(B)
6.	(B)	7.	(A)	8.	(B)	9.	(A)	10.	(C)

Chapter - 5 Force and Energy

1.	(B)	2.	(A)	3.	(C)	4.	(B)	5.	(A)
6.	(C)	7.	(C)	8.	(A)	9.	(D)	10.	(B)

Chapter - 6 Rocks and Soil

1.	(A)	2.	(C)	3.	(C)	4.	(B)	5.	(E)
6.	(D)	7.	(A)	8.	(C)	9.	(A)	10.	(B)

Chapter - 7 Our Environment

1.	(C)	2.	(C)	3.	(D)	4.	(C)	5.	(A)
6.	(B)	7.	(C)	8.	(C)	9.	(D)	10.	(B)

Chapter - 8 Universe

1.	(C)	2.	(A)	3.	(A)	4.	(A)	5.	(E)
6.	(B)	7.	(D)	8.	(A)	9.	(B)	10.	(A)

Practice Exercise-9
Reasoning and Aptitude

1.	(D)	2.	(B)	3.	(B)	4.	(C)	5.	(C)
6.	(A)	7.	(E)	8.	(D)	9.	(A)	10.	(D)
11.	(B)	12.	(D)	13.	(A)	14.	(C)	15.	(D)
16.	(C)	17.	(A)	18.	(C)	19.	(D)	20.	(C)

Practice Exercise Answers

Practice Exercise-1

1. (D) 2. (C) 3. (B) 4. (C) 5. (B) 6. (C) 7. (C) 8. (A)
9. (B) 10. (D) 11. (B) 12. (A) 13. (C) 14. (B) 15. (A) 16. (A)
17. (C) 18. (C) 19. (A) 20. (B) 21. (A) 22. (C) 23. (D) 24. (A)
25. (A) 26. (C) 27. (A) 28. (C) 29. (E) 30. (C) 31. (B) 32. (A)
33. (B) 34. (D) 35. (A) 36. (B) 37. (A) 38. (A) 39. (D) 40. (C)
41. (B) 42. (B) 43. (B) 44. (B) 45. (C) 46. (B) 47. (D) 48. (A)
49. (C) 50. (D)

Practice Exercise-2

1. (A) 2. (A) 3. (E) 4. (D) 5. (B) 6. (B) 7. (B) 8. (B)
9. (C) 10. (B) 11. (A) 12. (D) 13. (D) 14. (B) 15. (B) 16. (D)
17. (D) 18. (A) 19. (C) 20. (C) 21. (A) 22. (B) 23. (C) 24. (C)
25. (B) 26. (B) 27. (A) 28. (C) 29. (A) 30. (A) 31. (D) 32. (B)
33. (C) 34. (D) 35. (C) 36. (C) 37. (B) 38. (A) 39. (B) 40. (D)
41. (C) 42. (A) 43. (A) 44. (C) 45. (D) 46. (D) 47. (A) 48. (B)
49. (D) 50. (A)

Practice Exercise-3

1. (A) 2. (A) 3. (D) 4. (D) 5. (B) 6. (A) 7. (B) 8. (C)
9. (A) 10. (C) 11. (D) 12. (D) 13. (B) 14. (A) 15. (B) 16. (C)
17. (C) 18. (A) 19. (A) 20. (B) 21. (D) 22. (B) 23. (D) 24. (C)
25. (B) 26. (A) 27. (B) 28. (A) 29. (D) 30. (A) 31. (D) 32. (C)
33. (A) 34. (B) 35. (D) 36. (A) 37. (B) 38. (D) 39. (C) 40. (B)
41. (E) 42. (A) 43. (A) 44. (A) 45. (B) 46. (B) 47. (D) 48. (D)
49. (A) 50. (C)

Practice Exercise-4

1. (B) 2. (A) 3. (A) 4. (D) 5. (A) 6. (B) 7. (C) 8. (A)
9. (C) 10. (C) 11. (A) 12. (A) 13. (A) 14. (C) 15. (B) 16. (D)
17. (B) 18. (B) 19. (A) 20. (B) 21. (C) 22. (A) 23. (B) 24. (C)
25. (B) 26. (B) 27. (A) 28. (A) 29. (D) 30. (C) 31. (D) 32. (A)
33. (A) 34. (B) 35. (A) 36. (D) 37. (B) 38. (C) 39. (C) 40. (A)
41. (D) 42. (D) 43. (A) 44. (B) 45. (A) 46. (B) 47. (D) 48. (A)
49. (C) 50. (B)

Practice Exercise-5

1. (B) 2. (D) 3. (B) 4. (D) 5. (B) 6. (A) 7. (C) 8. (D)
9. (C) 10. (A) 11. (D) 12. (C) 13. (D) 14. (A) 15. (B) 16. (D)
17. (B) 18. (C) 19. (D) 20. (C) 21. (D) 22. (B) 23. (C) 24. (D)
25. (A) 26. (D) 27. (C) 28. (A) 29. (A) 30. (A) 31. (C) 32. (C)
33. (B) 34. (A) 35. (B) 36. (A) 37. (D) 38. (D) 39. (C) 40. (A)
41. (D) 42. (C) 43. (A) 44. (B) 45. (C) 46. (C) 47. (D) 48. (C)
49. (D) 50. (A)

Model Test Paper–Answers

1. (C) 2. (B) 3. (B) 4. (D) 5. (B) 6. (A) 7. (A) 8. (B)
9. (A) 10. (D) 11. (A) 12. (C) 13. (D) 14. (D) 15. (A) 16. (A)
17. (D) 18. (B) 19. (D) 20. (C) 21. (A) 22. (D) 23. (C) 24. (A)
25. (C) 26. (D) 27. (A) 28. (C) 29. (D) 30. (B) 31. (B) 32. (C)
33. (D) 34. (A) 35. (B) 36. (A) 37. (B) 38. (D) 39. (A) 40. (C)
41. (D) 42. (A) 43. (B) 44. (A) 45. (C) 46. (D) 47. (D) 48. (D)
49. (B) 50. (A)

10001

OMR - ANSWER SHEET

PLEASE SEE INSTRUCTIONS OVERLEAF BEFORE FILLING THE ANSWER SHEET

SILVER ZONE FOUNDATION

PARTICIPANT'S NAME

FATHER'S NAME

SCHOOL NAME

PARTICIPANT'S ENROLLMENT NUMBER

A B C D E F G H I J K L M N O P Q R S T U V W X Y Z –

0 1 2 3 4 5 6 7 8 9

PARTICIPANT'S CLASS

WRITE CLASS
Exp. 06 for class 6th

CLASS 01
CLASS 02
CLASS 03
CLASS 04
CLASS 05
CLASS 06
CLASS 07
CLASS 08
CLASS 09
CLASS 10
CLASS 11
CLASS 12

MOBILE NUMBER

0 1 2 3 4 5 6 7 8 9

TEST PAPER TYPE

Check 'Type' on Question Paper

A B C D

OLYMPIADS - SELECT YOUR SUBJECT

- (I) Informatics Olympiad (iiO)
- (M) Mathematics Olympiad (iOM)
- (S) Science Olympiad (iOS)
- (E) English Language Olympiad (iOEL)
- (G) GK Olympiad (SKGKO)
- (F) French Language Olympiad (iFLO)
- (T) Talent Hunt Olympiad (iTHO)
- (H) Hindi Olympiad (ABHO)

STREAM FOR CLASS XI & XII OLYMPIAD - iiO ONLY

- COMPUTER SCIENCE (C++) (S)
- INFORMATICS PRACTICES (JAVA) (J)
- COMPUTER SCIENCE (PYTHON) (P)
- MULTIMEDIA & WEB TECHNOLOGY (M)

STREAM FOR CLASS XI & XII OLYMPIAD - iOS ONLY

- PCB (B)
- PCM (M)

MARK YOUR ANSWERS WITH HB PENCIL/BALL POINT PEN (BLUE/BLACK)

1	A B C D E	11	A B C D E	21	A B C D E	31	A B C D E
2	A B C D E	12	A B C D E	22	A B C D E	32	A B C D E
3	A B C D E	13	A B C D E	23	A B C D E	33	A B C D E
4	A B C D E	14	A B C D E	24	A B C D E	34	A B C D E
5	A B C D E	15	A B C D E	25	A B C D E	35	A B C D E
6	A B C D E	16	A B C D E	26	A B C D E	36	A B C D E
7	A B C D E	17	A B C D E	27	A B C D E	37	A B C D E
8	A B C D E	18	A B C D E	28	A B C D E	38	A B C D E
9	A B C D E	19	A B C D E	29	A B C D E	39	A B C D E
10	A B C D E	20	A B C D E	30	A B C D E	40	A B C D E

SIGN. OF THE CANDIDATE & DATE OF EXAMINATION

SIGNATURE OF THE INVIGILATOR